THE DYNAMIC WORD

THE DYNAMIC WORD

New Testament Insights
for Contemporary Christians

Karl Paul Donfried

Harper & Row, Publishers, San Francisco

Cambridge, Hagerstown, New York, Philadelphia
London, Mexico City, São Paulo, Sydney

1817

For Raymond E. Brown
Friend
Scholar
Priest

THE DYNAMIC WORD: *New Testament Insights for Contemporary Christians.* Copyright © 1981 by Karl Paul Donfried. All rights reserved. Printed in the United States of America. No part of this book may be used or reproduced in any manner whatsoever without written permission except in the case of brief quotations embodied in critical articles and reviews. For information address Harper & Row, Publishers, Inc., 10 East 53rd Street, New York, NY 10022. Published simultaneously in Canada by Fitzhenry & Whiteside, Limited, Toronto.

FIRST EDITION

Designer: Jim Mennick

Library of Congress Cataloging in Publication Data
Donfried, Karl.
THE DYNAMIC WORD.

Includes bibliographical references and index.
1. Bible. N.T.—Criticism, interpretation, etc.
I. Title.
BS2361.2.D66 1981   225.6   80–8905
ISBN 0–06–061945–7   AACR2

81 82 83 84 85 10 9 8 7 6 5 4 3 2 1

Contents

Preface

This book is written to introduce and to share with laity and clergy alike some of the creative insights that have emerged from recent New Testament scholarship, as well as some of the excitement that can result from those insights. I hope that the material, presented in necessarily sketchy form, will stimulate further reflection and study. While this book attempts to share certain perspectives, it also includes with thanks many of the insights gained from the audiences and groups to whom much of it was originally given: my students at Smith College, meetings of clergy throughout the United States, the Ecumenical School of Theology of Christ Church Cathedral, Springfield, Massachusetts, ecumenical gatherings of many types but with special affection for the Ecumenical Institute of Assumption College in Worcester, Massachusetts, and to the many faithful congregations to whom I have had opportunity to proclaim the gospel. It is my hope that the discussion and further deliberation that these thoughts about the New Testament provoke might mutually encourage our faith in Jesus Christ as Lord in this unique and challenging period of history.

There are many friends and scholars from whom I have learned much and to whom I am deeply indebted—Raymond Brown is one of these. Although we both grew up in the Bronx, we first met in Cambridge, England, in 1966. His kindness, his sense of the church, and his scholarly accomplishments have enriched my life since. Our work together on the teams that produced *Peter in the New Testament* and *Mary in the New Testament* not only provided for me keen new biblical insights, but also a broader understanding of the church universal and the important ecumenical responsibility that Scripture scholars have.

I am especially grateful to my wife, Kathy, and to our children, Paul Andrew, Karen Erika, and Mark Christopher, for their understanding and kindness in letting me spend time on this manuscript when they certainly felt in their hearts that I should be doing less work and not more. A particular word of appreciation must be expressed to Karen and Kathy for their long hours of skillful typing and to my research assistant, Glenn Elizabeth Pharr, for her excellent work. Also, my sincere thanks to my distinguished colleagues and friends, Harvey McArthur, Patricia Skarda, and Richard Koenig, for their helpful and critical comments, and to John Shopp of Harper & Row for his encouragement and patience.

Some portions of the text that follows are dependent on articles published elsewhere. The reader may wish to pursue the arguments more fully and in more detail in their original location: "The Allegory of the Ten Virgins (Matt. 25:1–13) As a Summary of Matthean Theology," *Journal of Biblical Literature* 93 (1974): 415–428; "Justification and Last Judgment in Paul," *Zeitschrift für die Neutestamentliche Wissenschaft* 67 (1976): 90–110; "Justification and Last Judgment in the Theology of Paul," *Interpretation* 30 (1976): 140–152; "Ecclesiastical Authority in 2–3 John," in *L'Evangile de Jean,* ed. M. deJonge (Gembloux: J. Duculot, 1977), pp. 325–333.

Mary, Mother of Our Lord, August 15, 1981
Smith College
Northampton, Massachusetts

Introduction:
The Contemporary Challenge

Since World War II, biblical scholars have learned more about the development of early Christianity and the formation of the New Testament than the combined scholarship of the preceding nineteen centuries. Not only have new methodologies been developed, commonly referred to under the umbrella title "the historical-critical method," but significant new documents have been found in Qumran and Nag Hammadi.[1]

When one asks what captures best the basic thrust of the insights achieved in this century of New Testament research, perhaps the observation that the New Testament books were written by communities of faith for their own needs expresses it most succinctly. The recognition that these twenty-seven documents were written in the context of specific communities and addressed to the actual needs of these same audiences becomes critical for the proper understanding of these documents. In fact, the consequence of this insight is that without having some knowledge of the religious, sociological, and cultural factors that shaped the early Christian communities and without having some understanding of the specific needs and problems of the audiences addressed, one can interpret properly neither the original intention of these New Testament texts nor their meaning for the contemporary situation in which we live. Matthew and Mark share the common conviction that Jesus is the Christ, yet the way they shape their gospels and draw out the implications of their shared confession of faith is quite dissimilar. Why? Because the audiences to which they wrote were confronted with different sets of problems. Mark is attempting to present a picture of Jesus that serves as a corrective to possible distortions coming from his congregation's Hellenistic environment and Matthew is attempting to discuss the implications of the Christian ethic to an audience heavily shaped and influenced by Judaism as it appeared after A.D. 70. Paul's letters to the Corinthians are different from his letter to the Galatian Christians for the simple reason that the needs of each audience were different. Already we begin to perceive a very dynamic element in the writings of the New Testament, a phenomenon I will refer to as "dynamic actualization." By this I mean that there is no passing on of static, rigid principles in the New Testament, but rather a rich comprehension of the centrality of God's revelation in Jesus as the Christ and the application of that event to the actual and changing problems of the first communities of faith. It is precisely for this reason that we find not one, but four gospels in the canon of the New Testament. Each differs from the others because each is making the Christ event concrete in a situation that differs from the others chronologically, geographically, and theologically. In short, then, unless one grasps the necessity of audience criticism, that is, the concrete situation to which the author is writing, one cannot properly understand how New Testament texts functioned in their original context or how they can and should function in contemporary theology in its service of the Christian church.

As a corollary to the insight that the New Testament is written by the early church for its needs, New Testament scholars have come to recognize the multi-dimensionality of these writings.[2] The gospels, for example, are not one-dimensional biographies of Jesus that give day-to-day accounts of his activities; to see them in that way would be to severely limit the richness of both the intent and content of the gospels. Virtually every page of the gospels is multi-dimensional in that it includes: (1) words and deeds of Jesus of Nazareth; (2) the proclamation, interpretation, and expansion of these sayings and activities by the early Christian communities in light of the resurrection of Jesus and the needs of their communities; and (3) the literary and theological contributions of the evangelists themselves in the creation of their distinctive gospels. To recognize the presence of these three stages in the gospels of the New Testament is to recognize the richness and dynamism of early Christianity. The early church did not ask its followers to simply imitate or observe some static principles of Christianity, but rather to so comprehend the significance of the Christ event that they could dynamically actualize its implications in the situations in which they lived.[3] The freedom for this actualization and application to the concrete, existential situation can only be comprehended when one recognizes that these early Christians were not worshipping some dead prophet of Nazareth; rather, essential to their very existence was the conviction that this Jesus was raised from the dead by God, was now the Lord of the church, and present in its very life. It is this presence of the Risen One that both compelled and allowed the early church to engage in such vigorous and dynamic teaching and proclamation. Not only will we recognize this fact over and over again in the gospels, but in the writings of Paul as well. Why is it, one must ask, that Paul repeats no parables or miracles and at most only a handful of the sayings of Jesus in his extant letters? Paul so understood the mind of this Jesus whom he proclaimed as the Christ that he did not have to imitate his language; rather, in confident and utter freedom he stated the centrality of Jesus' message in ways his congregations could understand and comprehend.

Before we continue it will be helpful to illustrate what we have referred to as the multi-dimensionality of the gospels. For the moment one illustration must suffice, Mark 4:3–20:

"Listen! A sower went out to sow. 4 And as he sowed, some seed fell along the path, and the birds came and devoured it. 5 Other seed fell on rocky ground, where it had not much soil, and immediately it sprang up, since it had no depth of soil; 6 and when the sun rose it was scorched, and since it had no root it withered away. 7 Other seed fell among thorns and the thorns grew up and choked it, and it yielded no grain. 8 And other seeds fell into good soil and brought forth grain, growing up and increasing and yielding thirtyfold and sixtyfold and a hundredfold."

9 And he said, "He who has ears to hear, let him hear."

10 And when he was alone, those who were about him with the twelve asked him concerning the parables. 11 And he said to them, "To you has been given the secret of the kingdom of God, but for those outside everything is in parables; 12 so that they may indeed see but not perceive, and may indeed hear but not understand; lest they should turn again, and be forgiven." 13 And he said to them, "Do you not understand this parable? How then will you understand all the parables? 14 The sower sows the word. 15 And these are the ones along the path, where the word is sown; when they hear, Satan immediately comes and takes away the word which is sown in them. 16 And these in like manner are the ones sown upon rocky ground, who, when they hear the word, immediately receive it with joy; 17 and they have no root in themselves, but endure for a while; then, when tribulation or persecution arises on account of the word immediately they fall away. 18 And others are the ones sown among thorns; they are those who hear the word, 19 but the cares of the world, and the delight in riches, and the desire for other things, enter in and choke the word, and it proves unfruitful. 20 But those that were sown upon the good soil are the ones who hear the word and accept it and bear fruit, thirtyfold and sixtyfold and a hundredfold."

Essential to understanding these verses are the insights achieved by parable researchers in this century. One of the great contributions made by Adolf Jülicher[4] is the essential point, which has been accepted by virtually all subsequent scholars with only minor modification, that Jesus spoke in parables, not allegories. Allegories differ from parables insofar as they use an assigned system of symbols and tell a story with more than one point. Unless the audience knows or can decode the symbol system in an allegory, the message or messages remain obscure. In fact, an allegory presupposes that the reader already knows the essentials and these are now being reinforced via symbolic storytelling.[5] In using parables, on the other hand, as the work of Joachim Jeremias[6] and John Crossan[7] allows us to show, Jesus tries to make one essential point by way of analogy, using the most ordinary examples from daily life. While elements of allegory are present in the teaching of Jesus, the point to be made in this context is that parables are revelatory—they communicate something new about God and his kingdom to the hearers.

In light of these scholarly contributions, we can avoid the danger of overinterpreting verses 3–8. If this is an authentic parable of Jesus belonging to Stage 1, then we are looking for essentially one straightforward point, rather than a multiplicity of points that must first be desymbolized as in allegory. This parable deals with a reality factor: the ministry of Jesus will not find instant success; it will be accompanied by rejections, hindrances, and misadventures. Despite that, the results of the proclamation of the kingdom will be considerable.

This parable makes eminently good sense in the context of Jesus' ministry. But how should the early church some thirty or so years after the death and resurrection of Jesus (Stage 2) proclaim this parable? To simply repeat it without application would not have been enough—much as if a preacher today stepped into his pulpit, read a parable of Jesus, and then ended his sermon. The words and deeds of Jesus yearn for interpretation in light of his death and resurrection and in light of the creation of the church as a direct result of these events. The scholarly methodology known as "form criticism"[8] is particularly concerned with this creative period after the death and resurrection of Jesus in which the new communities of faith are proclaiming, teaching, and applying the message of Jesus. The form critic is concerned with the real-life setting in which these teachings and activities of Jesus are transmitted and interpreted. How, in what ways are they transmitted, and what motivating forces led early Christians to expand and interpret these words of him who for them was present as their Risen Lord? Although these observations and questions can only be dealt with more adequately in the following chapters, they already contribute to our understanding of verses 14–20, which function as an allegorical interpretation by the early church of a Jesus parable; in this way the parable became actualized for the new situation. That this portion of the parable stems from the early church (Stage 2) rather than from Jesus' life (Stage 1) is evident by its thoroughgoing allegorical style and its employment of terms that are only used by early Christians, for example, the repetition of the term "word" throughout verses 14–20 as a description of the Christ event.

Most New Testament scholars would attribute verses 10–13 to Stage 3, that of the evangelist or redactor. The methodology that deals with this stage is referred to as "redaction criticism," a methodology only developed in the early 1950s.[9] Redaction criticism has taught us that the authors of these gospels were authors in the genuine sense of the word. Not only did they collect, arrange, and shape material received from church tradition, but they also placed all of this within their own theological perspective. Matthew, Mark, Luke, and John are all addressing the needs of their specific congregations. Therefore they are anxious to stress certain elements as a way of correcting possible misunderstandings and as a way to positively exhort their fellow Christians. To do this effectively they not only rearranged material received from the tradition, but they also added to it as any good preacher or teacher would do. They are concerned that their audiences understand in no unclear terms the themes that need to be heard. Because these authors have made significant contributions of their own it becomes possible to speak, for example, of the theology of Mark or the theology of John. The evangelists are theologians in their own right.

Verses 10–13 undoubtedly contain many primitive elements, perhaps even some that may go back to the historical Jesus, but in their present context Mark shapes them to fit his theological presentation to his congregation. Throughout Mark's gospel, as we shall have opportunity to examine later, there is a concern for understanding and misunderstanding (v. 13, "And he said to them, 'Do you not understand this parable? How then will you understand all the parables?' "; also 6:52; 8:21) and these verses can only properly be understood in that wider context of Mark's theology. These verses provide a good example of why it is simply impossible to interpret selected verses apart from the context in which they appear.

We have just had one glimpse of the multi-dimensionality of the gospels and we have observed the intriguing way in which

Mark takes up earlier material and shapes it in such a way that it will speak to and become meaningful for his congregation. At this point we can suggest, in a preliminary way, that the challenge of the New Testament is the challenge to understand God's revelation in Christ in such a profound way that we will be able to proclaim this redemptive event dynamically and creatively and make it speak with relevance, meaning, and specificity to the human situations we are attempting to address. The pattern and example for effective response to this challenge are the writings of the New Testament themselves which, in the most exemplary fashion, contain this impulse to dynamic actualization of the Christ event.

In attempting to effectively respond to this challenge, at least three dimensions of the Christian life must be reviewed and examined with great care, and our deepened understanding of the formation of the New Testament is bound to lead to a new understanding and appreciation of these areas. These include, at the very least, the educational, theological, and ecumenical dimensions of the Christian community.

Educational Dimensions

If in the past four decades our knowledge about the formation of the New Testament has expanded so dramatically, then it follows that the contemporary church must acquaint itself with the basic insights of contemporary biblical scholarship, and through acquaintance with these insights come to a new awareness of the message of the New Testament. In so doing, it will discover that several of the methodologies developed throughout this century have become enormously useful in rediscovering the intention of the books of the New Testament. This in turn becomes especially helpful for the preaching, nurturing, and theological task of the church. The church will recognize in a new way the rich resources present in Scripture for dealing with many contemporary issues. One discovers over and over again that the difficulties first-century congregations faced really

are not so diffferent from those of their contemporary counter-
parts.

Theological Dimensions

For many, comprehension of the historical-critical approach
involves a different and more effective way of doing theology.
There has been a tendency, especially in Protestantism, to look
in Scripture for answers to contemporary situations without
clearly understanding the context in which these documents were
written. Thus, it was not infrequent that many cited Romans 13:1,
"Let every person be subject to the governing authorities," as
a text for noninvolvement in the tumultuous political situation of
the 1960s and early 1970s. But is Paul's advice, written to an early
Christian audience sometime about the mid–first century, a gen-
eralizing statement valid for all times? Or, was this exhortation
addressed to a very specific situation and with a very limited
application in mind? In order to answer that question, one must
first determine why Paul wrote Romans and to what precise situation it was being addressed. On that very point a lively discussion
is taking place in the circles of New Testament scholarship.[10]

The inadequency of a "proof-texting" theology becomes evident today at many points, not least in the discussions concerning
the ordination of women. Those supporting such ordination cite
Galatians 3:28, "There is neither . . . male nor female; for you are
all one in Christ Jesus"; and those in opposition cite 1 Timothy
2:12, "I permit no woman to teach or to have authority over men;
she is to keep silent." But is the matter as simple as picking and
choosing texts that support one's position? To do that is to play
"the game of first-century Bible-land."[11] In order to respond
thoughtfully to such an issue, does one not have to assemble all
the relevant texts and seek their original context and their interrelationship? Such a task is mandatory and it involves all the tools
and principles available to the historical-critical method. The
process involves careful study and analysis, including especially
the attitudes of the non-Christian world toward women, the atti-

tudes of Jesus and Paul, the attitudes of the earliest Christian communities and then, of course, the subsequent tradition of the church. Such diligent study will reveal no simplistic answers, but a complex progression of ideas involving the freedom of the Christian woman, but always within the exigencies of real history. The development of the early church's understanding of the role and function of women in its life can only be understood when it is seen that its positions are developed out of the juxtaposition of the liberation granted women in Christ with the realities of their community situation.

Theology, in short, will profit enormously not by imitating "biblical language" or "proof-texting" certain positions in a naive way, but by taking seriously the principle of "dynamic actualization." The task of theology is to so understand the Word of God as witnessed to in Scripture that it can apply the message in a radically new and relevant way from age to age. In that way it will truly be faithful to the *dynamic* Word. As highlighted by Paul Tillich's method of correlation, the Word of God (which for the New Testament is in its primary sense Jesus) must always be addressed to a specific cultural situation.[12] Thus, the effective theologian and preacher must both understand the Given and the situation into which that Given is to be proclaimed. That is what incarnation is all about—to make the Word become real within the realities of the world of individuals and nations. Then the correct question is not whether Scripture is the revealed Word of God, but whether it is revealing the Word of God to all of God's creation.

Further, the challenge to theology and preaching provided by New Testament criticism today is to recover the gift of clear, simple, and complete communication. There is always the danger of using "ghetto" language, "religious" or "biblical" language that may be clear to some on the inside, but to virtually none outside the Christian community. The question Paul raised with the Corinthians is just as relevant today: "And if the bugle gives an indistinct sound, who will get ready for battle?" (1 Cor. 14:8). The danger of indistinct and imprecise language comes from at

least two areas: simplistic "evangelical" preaching and abstract
academic theology. In the former, although often well intended
and motivated by sincere commitment, there is a way of using
biblical categories in such a manner that their rich content and
their original context is lost or simplified. Repentance from "sin"
is often seen in highly individualistic and psychological terms, so
that the biblical category of sin as being a demonic force present
in all the structures and institutions of society is not sufficiently
comprehended. Thus, it is stressed that "one should not steal,"
but little is said about the structure of sin that may be operating
in some of our businesses and institutions that permit many to
be "ripped off " and others to remain trapped in the gutters of
poverty. Biblical scholarship is challenging all involved in theology to understand the full range of the message of the kingdom
of God proclaimed by Jesus. That proclamation involves not only
Jesus, but the message of the kingdom, the kingdom of God.[13]
Once again we are challenged to full dimensionality.

Many in the academic study of theology fall into opposite dan-
gers of abstraction and "neutrality" in their reaction to the na-
ivete and overzealousness just described, and this tendency often
leads to irrelevance. When the historical-critical method serves
only to foster more and more academic books, articles, and con-
ferences it becomes self-serving and arrogant. While some of
these activities may be important for the advance of scholarship,
their true meaning and value only become manifest when they
lead to the "upbuilding and encouragement and consolation" of
the church (1 Cor. 14:3). When theology loses its churchly context it no longer edifies the people of God in carrying out their
responsibility.

In view of these divergent tendencies it is important to listen
to the advice Paul gives the Corinthian Christians: "I will pray
with the spirit *(pneuma)* and I will pray with the mind *(nous)* also;
I will sing with the spirit and I will sing with the mind also" (1
Cor. 14:15). Paul calls for a combination of the Spirit and the
mind: this balance between the experiential and the intellectual
must be applied not only to praying and singing, but also in the

doing of theology. The Spirit allows theology to be faithful to its task of relevant proclamation, and the mind exercises the critical check so that theology does not speak superficial nonsense and trivia in the name of the Word of God. As Paul reminds his audience in the next two verses, only when proclamation is carried out with the help of the Spirit *and* with the help of the mind does it communicate to the "outsider" in such a way that that person is "edified." It is noteworthy that Paul stresses the matter of communicating intelligibly to the person outside of the Christian community; it is this focus that sought to prohibit the kind of introverted "ghetto" language that some of these Corinthian Christians were using.

Briefly, then, New Testament scholars are attempting to assist the whole people of God to blow the trumpet more distinctly so that its sound will be heard precisely and in the rich fullness of the proclamation of the kingdom.

Ecumenical Dimensions

Much of the fragmentation within Christianity today has been caused because a good deal of our speech has not been as intelligible, distinct, or as complete as it might have been. Why major church bodies are distinctive entities today is quite blurred in the mind of many sincere believers. And even when one is aware of some of the unique stresses of each denomination and how they have been historically determined, the question must be raised whether they are still so distinctive today as to support the continued fragmentation of Christ's church? In this situation of confusion, questioning, and rethinking the historical-critical method has an enormous contribution to make. In fact, the foundation for the continuance of the ecumenical movement has been laid anew by contemporary New Testament studies.

"Christ wills for his church a unity which is not only spiritual, but must be manifest in the world."[14] This statement made by an ecumenical commission is supported by the current discussions concerning the historical context of the New Testament. Repeatedly one can observe how the earliest Christian churches were threatened by disunity. Already in one of the earliest New Testament writings, Paul urges the Corinthians "that all of you agree and that there be no dissensions among you, but that you be united in the same mind and the same judgment. 11 For it has been reported to me by Chloe's people that there is quarreling among you, my brethren" (1 Cor. 1:10b–11). Or, to cite one other example, John 17, which is a prayer for the unity of Christ's disciples: "I do not pray for these only, but also for those who believe in me through their word, 21 that they may all be one . . ." (vv. 20–21). This same emphasis is sharpened in verses 22–23: "The glory which thou hast given me I have given to them, that they may be one even as we are one, 23 I in them and thou in me, that they may become perfectly one, so that the world may know that thou hast sent me and hast loved them even as thou hast loved me." By examining the context of Johannine Christianity it becomes evident that this church was in real danger of fragmentation. This is especially to be seen in 2 and 3 John. In light of this situation illuminated so carefully by contemporary scholarship, one can see how acutely relevant John 17 is to an actual situation in the Johannine church of the first century.[15] The reality of that plea for Christian unity has been brought to light in a new way through the historical-critical method.

While recognizing a major concern for the unity of the church in the New Testament, biblical scholars have also rediscovered the diversity of the writings contained in the New Testament. Unity clearly does not mean homogeneity; it is not defined in any narrow, rigid way in these books of the early church. Rather the unity represented in the confession that Jesus is Lord can be actualized in a wide range of different church styles. Precisely for that reason we do not have one gospel, but four. The Johannine congregation simply is not a duplicate of the Marcan; similarly, Hebrews is decidedly different than 1 Corinthians, and the problems encountered in Revelation are of a different order than those in Romans.

When this principle of diversity within unity is recognized, a whole series of questions is raised about the validity of certain rigid ecclesiastical distinctions that have been made since the Reformation. It simply can no longer be maintained that the Congregational or the Presbyterian or the Episcopal form of church government is more biblical. The fact is that all three are biblical and that all three can be found in the first century of Christianity. The much more cogent question is why early Christianity increasingly opted for the episcopal form of ecclesiastical government. As we shall see, it was this type of structure that best allowed the church to maintain unity, to effectively combat the spiritualizing threat of gnosticism and to protect itself from persecutions by the state.[16]

Not only has contemporary New Testament scholarship helped make our understanding of the New Testament less provincial and less rigid by recognizing the diversity and manifold richness of its witness, but it has drawn to our attention the central significance of the church and its traditions. In our current understanding of the development of early Christianity this fact becomes so self-evident as to be taken for granted. Let us reflect on these categories of church and tradition just a little.

If Jesus died about A.D. 30 and the earliest gospel, Mark, was written about A.D. 65–70, how was the gospel material transmitted and preserved? Who collected these materials together so that they could eventually be shaped into a gospel? The answer is the church. These books were not hand delivered from heaven as complete summaries of the faith for all time; they were, as we have just seen, written by and for the church. It was the earliest Christian communities that preserved, transmitted, interpreted, shaped, produced, and collected these writings. This is evident in the remainder of the New Testament as well. Paul writes to the Corinthians: "For I delivered to you as of first importance what I also received, that Christ died for our sins in accordance with the scriptures . . ." (1 Cor. 15:3). Paul is passing on the early Christian tradition from one generation to the next.[17]

Throughout the history of the church, the terms "tradition," "Scripture," and "church" have been related to one another in

various ways by different Christian communities.[18] In many Protestant contexts Scripture has been given a chronological priority
over both church and tradition. Once again the historical-critical
method would urge that matters are not quite so simple. A study
of the New Testament and early Christian writings suggests the
following relationship with regard to such terms as "gospel"
"tradition," "Scripture," and "church": primacy is given to the
gospel of God about Christ, including the formation of the new
community, the church; this is then followed by traditions transmitted by the church concerning the Christ event, and only then,
as a consequence of these prior developments, does the New
Testament eventually emerge as Scripture. It is in the context of
the church that what is subsequently called "the New Testament"
originates.[19] It is the church that transmits, shapes, and collects.
One should also not forget that it was the church, in several
councils, that defined the canon of the New Testament. It is the
church in council that finally said these twenty-seven books and
not the others (which today can be found in the New Testament
apocrypha) belong to the canon.

This discussion, in addition to reminding us of the centrality
of the church in the formation of the New Testament, should
make us aware of three other self-evident, but easily overlooked
facts: (1) When early Christians refer to "the Scriptures" they are
referring to the Old Testament.[20] Because this is their Scripture,
the Old Testament is crucial for their understanding and interpretation of the Christ event. Given this fact, no one today can
hope to come to a serious understanding or appreciation of the
New Testament unless there is a prior understanding of the Old
Testament as well as the various forms of Judaism present in the
first century. (2) In the first century there is no New Testament
as we know it. The New Testament only begins to take its present
shape in the mid-second century in response to certain heretical
abuses. Thus, in our discussions of the first Christian century it
is important to realize that the New Testament canon did not
exist at this point. (3) The books that were eventually collected
into the canon do not represent the full range of Christian writ-

ings in this period. Many groups that were eventually declared to be heretical wrote gospels, acts of apostles, and epistles of their own. These writings should also make us sensitive to the fact that in the first century there was not yet a precise distinction between what are later referred to as heresy and orthodoxy.[21] They existed intermingled, the followers of each claiming to be the faithful followers of Jesus. Many of the New Testament writings arose out of these situations of confusion and they, each in their context, attempt to describe who Jesus was and what it means to be his follower over against deviant interpretations.

This new understanding of the relationship of the church to the formation of the New Testament is bound to have positive and serious implications for the long divisive issue between Roman Catholics and Protestants, Scripture and tradition. In addition to these issues just discussed, the historical-critical method allows a new reassessment of other neuralgic theological divisions that have separated Roman Catholics and Protestants, such as justification and good works,[22] Peter and papacy,[23] Mary and the role of women.[24] The careful and dedicated work of ecumenical teams of New Testament scholars has shown that a new examination of these issues can assist in eliminating some of the falsely erected barriers of the past. Once again the challenge of the New Testament forces men and women of good will to reexamine whether or not the current divisions in Christianity may not be largely due to an oversimplification of some very complex issues and whether a position more faithful to the biblical text will not attempt to bring some of these elements back together into a better balance. When "Catholic substance" and "Protestant principle" come closer together, one may find that one is responding more faithfully to the challenge of the New Testament.[25]

Before proceeding to the first chapter, a few words must be said about the phrase "dynamic Word." Although I have already made several specific references to the concepts "dynamic" and "dynamic actualization," "Word" is still in need of greater precision. What is meant by "Word," and how does it relate to such common terms as "Word of God," "gospel," and "Christ event"? What is this "Word" that is being dynamically actualized?

"Word" as it is used in the title of this book means "Word of God" in the sense of gospel, the proclamation of good news of what God has done in Christ. These two terms are set side by side and used interchangeably by the apostle Paul in his letter to the church at Philippi.

I want you to know, brethren, that what has happened to me has really served to advance the gospel, 13 so that it has become known throughout the whole praetorian guard and to all the rest that my imprisonment is for Christ; 14 and most of the brethren have been made confident in the Lord because of my imprisonment, and are much more bold to speak the word of God without fear. (1:12–14)

In some of the subsequent chapters I point out that the gospel in early Christianity originally meant the oral proclamation of what God had done in Jesus Christ, the good news of God's salvation. Although the articulation of the gospel varies with the audience, it does have some definite features. Paul, in a passage we will examine more closely in the next chapter, gives a summary of the essential contents of the gospel as he proclaimed it to the Corinthian church:

For I delivered to you as of first importance what I also received, that Christ died for our sins in accordance with the scriptures, 4 that he was buried, that he was raised on the third day in accordance with the scriptures, 5 and that he appeared to Cephas, then to the twelve. 6 Then he appeared to more than five hundred brethren at one time, most of whom are still alive, though some have fallen asleep. (1 Cor. 15:3–6)

Although there are various ways by which the content of the gospel is expressed, its normative character is expressed by Paul when he concludes this section in verse 11: "Whether then it was I or they, so we preach and so you believed." Precisely in this Corinthian church that had known not only Paul as preacher, but others as well, it is stressed that the same gospel is proclaimed by all. It is a gospel of good news and joy, because it is a message declaring God's mercifully gracious and free act in offering redemption and new life to a lost world. To proclaim this gospel of God's mercy lies at the center of the entire New Testament.

To return for a moment to the Philippian text cited earlier, we notice that Paul uses the term "Word of God" interchangeably with "gospel." It is a Word about what God has done in the salvific event of Jesus Christ, a word that changes the lives of those who believe it, a word that creates new community. This is exactly what Paul is expressing to the Christians at Thessalonica:

> And we also thank God constantly for this, that when you received the word of God which you heard from us, you accepted it not as the word of men but as what it really is, the word of God, which is at work in you believers. (1 Thess. 2:13)

The Dynamic Word intends to demonstrate how this Word of God, this gospel, was proclaimed and articulated by different authors in different communities. To witness this process of actualization in the literature of the New Testament is both challenging and exciting.

Although I will be using the term "Word" in the way just described, we need to be clear that there are two other common ways in which the phrase "Word" or "Word of God" is understood. One, explicitly biblical, I referred to briefly above: the identification of Jesus as the Word (in the opening of John's gospel and at the closing of the book of Revelation, for example). In this latter case we read about Jesus "clad in a robe dipped in blood, and the name by which he is called is The Word of God" (Rev. 19:13). Without question, this usage of the concept "Word of God" is the primary one in the New Testament: Jesus is the expression, the revelation, of the reality of God. Therefore, the reference to the Word of God as gospel, as dynamic Word, is subsidiary to this primary meaning, because it is always a word about what God has accomplished in the Christ event.

A final way in which "Word of God" is used by many is in relation to Scripture. The Old and New Testaments are seen as a witness to Christ, so the Bible too is referred to as the Word of God. While such a confession can be made with integrity, one must guard against the distortion that paper and ink are identical to the Word of God in its primary sense. Only as the Word is proclaimed and uttered in the radicality of each new situation does it become a dynamic Word. Scripture contains the Word of God, witnesses to the Word of God, and proclaims the Word of God only as the risen Lord inspires his servants to proclaim the Christ event anew in each generation. Particularly helpful in this regard is a discussion between Jesus and nonbelievers in John 5. In the midst of an exasperating dialogue in which they refuse to understand and accept who Jesus is, he responds to them: "You search the scriptures, because you think that in them you have eternal life; and it is they that bear witness to me; 40 yet you refuse to come to me that you may have life" (John 5:39–40). Eternal life is not found in the texts of Scripture, but only in him to whom they bear witness; only in this sense can one speak properly of Scripture as the Word of God.

To summarize these observations, the concept "Word of God" in the New Testament refers in its primary sense to Jesus Christ, the center of God's revelation. The good news about this Christ event, which is always proclaimed anew, is also referred to in the New Testament as the Word of God; it is a dynamic Word spoken concretely amid a wide diversity of situations to which the New Testament bears witness. And, finally, all Scripture, Old and New Testament, can be referred to as the Word of God, since it bears powerful witness to *the* Word—Jesus—and to the continued and repeated proclamation of the Christ event as a dynamic Word.

I. PAUL THE APOSTLE
IN THE EARLY CHURCH

1. Theology and Praxis: 1 Corinthians

The earliest extant literature of the New Testament is the Pauline corpus of letters (ca. A.D. 48–55).[1] While the gospels refer to events prior to Paul, that is, to Jesus and his ministry, they are actually written in their present form at a considerably later time (ca. A.D. 65–95).[2] In this chapter I hope to show how Paul applies with consistency the principle of dynamic actualization. In virtually every one of his letters he is attempting to clarify and actualize the dynamic Word as he had proclaimed it previously in oral form to his congregatons. It is evident from these letters that Paul never preaches some nebulous gospel to a nonexistent audience, but that he is always attempting to communicate the gospel of God (Rom. 1:1; 1 Thess. 2:2) relevantly to the specific needs of the congregation addressed. It is the matter of taking each of his audiences and their needs seriously that gives Pauline theology its power and its biting concreteness.

This process of dynamic actualization can be witnessed in all the Pauline letters and especially in 1 Corinthians, one of many letters Paul writes to the congregation he founded in Corinth. Throughout this communication Paul is concerned not with merely repeating the gospel and the tradition of the church, but with explaining their meaning and relevance for day-to-day Christian existence. One specific example of this process can be vividly witnessed in 1 Corinthians 15.

A familiarity with the Greek city of Corinth and its setting in Hellenistic culture is helpful to our understanding of 1 Corinthians 15. Situated on the Isthmus of Corinth and serving as the capital of the Roman province of Achaia, Corinth was a great seaport and commercial center linking east with west. The Romans destroyed the city in 146 B.C., but after some 100 years Julius Caesar refounded the city as a Roman colony. The old Corinth was often referred to in literature as a center of immorality and vice, and from Paul's correspondence with the Corinthian church, we have every reason to believe that this reputation was carried on by the new Corinth. The well-known proverb "Not for every man is the voyage to Corinth"[3] became synonymous with such practices as fornication. These features, together with the biannual celebration of the Isthmian games, indicate the cosmopolitan nature of Corinth.

In many ways Corinth was influenced by Roman Hellenism, that civilization which spread throughout the Mediterranean world as a result of Alexander the Great's military adventures and conquests in the period 334–325 B.C. One of the characteristics of this period was religious individualism; the state no longer controlled worship, so citizens chose their own gods. Foreign deities became commonplace, and the identification of Greek gods with foreign deities was not unusual. Such foreign gods as Isis and Serapis were common in Corinth, as were such Greek deities as Apollo and Aphrodite. The ruins of the temple of the goddess Aphrodite can still be seen on the acropolis (highest point) of Corinth, and the remnants of the majestic temple to the god Apollo can still be seen adjacent to the *agora* (marketplace) of ancient Corinth. From an important inscription we now know also that there was a Jewish synagogue in the city. In short, the Corinth Paul knew was a place of religious pluralism and syncretism. It is precisely this environment that led to so many of the ethical dilemmas that confronted the Corinthian Christians.

1 Corinthians 15: Resurrection of the Body, Not Immortality of the Soul

In this chapter Paul must address some in the Corinthian church who either deny or fundamentally misunderstand the significance of bodily resurrection for the Christian believer. It is interesting to observe how he deals with this problem. Does he simply tell them they are wrong and that they ought to believe what they were first taught? No, he reminds them in only seven verses about the gospel as he preached it to them and then continues with fifty-one verses of explanation! A closer look at the opening of this chapter will be instructive.

1 Corinthians 15 is a classic example of how Paul tries to actualize the contents of the gospel to a particular situation, in this case a misunderstanding about resurrection.[4] Paul begins: "Now I would remind you, brethren, in what terms I preached to you the gospel, which you received, in which you stand, 2 by which you are saved, if you hold it fast—unless you believed in vain" (vv. 1–2). For Paul, the way to tackle the problem is not in the first place to listen to everyone's opinion on the matter, or to give his own opinion; the starting point is the gospel he proclaimed to them and they received. Their existence as Christians is rooted in this gospel and only as they hold fast to it will the salvation already initiated and experienced be culminated on the last day. Typical of Paul's understanding of Christian existence is the realization that one can believe in vain, a state of affairs that develops when one no longer clings to the content of the gospel in a steadfast manner. In short, there is no guaranteed conclusion to the salvific process begun in baptism.

Paul, having indicated to the Corinthians that the starting point for a discussion of the current situation must be the gospel, proceeds to give a summary of the gospel as it was common in wide areas of primitive Christianity. That Paul himself did not write this summary is indicated by his use of the technical terms "to receive" and "to deliver," terms used in Judaism to indicate the transmission of tradition.[5] Paul continues: "For I delivered to you as of first importance what I also received, that Christ died for our sins in accordance with the scriptures, 4 that he was buried, that he was raised on the third day in accordance with the scriptures, 5 and that he appeared to Cephas, then to the twelve . . ." (vv. 3–5). According to this account, which we have already stressed in the Introduction, the foundation of the Christian proclamation is Jesus' death, burial, resurrection and post-resurrection appearances, with death and resurrection standing at the center. As we shall see, virtually every element of this traditional confession is explained in the remainder of chapter 15. But before Paul proceeds to a further elaboration, he adds in verse 11: "Whether it was I or they, so we preach and so you believed." Not only Paul, but also the other Christian leaders with whom the Corinthians were acquainted (Apollos and Peter), proclaim this identical gospel. Perhaps Paul even wishes to include under "they" all those Christian leaders to whom he has just referred in the preceding verses.

What groups of early Christians would have asserted that "there is no resurrection of the dead" (v. 12)? There are two possibilities: (1) Some Christians in Corinth might have been influenced by the general Hellenistic anti-body attitude that would look at a concept such as physical resurrection as absurd. Virtually every church father in the early centuries of Christianity had to write a tract in defense of the resurrection because of this widespread dualistic attitude, which argued that the body was an evil prison from which the soul would be liberated at death. (2) Alternatively, some Corinthians might have been attracted to a perspective that developed more fully in the second century, a heresy commonly referred to as gnosticism.[6]

Although gnosticism was a pre-Christian movement, it rapidly merged with aspects of early Christian thought and became a major deviant movement. The development of a canon, ecclesiastical authority, creeds, and doctrines, just to cite a few examples, was in direct response to the threat of gnosticism by what eventually becomes the catholic and orthodox church. Since the term *gnosticism* is a catch-all term that covers widely divergent movements that are syncretistic in nature, it is difficult to give a precise definition. Features characteristic of some gnostic movements include a sharp dualism between the heavenly worlds and this evil world, and the belief that this world came into being accidentally or by an inferior god, that some humans contain a divine spark in the midst of their evil, corrupt bodies, that a heavenly redeemer, often Jesus, descends from above to rescue through knowledge (*gnosis*, thus "gnosticism") those who have this spark, that since this world and the body are evil, ethics are of no consequence. In view of such beliefs most gnostic Christians would be reluctant to assert that the present physical body would be transformed at some future point. This perspective may have influenced some in the Corinthian church.

This second group is the more likely since it is against such a perspective that Paul appears to be arguing in the remainder of chapter 15. After initiating his argument in verses 12–19 with reference to the fact of Christ's resurrection as previously summarized in the confession and then developing its implications, Paul proceeds to dwell on primarily two facts, the first of which is that the resurrection of the Christian has not yet taken place but will take place in the future. This argument is contained in verses 20–34, and we receive good insight into his perspective in verse 23: "But each in his own order: Christ the first fruits, then at his coming those who belong to Christ." Not in the present, not immediately after death, but at the consummation of history is the moment of resurrection for those who have died in Christ. In other words, Paul is stressing the futurity of the resurrection. Paul, in verses 35–37, argues against the idea of the immortality of the soul; he attempts rather, to demonstrate to these Corinthian Christians that the future resurrection will be a resurrection of the body. The second basic stress then, is that of a future *bodily resurrection.* Representative of Paul's thinking is verse 46: "But it is not the spiritual which is first but the physical, and then the spiritual."

The thrust of the argument makes more sense when we take note of a passage in 2 Timothy 2:17 and following where the writer refers to "Hymenaeus and Philetus, 18 who have swerved from the truth by holding that the resurrection is past already." When one reads this together with a noncanonical document known as the *Letter to Rheginus,* [7] one realizes that there were Christians in the first and second centuries who, difficult as it may seem to us, believed that they had already experienced a *spiritual resurrection;* for many this experience of a spiritual resurrection was conflated with the moment of baptism. To such a distortion Paul responds: By no means! Resurrection is future and it is to be bodily. We need to look at both these dimensions somewhat more carefully.

Paul's stress on the future consummation of salvation is consistent throughout his correspondence. Particularly relevant to the theme of future resurrection is Philippians 3:8 and following, especially verses 10–11: "that I may know him and the power of his resurrection, and may share his sufferings, becoming like him in his death, 11 that if possible I may attain the resurrection from the dead." Paul stresses that the gift of resurrection is future and it is not something immediately guaranteed, a point underscored by his use of the subjunctive (indicating something indefinite, possible, rather than a fact) in this verse and his further elaboration in verses 12–14: "Not that I have already obtained this or am already perfect; but I press on to make it my own, because Christ Jesus has made me his own. 13 Brethren, I do not consider that I have made it my own; but one thing I do, forgetting what lies behind and straining forward to what lies ahead, 14 I press on toward the goal for the prize of the upward call of God in Christ Jesus." As I shall explain further in the next chapter, the beginning of the Christian life is marked by justification; but that is only the *beginning* of a process. The first fruits of salvation that are experienced in the process of justification/baptism continue to be worked out in the process of living the Christian life ("Work out your own salvation with fear and trembling," Phil. 2: 12c) but are only consummated and brought to fulfillment on the last day.

As a corollary to this stress on the futurity of resurrection, then, is the emphasis that it will be bodily. At this point there is clear tension between Paul and the Platonic conception, according to which the soul leaves the physical body at death. The apostle is not teaching separation, but transformation. Two verses in 1 Corinthians 15 in particular deserve some further comment: verse 35, "But some one will ask, 'How are the dead raised? With what kind of body do they come?' " and verse 44, "It is sown a physical body, it is raised a spiritual body. If there is a physical body, there is also a spiritual body." Paul is stressing both a continuity between our present and future existence by his use of the term "body" (Greek: *sōma*) as well as a discontinuity, a fact suggested by the distinction made between "physical" and "spiritual."

If one follows the argument from verses 35–37 carefully, Paul appears to be saying that there is a continuity of our individual existence (body) although the form of that existence will be transformed from a physical to a spiritual body on the last day: "For the trumpet will sound, and the dead will be raised imperishable, and we shall be changed. 53 For this perishable nature must put on the imperishable, and this mortal nature must put on immortality" (vv. 52–53). Upon further reflection this thought process is not really so unbelievable. Just think of yourself for a moment at ages five, twenty, forty-five, and seventy. Quite obviously your physical appearance will be substantially different from decade to decade, yet those who have known you well as a child would readily recognize your unique personality at age seventy. Despite the fact that virtually all the cells in your body have been replaced with new cells, there is still something distinctively recognizable about you. It is likely that this is what Paul means by the term "body." To use more contemporary language, each of us has a unique genetic program from the moment of conception that remains the same despite fairly radical physical changes during growth. This program determines a specific development that makes us uniquely us, but who has not wondered at the overwhelming and momentous transition from *in utero* to *ex utero* that makes manifest the miracle of human life? Paul appears to be suggesting that, although there is continuity of individual existence which can be likened today to the genetic program, after death, at the resurrection, there will be a further transformation and at that time we will receive a new spiritual body. In a way parallel perhaps to the change between *in utero* and *ex utero* will be the change from this physical, in the world, existence to a

spiritual, with the Lord, existence. At that point of consummation
the words of the prophets Isaiah and Hosea will be fulfilled:

> "Death is swallowed up in victory."
> 55 "O death, where is thy victory?
> O death, where is thy sting?"
> . . . 57 But thanks be to God, who gives us the victory through our
> Lord Jesus Christ.

(1 Cor. 15:54–57)

Thus far, then, we have attempted to show how Paul creatively
and dynamically actualizes the gospel message so as to meet the
specific needs of the Corinthian church with regard to the meaning of the resurrection. Chapter 15 is not, by any means, an
isolated example of this process. All of 1 Corinthians, from beginning to end, is an illustration of this process of dynamic actualization. In the remainder of this chapter we shall review some
further examples of this process.

Arrogance and the Cross of Christ

Another dimension of the gospel that Paul preached to the
Corinthians was "that Christ died for our sins . . ." (1 Cor. 15:3).
The fact that their Lord suffered and died should have had important ethical implications for his followers, central among such
implications being the characteristic of humility and openness
toward the need of the neighbor. However, due to a high degree
of immaturity and arrogance in the Corinthian church, a sizeable
proportion in this congregation misunderstood the gospel as a
message that allowed them to think of themselves as superior
human beings; they understood the gospel as giving them insight
and knowledge that elevated them above ordinary folk, a misin-
terpretation quite comprehensible in light of their Hellenistic
philosophical background. For this reason Paul states: "Your
boasting is not good" (1 Cor. 5:6a). Elsewhere he warns them:
"Some are arrogant, as though I were not coming to you. 19 But
I will come to you soon, if the Lord wills, and I will find out not

the talk of these arrogant people but their power. 20 For the kingdom of God does not consist in talk but in power" (1 Cor. 4:18-20).

This arrogance leads to a view of the Christian life as already perfected, a view Paul does not share and one he refutes sharply and at times quite sarcastically. "Already you are filled! Already you have become rich! Without us you have become kings! And would that you did reign, so that we might share the role with you!" (1 Cor. 4:8). What a pity it is, Paul laments, that you really are not perfected, because I would like to share in that kind of existence myself! Instead, the reality of the situation is that we "are fools for Christ's sake, but you are wise in Christ. We are weak, but you are strong. You are held in honor, but we in disrepute" (1 Cor. 4:10). These divergent understandings of the practical implications of the Christian gospel become the subject of many discussions in 1 Corinthians.

This position of boasting and arrogance is not limited to the realm of abstract pronouncements and theologizing; it has definite implications for the day-to-day behavior of these Corinthian Christians. Their arrogance leads to dissension bordering on disunity, criticism of Paul himself for his lack of oratorical eloquence, immorality, selfishness, disregard of the lesser brother or sister, misunderstanding of the gifts and grace of God, failure to understand the church as a community, and the distorted view of the resurrection we have already noted. It is into this concrete situation that Paul must actualize the gospel message. This Corinthian church has real needs and problems and Paul must now address them precisely, relevantly, and cogently. Before we can witness Paul's process of actualization, we must first examine the negative consequence of the Corinthians' arrogance and then Paul's response to it.

Pride, which lies at the root of arrogance, is hardly a characteristic that leads to community building. By its very definition it elevates an individual or a small group above others and this has a splintering and divisive effect. As Reinhold Niebuhr so often stresses, pride is nothing other than putting yourself into a position where you can spit down on your neighbor.[8] And so it is not surprising to find arrogance causing a tendency toward disunity in the fifties of the first century. In his opening remarks in 1 Corinthians 1, Paul appeals to them "that there be no dissensions among you" since he has heard from Chloe's people "that there is quarreling among you" (vv. 10–11). "What I mean is that each one of you says, 'I belong to Paul,' or 'I belong to Apollos,' or 'I belong to Cephas,' or 'I belong to Christ' " (v. 12). Then Paul comes to the heart of the matter with the question "Is Christ divided?" to which the obvious response must be a negative one (v. 13).

The notion that early Christianity is a perfect model that all successive followers of Jesus Christ should imitate is clearly undermined in 1 Corinthians, and elsewhere in the New Testament as well. The early church, as we shall repeatedly see, had the same frailties and difficulties as every other subsequent Christian generation. Since this is the case, the way in which such difficulties are resolved should be particularly illuminating for the contemporary church, where many of these same issues are reflected, not least of which is the problem of the disunity and fragmentation of Christianity.

Already in the mid–first century this same group of Corinthian Christians is rallying around different heroes: Paul, Apollos, Cephas, Christ. For this reason Paul writes in a sense of despair that "when you come together it is not for the better but for the worse. 18 For . . . when you assemble as a church, I hear that there are divisions among you" (1 Cor. 11:17b–18). What is the logic for these divided loyalties? Some wished to elevate Paul as their leader/hero for the obvious reason that he was both an apostle and the founder of the community. Apollos, Paul's successor, apparently possessed oratorical skills that pleased many in this Hellenistic environment, skills that Paul by his own testimony did not possess (1 Cor. 2:1–5), but for the absence of which he was roundly criticized (cf. 2 Cor. 10:10). Acts 18:24 describes Apollos as "an eloquent man, well versed in the scriptures." The references to Cephas and Christ are more difficult. Cephas, the Aramaic surname given to Peter by the resurrected Jesus meaning "rock," was clearly the most important figure in Christianity at this time and perhaps even had visited Corinth; either way he was well known.[9] If one is going to select a hero, some are undoubtedly asking, "Why not go directly to the head man in Jerusalem?" This group may also have been attracted to Peter's more conservative Jewish-Christian background. Whether the reference to Christ represents the leader of a fourth party of arrogant elitists or represents those disgusted with the party strife is difficult to determine. Given the tone of the remainder of 1 Corinthians, there is much to be said for the position of two recent commentators that the "Christ party" is a fourth group of arrogant, elitist Christians to whom much of the remainder of the letter is addressed.[10]

"Is Christ divided? Was Paul crucified for you?" (1:13). In demonstrating the absurdity of a positive answer to these questions, Paul must defend the message he proclaims and himself, as well as deflate the boasting of the Corinthians and clarify the relationship of apostles and servants to Jesus Christ. The task for Paul is not an easy one since he has to contend with religious presuppositions and philosophical categories of thought alien to his understanding of the gospel.

Paul forcefully points out that their arrogance is at odds with the gospel as it was originally proclaimed to them. The content of this gospel is not a way to religious perfection, but the power of the cross of Christ. The religious hero of Christianity is not some divine being who is elevated above ordinary men and women, but one who was crucified.[11] At this point Christianity breaks sharply with its culture. "For Jews demand signs and Greeks seek wisdom, 23 but we preach Christ crucified, a stumbling block to Jews and folly to Gentiles, 24 but to those who are called, both Jews and Gentiles, Christ the power of God and the wisdom of God" (1 Cor. 1:22–24). The ethical consequence that the religious hero for early Christians is a crucified messiah will be drawn throughout 1 Corinthians. Essentially it will issue in a repeated call to humility, concern for the weaker brother, and the upbuilding of the church.

Already here in chapter 1, Paul draws some conclusions from

the fact that the messiah whom the Corinthians proclaim is a crucified messiah. When one says yes to the call of Christ, it implies neither immediate perfection nor an automatic guarantee of salvation. Rather, the Christian life is a process and here in 1:18 it is appropriately expressed in participial form: "For the word of the cross is folly to those who are perishing, but to us who are being saved it is the power of God." Note well the phrase "to us who are *being* saved." This understanding of the Christian life as a process of growth in obedience to the will of God is a dimension many of the Corinthians overlooked and an element Paul deals frequently with in varied ways throughout this first letter to the Corinthians.

Paul must also challenge the Corinthian's perception of what it means to be an apostle. Here, too, he must demonstrate that the call to be a Christian apostle is not at all similar to the expectations of Hellenistic culture. The criteria for evaluation are not philosophical erudition or rhetorical skill, but faithfulness to the gospel of the crucified Lord. "When I came to you, brethren, I did not come proclaiming to you the testimony of God in lofty words of wisdom. 2 For I decided to know nothing among you except Jesus Christ and him crucified" (1 Cor. 2:1–2).

The Corinthian view of apostleship, significantly influenced by Hellenistic culture, leads them to misunderstand the relation of Christian workers to one another. The relationship is not marked by competition in trying to outdistance one another as is the case among the wandering preachers and apostles in their environment. Rather, all Christian teachers and preachers are subject to the Lord and to do as he assigns to each. "What then is Apollos? What is Paul? Servants through whom you believed, as the Lord assigned to each. 6 I planted, Apollos watered, but God gave the growth. 7 So neither he who plants nor he who waters is anything, but only God who gives the growth" (1 Cor. 3:5–7). Furthermore, Paul must indicate that the foundation of the Christian church is Jesus Christ, that fact alone reduces to absurdity the rivalry that is developing in Corinth. Appropriately Paul concludes the chapter with this exhortation: "So let no one boast of men" (1 Cor. 3:21).

It is becoming apparent that when Paul first proclaimed the gospel to these Corinthians they perceived it through the religious, philosophical, and cultural glasses of their situation. This led to misunderstandings and distortions. Paul's task, having been alerted to these problems by Chloe's people and a letter from some in the Corinthian congregation (1 Cor. 7:1), is to clarify, redefine, and make concrete the gospel of the cross for these Corinthians in their very specific cultural situation. We must now examine more closely the consequences of this Corinthian arrogance in specific acts of immortality, selfishness, disregard for their brothers and sisters in Christ, and how Paul applied the gospel to these deviations.

Individualistic Freedom and the Community of Love

The arrogance of the Corinthian Christians that led to a false view of Christian perfection also resulted in a totally distorted understanding of the individual, especially in his or her relationship to the community and with regard to the concept of freedom.

As we shall explore more fully in our discussion of Paul's use of the term justification, the apostle essentially viewed humans as belonging to one of two specific social institutions: the world or the body of Christ, the church. The world is dominated by the power of sin, and this life in Adam results in a lifestyle characterized by "fornication, impurity, licentiousness, 20 idolatry, sorcery, enmity, strife, jealousy, anger, selfishness, dissension, party spirit, 21 envy, drunkenness, carousing, and the like" (Gal. 5:19–21). The church is dominated by the power of the Holy Spirit, and this life in Christ results in a lifestyle characterized by "love, joy, peace, patience, kindness, goodness, faithfulness, 23 gentleness, self-control . . ." (Gal. 5:22–23).

In the first place, then, there is no such thing as "individual" freedom since every human being is bound to one of these two groups: this immediately puts a severe limitation on the category of "freedom" and specifically eliminates the view that an individual is free to do anything as a being in isolation from others. In fact, Paul argues that men and women are totally unable to, in other words lack the freedom to, move from life under the power of sin to life under the power of the spirit. The agonizing cry in Romans 7:15 ("I do not understand my own actions. For I do not do what I want, but I do the very thing I hate") refers precisely to this human dilemma. The ability to move from Adam to Christ, from the world to the church, is a gift given by Jesus Christ and received by the believer. Freedom for Paul has clearly defined limits—it involves movement from one well-defined social realm to the other. The transition from one to the other is freedom, and this is a gift; it is not and can never be claimed as a human achievement.

Does not Paul then use the term "freedom" as a description of human possibility in day-to-day activities? Quite definitely not. The term used is "slave." One is a slave either to the power of sin or to the power of the Spirit; freedom is the transition from one form of slavery to the other, from a type that leads to death to one that leads to life. This perspective of Paul should not really startle us if we have some acquaintance with Paul Tillich's phrase "ultimate concern."[12] Every human being, argues Tillich, has an ultimate concern—for example, power, wealth, God—and it is this ultimate concern that shapes our decisions and activities. We are free to act only within the parameters of our ultimate concern; we are, in fact, slaves to our ultimate concern. It is exactly this that Paul expresses in Romans 6:16: "Do you not know that if you yield yourselves to any one as obedient slaves, you are slaves of the one whom you obey, either of sin, which leads to death, or of obedience, which leads to righteousness?"

The Corinthians misunderstood Paul's initial preaching and held a view of freedom quite the opposite of the apostle's. They held that their new religion released them from all limitations and empowered them to do virtually anything they desired. This view not only so elevated the individual above the community so as to make him arrogant, but also made an existence of shared responsibility and concern within the new community of the church most difficult, if not impossible. Let us now turn to these problems that stem from a distorted view of freedom and also to Paul's reaction to them on the basis of the gospel.

The problems resulting from this misunderstanding of freedom and responsibility of the individual within the community dominate much of the discussion from chapter 5 to 14 of 1 Corinthians. Chapter 5 begins with a man who so misunderstands his life in Christ that he believes he is now free to do anything. All restraints have vanished, and so he is having sexual relations with his father's wife! The apostle is incensed at this behavior for at least two reasons: the flagrant violation of the Christian ethic and the utter disregard for the community. The only appropriate response the gospel allows Paul is that of judgment and excommunication.

Those of us who have been influenced by a permissive culture might well ask, Is this not a rigid and narrow understanding of Christianity? What about mercy and grace? Is not Paul's attitude incongruent with the teaching of Jesus? Paul would certainly respond in the negative and if he were alive today he might even share Dietrich Bonhoeffer's distinction between cheap and costly grace, between a cheap and costly form of Christianity.[13] Costly grace attempts to be obedient to the will of God and understands that growth in grace requires discipline. As we have already noted briefly in our reference to Galatians 5 above, Paul affirms that the believer in Christ is now, in the present, enabled by the Spirit to do the will of God and to break with the behavior of the world. Consequently, he writes in 1 Corinthians 5:11, "But rather I wrote to you not to associate with any one who bears the name of brother if he is guilty of immortality or greed, or an idolater, reviler, drunkard, or robber—not even to eat with such a one." Those in Christ have broken with a lifestyle dominated by the power of sin and a return to that lifestyle cannot be tolerated in the new community since it would violate the very purpose of its existence. Here again this dual understanding of life, either Adam or Christ, world or church, is the basic presupposition of Pauline theology. He underscores this in 1 Corinthians 6:9–11, in all probability incorporating some traditional language of the church. "Do you not know that the unrighteous will not inherit the kingdom of God? Do not be deceived; neither the immoral, nor idolaters, nor adulterers, nor sexual perverts, 10 nor thieves, nor the greedy, nor drunkards, nor revilers, nor robbers will inherit the kingdom of God. 11 And such were some of you. But you were washed, you were sanctified, you were justified in the name of the Lord Jesus Christ and in the Spirit of our God." Precisely because Christians have been "washed," "sanctified," and "justified" the kind of immoral behavior referred to in 1 Corinthians 5 cannot be tolerated. And if persons persist in such behavior as is apparently the case in chapter 5, they must be removed from the community, not only because a contradiction exists between their confession and their behavior, but because their actions actually do damage to the community.

How can one person's immorality affect the whole community to the point that this person must be removed? Essential here is Paul's understanding of the church as the body of Christ. For the apostle the new community in Christ is so tightly knit, such a cohesive social unit, that he can compare it to the human body in 1 Corinthians 12. The human body is made up of many parts —fingers, eyes, ears, feet, and so forth. These cannot function alone and if they do not all work together, there is no body. When one is sick, the entire body is affected. So in the Christian community the believer is a part of the body and has been given a distinctive function in it. The point being stressed is that the whole affects the individual as the individual affects the whole. The Christian ought, therefore, to be so intertwined with the others that if "one member suffers, all suffer together; if one member is honored, all rejoice together" (1 Cor. 12:26).

In light of this it should become apparent to us that in 1 Corinthians 5 Paul is not only concerned about the one person who has disobeyed God's will but also with the effect of that person's actions upon the whole. In the same way that a cancerous tumor affects the whole body in a negative way, so the immoral behavior of the one affects the entire community. So Paul writes to the Corinthians in 5:6b–8: precisely because the church is God's new lump, "the leaven of malice and evil" that belongs to the realm of the flesh and not to the Spirit must be removed from its midst.

Implicit in our discussion thus far is that Paul takes very seriously the matter of discipline as an intrinsic part of the Christian growth process. The apostle and the community must provide correction and admonition so that each Christian, and the congregation as a whole, will be assisted in obeying the will of God. Again the apostle underlines the fact that the Christian is not perfected at baptism and that it is possible when discipline and mutual support are absent to fall back into the old way of life and therefore to have believed in vain. Paul summarizes this matter well in 1 Corinthians 11:32: "But when we are judged by the Lord, we are chastened [literally, disciplined] so that we may not be condemned along with the world." It is increasingly apparent how crucial it is for the apostle that the gospel be actualized and made relevant to every dimension of the Christian life.

The problem of individual freedom in relation to one's participation in the community of Christ can be seen from another dimension in 1 Corinthians 6:1–8:

When one of you has a grievance against a brother, does he dare go to law before the unrighteous instead of the saints? 2 Do you not know that the saints will judge the world? And if the world is to be judged by you, are you incompetent to try trivial cases? 3 Do you not know that we are to judge angels? How much more, matters pertaining to this life! 4 If then you have such cases, why do you lay them before those who are least esteemed by the church? 5 I say this to your shame. Can it be that there is no man among you wise enough to decide between members of the brotherhood, 6 but brother goes to law against brother, and that before unbelievers?

7 To have lawsuits at all with one another is defeat for you. Why not rather suffer wrong? Why not rather be defrauded? 8 But you yourselves wrong and defraud, and that even your own brethren.

For those of us who live in a litigious society where many relationships of trust have broken down, these words must sound as strange as they did to the Corinthians living in the midst of a very

pagan society. Paul has at least two objections with regard to
Christians having lawsuits against one another: (1) It is an exercise in pride that is bound to create animosity rather than reconciliation. When Paul argues in verse 7 that to "have lawsuits at
all with one another is defeat for you," it is quite likely that he
has in mind the words of Jesus about turning the other cheek. (2)
To have lawsuits against one another is a very direct violation of
the most important principle that serves as the fundamental criterion for all Christian decisions, *agape,* love, a theme further developed in 1 Corinthians 13. Lawsuits must by necessity be decided
in secular law courts and that undermines the very uniqueness of
the Christian community. In such situations the new ethic and
lifestyle of the body of Christ given to it by the Holy Spirit has
capitulated to the old ethic of the world; for Paul such compromise cannot be tolerated. For Christians to believe that they are
free to step outside the bounds permitted by life in the new
community for the sake of serving their self-interest must be
repudiated. It is not accidental that the next verse reads: "Do you
not know that the unrighteous will not inherit the kingdom of
God? Do not be deceived . . ." (v. 9a). It is simply a contradiction
to claim allegiance to the Christian community and then to violate its principles when it suits one's individual needs. That is
nothing other than using "unrighteous" rather than "righteous"
means and God will not be deceived on the last day when all
secrets are revealed before him.

Toward the middle of 1 Corinthians 6 we receive very specific
insight into the Corinthians' misunderstanding of the gospel.
Their slogan is, "All things are lawful for me" (v. 12), to which
Paul responds that "not all things are helpful." The Corinthian
slogan is repeated in the next verse and again in 10:23. In verses
23 and 24 we come to the heart of the misunderstanding between
individual freedom and community responsibility: " 'All things
are lawful,' but not all things build up. 24 Let no one seek his own
good, but the good of his neighbor." For the apostle the sign of
being a Christian is not talk, but action—action that is concerned

with the common good of the community in general, and of its members specifically.

The Corinthians tried to justify all kinds of activity under the slogan that now in Christ "all things are lawful," including such things as temple prostitution. Let us examine only one of these activities, eating idol food, together with Paul's response to it in 1 Corinthians 8. (Eating idol food is the practice of eating the meat from an animal sacrificed to a heathen god as part of cultic worship.) The freedom to eat food offered to idols is defended by the Corinthians with reference to the concept of "knowledge." In all likelihood Paul is repeating a Corinthian slogan in 8:1: "All of us possess knowledge." As we know from 1 Corinthians 12:8, Paul recognizes the importance of knowledge as a gift of the Spirit, but it, like all gifts of the Spirit, is subservient to the most important gift of all, love *(agape),* a concept we examine in great detail shortly. Knowledge "puffs up" whereas love "builds up" (8:1). Knowledge has the tendency to make the individuals arrogant insofar as they believes that they have greater knowledge than others and are therefore superior. Love, however, is concerned with others, especially the weak neighbor in Christ, and it is such compassion that leads to the upbuilding of the community. The incompleteness of knowledge is also referred to in verse 2: "If any one imagines that he knows something, he does not yet know as he ought to know." A little knowledge has the tendency to make one heady and to make one imagine that one knows more than one really does. To "know as one ought to know" is to be truly wise and to recognize that the more one knows, the more one is aware of how little one really knows. True knowledge leads to humility. For as Paul correctly suggests in 1 Corinthians 13:9, our present knowledge is imperfect. These, then, are some of the reasons why Paul does not place knowledge in a central position in his efforts to advise the Corinthians on food offered to idols.

But what is the content of this knowledge to which the Corinthians refer? Paul apparently repeats their language in 8:4: "We know that 'an idol has no real existence,' and that 'there is no God but one.' " On this basis some of the members of the congregation argued that it was perfectly acceptable to eat food that had been offered to pagan idols since a Christian knows that such idols really do not exist, since "there is one God, the Father, from whom are all things and for whom we exist, and one Lord, Jesus Christ, through whom are all things and through whom we exist" (v. 6). Theoretically, Paul has no problem with this theological position; it is a correct assertion about the Lordship of Christ. But to use this theological insight to support eating food offered to the idols overlooks one important human dimension: "Not all possess this knowledge" (8:7). Some members of the Christian church in Corinth are weak; their consciences are not yet fully mature in Christ and so it is possible that they would be tempted to think that if they ate food that had been offered to an idol it would in fact be an act of worship to such idols. And the result for such weak persons would be that "their conscience, being weak, is defiled" (v. 7).

The heart of the matter is expressed by the apostle in 8:9: "Only take care lest this liberty of yours somehow become a stumbling block to the weak." Christian freedom and Christian knowledge do have a specific boundary beyond which they become demonic; that boundary is the point at which they cause the weak brother or sister to stumble. Thus, while sitting at table in an idol's temple is abstractly a Christian possibility, it is to be avoided because "if any one sees you, a man of knowledge, at table in an idol's temple, might he not be encouraged, if his conscience is weak, to eat food offered to idols?" (v. 10). The result of such action is that "by your knowledge this weak man is destroyed, the brother for whom Christ died" (v. 11).

The weak man is not simply some computerized number, but the brother for whom Christ died. Therefore he is of infinite value and dare not be disregarded, overlooked, or trampled upon. In verse 12 Paul intensifies the value of the weak man. He urges the Corinthians to remember that when their personal freedom becomes more important than their concern for the weak man, they are involved in sinning against their brethren and "wounding their conscience when it is weak," and thus they "sin against Christ" (v. 12). This identification of the brother with Christ in 1 Corinthians is quite similar to the point being made in Matthew 25:40, "Truly, I say to you, as you did it to one of the least of these my brethren, you did it to me."

Paul's final conclusion to the argument in chapter 8 is this: "Therefore, if food is a cause of my brother's falling, I will never eat meat, lest I cause my brother to fall." A modern analogy might be: if I am at a cocktail hour and I am with a friend who has a problem with alcohol, while I am at liberty to drink my martini, I will forego this liberty for the sake of the weak brother and request a ginger ale. My freedom and my knowledge must never violate the law of love; to do so would allow my brother or sister to fall.

Just as we have seen Paul actualize the event of the resurrection in order to clarify the misunderstandings of the Corinthian Christians with regard to that matter and just as we have witnessed how Paul applies an important dimension of the gospel tradition to the problem of whether or not to eat idol meat, so in 1 Corinthians 11 we observe how Paul takes up the tradition of the Lord's supper and actualizes it in the midst of the Corinthian abuse of that communal meal.

Paul's irritation at the Corinthian practice of the Lord's Supper is evident in 11:17: "In the following instructions I do not commend you, because when you come together it is not for the better but for the worse." When they gather together there are "divisions" and "factions" (11:18). Because of this, Paul is bold enough to tell the Corinthians that when they meet together "it is not the Lord's supper that you eat" (v. 20).

In order to understand the nature of Paul's concern one must realize that early Christians originally celebrated what is today referred to as the eucharist as a common meal. It was a supper but because it was done in the name of their Lord it was quite naturally called "the Lord's supper." The abuse set in when some members of the congregation set aside the communal nature of the meal and simply ate and drank their fill quite unmindful that by so doing there would not be enough for all. It almost appears as if members of the leisure class got there first and immediately began filling themselves without any regard for the poor working man who could only get there upon the completion of his job. Thus Paul chides them in verse 22: "What! Do you not have houses to eat and drink in? Or do you despise the church of God and humiliate those who have nothing? What shall I say to you? Shall I commend you in this? No, I will not."

1 Corinthians 11:23–26 contains the earliest account of the words of institution. Paul adds in verse 26: "For as often as you eat this bread and drink the cup, you proclaim the Lord's death until he comes." Participation in the Lord's supper is not an opportunity for overeating or a magical guarantee of salvation (so the tendency in 1 Cor. 10) or merely a meaningless religious rite, but it is a participation in and remembrance of the death of their Lord. Participation in his death means participation in his community, the lifestyle of which is not an individual ego trip leading to boasting, but a humility that results in service to others. It is this latter lifestyle that must be proclaimed and lived "until he comes" (11:26). As the apostle already made clear in chapter 1, the Christian lives in anticipation of God's final judgment and the fulfillment of his promises.

Since the confession of Christ's name alone is not an automatic guarantee of God's favor on the last day, Paul adds some firm warnings in verse 27 and following in a manner similar to his warnings in chapter 10. Having briefly reviewed the history of Israel, he concludes in 10:5–6, "Nevertheless with most of them God was not pleased; for they were overthrown in the wilderness. 6 Now these things are warnings for us, not to desire evil as they did." And then in verse 12 we read, "Therefore let any one who thinks that he stands take heed lest he fall." In like manner Paul exhorts this congregation in 11:28–29: "Let a man examine himself, and so eat of the bread and drink of the cup. 29 For any one who eats and drinks without discerning the body eats and drinks judgment upon himself." To participate in the Lord's supper is not a neutral affair—its consequences are either blessings or curses, salvation or condemnation. Since there are these two possibilities, the Christian must examine himself to be certain that he does not partake in "an unworthy manner" since the consequence of such participation would lead them to "come together to be condemned" (v. 34).

In 1 Corinthians 12 Paul discusses the nature of the church in the context of spiritual gifts. As is evident from 1 Corinthians, these Christians prided themselves in having received spiritual gifts. Paul must remind them that gifts of the Spirit are not to be used for vain self-glorying but for the "common good." God is the giver, and God gives different gifts to different persons for the upbuilding of the church and not as a source of individual boasting over each other. "To each is given the manifestation of the Spirit for the common good" (v. 7). To further illustrate the "common good" Paul develops the analogy of the church as the body of Christ.

"For the body does not consist of one member but of many" (v. 14). While such an assertion may strike us as obvious, it is essential for the Corinthians to have this stressed because of their hyper-individualism and their failure to grasp that their existence in Christ involves participation in a new social relationship. Obviously some are going around boasting how great they are because, for example, they can speak in tongues (1 Cor. 13:1; 14). Precisely because of this tendency Paul writes: "If the foot should say, 'Because I am not a hand, I do not belong to the body,' that would not make it any less a part of the body. 16 And if the ear should say, 'Because I am not an eye, I do not belong to the body,' that would not make it any less a part of the body. 17 If the whole body were an eye, where would be the hearing? If the whole body were an ear, where would be the sense of smell? 18 But as it is, God arranged the organs in the body, each one of them, as he chose" (1 Cor. 12:15–18). Similarly, God chose what gift he was to give every member of the body of Christ and they are to be used in a cooperative and complementary way for the effective functioning of the church. The cohesive interaction must be such that "there may be no discord in the body, but that the members may have the same care for one another. 26 If one member suffers, all suffer together; if one member is honored, all rejoice together" (1 Cor. 12:25–26). Just as when one part of the human body is infected it affects the whole, or when we hear exciting news our entire body is ecstatic, so it must be in the life of the church. What a challenge Paul presents to the church in all ages!

We would argue that Paul's discussion of love *(agape)* in 1 Corinthians 13 is both the high point of his letter to the Corinthians as well as the basic criterion he uses in applying the gospel to the problems of this congregation. As we shall see not only in this chapter but in 1 Corinthians 14 as well, he expects that the gift of love is to be the criterion used in all decisions affecting the Christian life and church. In using the term *agape,* Paul uses the word used most frequently in the early Christian tradition to speak of that love for the other that has as its referent point God's self-giving and self-sacrificing love, as demonstrated in the suffering and death of his son. It is this gift of the Spirit, love, which excels all others and without which the other gifts of the Spirit are without value. If this love is anchored in the suffering and generous love of God in Christ, its constant concern is for the other—the neighbor, the weak person—so that it will lead to the "upbuilding, encouragement and consolation" (1 Cor. 14:3) of the body of Christ. *Agape* uses the individual as an instrument for the edification of the common good.

Paul begins chapter 13 by reviewing a number of spiritual gifts the Corinthian Christians held in high regard: speaking in tongues, having prophetic power, understanding mysteries and knowledge, having faith, being charitable, and even being willing to die as a martyr. If these gifts are not performed in the context of love, that is for the edification of the church rather than for self-boasting, they are empty and void. It is particularly noteworthy that Paul makes faith, even a faith that can "remove mountains" (1 Cor. 13:2), subservient to love. Faith, as the apostle says in Galatians 5:6, must always be active in love. Faith that does not manifest its own relationship with God in acts of concrete love is without value. This point is underlined in the conclusion to chapter 13: "So faith, hope, love abide, these three; but the greatest of these is love" (v. 13).

In verses 4–7 the characteristics of love are described, and in verse 8 and following the apostle gives support for the superiority of love to the other spiritual gifts. "Love never ends"—it has an enduring value whereas all other gifts have some temporal limit to their usefulness to the community (v. 8). Prophecies— that is, the critical application of God's Word to specific situations—whether they be of Amos, Jeremiah, or Martin Luther King, Jr., are limited and time-bound by the very specificity of their intention. The state of inspiration that allows one to speak in tongues does not continue without end. Knowledge, too, it is said, "will pass away" and "is imperfect" (vv. 8–9). All we have to do is to reflect upon the status of any scientific discipline, for example physics, at the beginning and the end of the twentieth century to realize how quickly our knowledge advances and revises previously held hypotheses. Paul concludes his great exposition on love with the reminder that Christian existence is still being lived in a situation of eschatological reservation, in the "already/not yet" situation. Already now we share in the good gifts of God's salvific action in Christ Jesus, but not yet in its final, fulfilled and consummated state, which is still before us. For that reason our knowledge is imperfect and our prophecy is imperfect (v. 10). "For now we see in a mirror dimly, but then face to face. Now I know in part; then I shall understand fully, even as I have been fully understood" (v. 12).

To make absolutely sure that his point about the necessity and primacy of love has not been misunderstood, Paul singles out one gift of the Spirit, speaking in tongues, for special attention in 1 Corinthians 14. It is a marvelous chapter because it is one of Paul's greatest attempts to actualize the gospel—in this case the relationship of love to speaking in tongues. Beyond that it contains a whole host of practical suggestions for the life of the church.

Already the first verse gives us much insight: "Make love your aim, and earnestly desire the spiritual gifts, especially that you may prophesy" (14:1). Here as in Galatians 5:22, love is preeminent over every other gift of the Spirit; in fact one might say that all other gifts of the Spirit flow from the greatest gift of all, love, and that they are actualizations of it. Of these various actualizations of love it is clear that Paul gives prophesy a very high rank, certainly in comparison with speaking in tongues. The basic problem of speaking in tongues is this: "For one who speaks in a tongue speaks not to men but to God; for no one understands him, but he utters mysteries in the Spirit" (v. 2). Here again we see clearly that the Christian's relation to God must always involve the other. There can be no private, individualistic Christianity that involves only the believer and God; it is precisely because speaking in tongues, a phenomenon with parallel in the Hellenistic religions of the day, involves only this singular relationship with God while overlooking the neighbor that Paul has serious reservations about it. One must underline at this point the word "reservations"; he does not reject it. The key to its acceptability is interpretation. If there are those who can interpret that which is normally unintelligible to the worshipping congregation, then and only then is it a useful contribution for the church. "If any speak in a tongue, let there be only two or at most three, and each in turn; and let one interpret. 28 But if there is no one to interpret, let each of them keep silence in church and speak to himself and to God" (vv. 27–28).

The reason the apostle speaks so highly about prophecy is that "he who prophesies speaks to men for their upbuilding and encouragement and consolation" (v. 3). As he further stresses in verse 26, *"all things"* must be done for the edification of the community. All activities of the Christian have one goal: the building up of the church in obedience to the call of God in Jesus Christ. Here as in several of the previous chapters we note the obvious tension between Paul's understanding of the church and the individualistic tendencies of the Corinthians.

As in 1 Corinthians 8 the freedom of the man of knowledge must be restrained by the concern for the weak brother, so in 1

Corinthians 14 the phenomenon of speaking in tongues must be interpreted so that the "other man," the man who cannot understand tongues, is edified. This is described with forcefulness in 1 Corinthians 14:13–19:

Therefore, he who speaks in a tongue should pray for the power to interpret. 14 For if I pray in a tongue, my spirit prays but my mind is unfruitful. 15 What am I to do? I will pray with the spirit and I will pray with the mind also; I will sing with the *spirit* and I will sing with the *mind* also. 16 Otherwise, if you bless with the spirit, how can any one in the position of an outsider say the "Amen" to your thanksgiving when he does not know what you are saying? 17 For you may give thanks well enough, but the other man is not edified. 18 I thank God that I speak in tongues more than you all; 19 nevertheless, in church I would rather speak five words with my mind, in order to instruct others, than ten thousand words in a tongue.

It is important to observe that when we sing or pray we do it with "the spirit . . . and the mind."[14] The Christian life is a combination of the Spirit and the mind for Paul. The apostle uses the classical Greek word *nous* for the critical, reflective principle, namely the mind. Life in the Spirit only would lead toward emotionalism; the life of the Spirit infused by the critical thinking of the mind allows the Christian to "test everything" (1 Thess. 5:21) and to critically judge whether his actions and those of the community are truly leading to the upbuilding of all. A Christian life guided only by the mind would lead to that arrogance and insensitivity to the other that Paul rejects in 1 Corinthians 8. The mind operating in the context of the Spirit allows the Christian to be critically sensitive to the neighbor and the common good. Both the gifts of the Spirit and the mind have their origin in God; working together they excel in building up the church, working without each other they lead either to emotionalism that is immature or to abstract theological activity that has no relevance to life. Others cannot be instructed, as Paul urges in verse 19, with unintelligible, sloppy nonsense; there must be solid content. Yet that content cannot be communicated effectively and with sensitivity if it is not presented in the context of love.

Once again we have seen how with insight and with simplicity Paul has actualized and applied the gospel to a unique situation in Corinth. In the same way that the apostle urges the individual members of the Christian church to look beyond themselves to the common good, he urges the Corinthian church to look beyond itself to the universal church. He does this at least twice. First, in 1 Corinthians 1:2 he reminds them that they are "called to be saints together with all those who in every place call on the name of our Lord Jesus Christ, both their Lord and ours." This, together with the reference to "the church of God which is at Corinth," is a clear indication that the Corinthian church is a part of a much larger plan (1:2). They are merely one part, an important part to be sure, but their group is not the total operation itself.

Second, in 1 Corinthians 16:1 and following Paul speaks about a "contribution for the saints." What is this contribution or collection for the saints?[15] In addition to this reference there are several others in the Pauline corpus. Especially helpful is the reference in Romans 15:25–27:

At present, however, I am going to Jerusalem with aid for the saints. 26 For Macedonia and Achaia have been pleased to make some contribution for the poor among the saints at Jerusalem; 27 they were pleased to do it, and indeed they are in debt to them, for if the Gentiles have come to share in their spiritual blessings, they ought also to be of service to them in material blessings.

From these remarks in 1 Corinthians and Romans, it becomes apparent that the "saints" are the Christians in the Jerusalem church who are having financial difficulties. Paul calls not only upon the Corinthian compassion for the weaker brother and sister as motivation for the contribution, but also upon a sense of obligation or, more accurately, mutual interdependence with the Jerusalem church. For "if the Gentiles [including the Corinthians] have come to share in their spiritual blessings, they ought also to be of service to them [the Jerusalem church] in material blessings" (Rom. 15:27). The Corinthians are indebted to the Jerusalem church for their spiritual blessings in the sense that it was from and through Jerusalem that the gospel was proclaimed to the nations. In this sense, Jerusalem had a gift that it shared with the Graeco-Roman world and the Corinthian Christians, along with others, were recipients of this gift. Now, in a new moment in history the Gentile Christians have a gift, financial means, that the Jerusalem Christians have need of—and Paul encourages them, based on the theological principle of mutuality and interdependence to give generously to "the poor among the saints," and in so doing to look beyond themselves to the world-wide church. Already in the earliest days of Christianity there is a social consciousness and a universal perspective.

2. Paul's Understanding of Salvation

The most important way Paul actualizes the significance of the Christ event in his theology is by use of the concept "justification." In his writings this term emerges explicitly, as in Galatians and Romans, or implicitly, but still as the basic substructure of his theology, as in 1 Corinthians. Since the concept of justification and its relationship to salvation and last judgment is so critical for an understanding of Pauline theology, it is well for us to devote a few pages to these themes.[1]

Justification

The starting point for any understanding of Pauline theology must be his understanding of justification. Ernst Käsemann is to be credited with igniting the current discussions on justification with his 1961 article, " 'The Righteousness of God' in Paul."[2] Käsemann argues vigorously and forcefully that justification, together with the corollary term "righteousness of God," is much more than simply God's gift to man. When understood in this limited way, as it appears in Bultmann's theology,[3] not only does the gift character become isolated, resulting in an unbalanced individualism, but the eschatological tensions in Pauline theology, particularly between beginning and end, are either reduced to insignificance or entirely ignored. For Käsemann, justification and the term "righteousness of God" certainly include the gift character, but they are viewed as part of a much broader historical and eschatological context: *"dikaiōsynē theou* [righteousness of

God] is for Paul God's sovereignty over the world revealing itself eschatologically in Jesus."[4] God's gift to man in Jesus Christ is a manifestation of the God who has been faithful to his people and who reveals himself in sovereignty and power. When this larger context of the sovereign God revealing himself is ignored, "the inevitable result is that the Pauline anthropology is sucked under by the pull of an individualistic outlook."[5] The value of Käsemann's approach to justification is that it avoids this danger of absolutizing the meaning of the term as "gift" in individualistic categories. Rather, justification is regarded as *Gabe und Aufgabe* (gift and responsibility). It contains a present and a future dimension—it is "a matter of promise and expectation."[6]

The gift involved in justification is not automatic; it remains a gift only as long as there is daily allegiance and obedience to Christ. For this reason Paul can speak of present and future judgment as an integral part of his theology. The righteousness of God which is revealed in Christ recaptures man for the sovereignty of God; this sovereign God acts not only in mercy but also in judgment to those who reject him, to those who no longer remain obedient, and who consequently fail to actualize his promise.

The Roman Catholic scholar Karl Kertelge has developed with rich insight some of Käsemann's pregnant suggestions. His excellent monograph, *Rechtfertigung bei Paulus* (Justification in Paul),[7] presents us with some fruitful suggestions for a clearer understanding of the relationship between justification and last judgment.

One of Kertelge's fundamental themes is based upon Käsemann's observation that when Paul speaks of the "gift of righteousness" in Romans 5:17, he is referring to a gift that is both present and future, already received and still expected.[8] For both Kertelge and Käsemann, God's righteousness is a gift in the present, but a gift that at the same time recognizes God's sovereign power and the fact that the redeemed man is placed under that power in obedient service. This grace and power of God as "promise" presupposes an eschatological framework of "al-

ready/not yet." For the justified man salvation is not yet completed in the present; it has still to be consummated and fulfilled
on the last day. Only as the Christian waits and hopes is he saved
(Rom. 8:23–25; Gal. 5:5). Kertelge suggests that both Bultmann
and Conzelmann have not properly understood this dimension
of Pauline thought.[9] Bultmann overstresses the present nature of
dikaiōsynē and Conzelmann dismisses the "not yet" dimension of
salvation as a polemic primarily directed against Corinthian en-
thusiasts. As a correction of this typical misunderstanding of
Paul, Kertelge argues that both the present *and* future dimension
of salvation must be taken seriously.[10]

What is the critical component or link between the already
realized dimension of salvation experienced in justification and
that which is yet to be actualized? Kertelge, again acknowledging
his dependence upon Käsemann, demonstrates in both a creative
and detailed way that the critical component is "obedience."[11]
"For Paul faith always means obedience to the saving will of God
and contains, therefore, an active element insofar as man responds to the expectation of God."[12] This interpretation is
demonstrated by a careful exegesis of Romans 6, particularly
verses 12–23. Sanctification (6:19, *eis hagiasmon*), the development and maturation of the Christian life in Christ, is an integral
part of justification and can only be accomplished in obedience
to the will of Christ (Rom. 6:16). Sanctification serves both to
elucidate and to preserve what has taken place in justification.
Only when this is carried out in obedience will God fulfill what
he has begun.

Thus far we have attempted to show that justification must be
the starting point for Paul's understanding of salvation and last
judgment, and we have reviewed two recent studies on justification that appear to have set the stage for a reevaluation of the
relationship of these categories in Pauline theology. Before we
proceed to discuss Paul's specific remarks about salvation and
last judgment, it will be helpful to review briefly his attitude
toward the entire scope of the Christian life, from beginning to
end.

Justification and the Christian Life

For Paul, justification marks the beginning of the Christian life. As man receives the revelation of the sovereign creator in Jesus Christ by faith, his broken relationship with God is restored and becomes whole. God now offers the new Christian, through the gift of his Spirit, the possibility of leading a new life that is both obedient to him and responsive to the needs of his fellow men. The Spirit permits man to live *en hagiasmos,* traditionally referred to as sanctification. As man continues to participate obediently in the process of sanctification granted him by God, this process will lead to the final fulfillment of that which began in baptism, namely, the gift of salvation to be consummated at the last day.

The fact that sanctification is the process of living out the Christian life between justification and the last day is made clear at several points, specifically Romans 6:19 and 22: "For just as you once yielded your members to impurity and to greater and greater iniquity, so now yield your members to righteousness for sanctification. . . . 22 But now that you have been set free from sin and have become slaves of God, the return you get is sanctification and its end, eternal life." Sanctification, based upon justification, leads to the final gift of salvation, eternal life.[13] That the life of the Christian is in fact a process that has a beginning and an endpoint is also made abundantly clear in 1 Corinthians and Philippians. In language very similar to the Synoptic logion "many are called but few are chosen," Paul warns the Corinthians that there is nothing automatic about the Christian life. He reminds them that not every athlete receives a prize (1 Cor. 9:24ff.) and that, in fact, God was not pleased with the behavior of Israel (1 Cor. 10:1ff.).[14] It is only the Christian who both competes in the race and who is pleasing to God (10:5) who will receive the prize. This is exactly Paul's point in Philippians 2:12 where he urges the Philippians to work out their "own salvation with fear and trembling." The seriousness with which Paul affirms that salvation is not yet a fully possessed gift is affirmed in Philippians 3:12 and following: "Not that I have already obtained this [the resurrection from the dead] or am already perfect; but I press on to make it my own. . . . 14 I press on toward the goal for the prize of the upward call of God in Christ Jesus." In short, the Christian life is a process that begins in justification, is actualized in sanctification, and is consummated with salvation. Critical for the final reception of salvation is man's continued obedience and openness to God's freely offered gift of the Spirit who is at work in the believer as a part of the body of Christ.[15]

This brief discussion should assist our understanding of a Pauline text that is of fundamental importance, Romans 5:9–10: "Since, therefore, we are now justified by his blood, much more shall we be saved by him from the wrath of God. 10 For if while we were enemies we were reconciled to God by the death of his Son, much more, now that we are reconciled, shall we be saved by his life." What is crystal clear from this text is that Paul, speaking to a Christian congregation, refers to justification as an event in which they have and continue to participate and to salvation as a future event in which they have yet to participate fully. In this particular text Paul expresses a strong confidence that the one who is justified shall also be saved on the day of wrath. But what is of interest is that despite Paul's strong confidence, he does not simply conflate salvation with justification. They remain two distinct points along the trajectory of the Christian life. Nor should one think that Romans 5:9–12 is a unique text. The regular pattern in the Pauline letters is that *dikaioō* (to justify) refers to the beginning of the life in Christ, and that *sōzō* (to save) and *sōtēria* (salvation) refer to an event yet to be consummated. A few examples must suffice. In his discussion of baptism in Romans 6, Paul writes in verse 7: "For he who has died is freed [*dedikaiōtai* (perfect)] from sin." Not only is the event of death with Christ and justification a past event, but Paul also is very careful to point out in this context that resurrection is a future possibility, not a present reality.[16] We died with Christ so that "we too might walk [*peripatēsōmen* (subjunctive)] in newness of life" (v. 4). Also important as a summary expression of Paul's intent in using *dikaioō* is the formula, perhaps pre-Pauline, in 1 Corinthians 6:11: "But you were washed, you were sanctified, you were justified [*edikai-ōthēte*] in the name of the Lord Jesus Christ and in the Spirit of our God." More important than observing the obvious, that is, that justification refers to a past event with continuing significance for the Christian, is the less frequently noted fact that for Paul *sōzō* and *sōtēria* have an explicitly future reference.

Two texts in particular support Paul's use of the future passive of *sōzō* in Romans 5:9 to indicate the futurity of the consummated gift of salvation: 1 Thessalonians 5:8, where he refers to the "hope of salvation" which is immediately followed by the thought that God has destined us to obtain salvation; and Romans 13:11, where the Romans are reminded that "salvation is nearer to us now than when we first believed." This clearly indicates that salvation is a future event toward which the Christian moves; it is not yet a present possession. It is unimaginable for Paul[17] that a Christian could properly confess, "I have been saved." At most the Christian can assert that he is in the process of being saved (*sozomenois*, 1 Cor. 1:18). The Christian can give thanks not because he is already saved, but "because God chose you . . . to be saved [*eis sōtērian*], through sanctification [*en hagiasmō*] by the Spirit . . ." (2 Thess. 2:13).

The Pauline pattern we have observed might be summarized in the following way as different nuances of a single process:

1. justification—an initiating event that is actualized and made concrete through sanctification;
2. sanctification—a present process, dependent upon justification, that has future implications, namely consummated salvation;
3. salvation—a gift to be consummated in the future, already anticipated and partially experienced in justification and sanctification and clearly dependent upon them.

Even in those occasional texts where Paul uses *sōzō* in a present tense, there is no ground for confusion suggesting that salvation is now fully possessed or that the process leading to it is automatic. This can be seen in 1 Corinthians 15:1–2: "Now I would remind you, brethren, in what terms I preached to you the gospel, which you received, in which you stand, 2 by which you are saved [*sōzesthe*], *if you hold it fast* [*ei katechete*]—unless you believed in vain." Yes, the gospel is the means of salvation—but only if one holds fast to its power, only if one is obedient to its claim (Rom. 6:16f.). When one does not hold fast, when one is not obedient, then one has believed in vain (1 Cor. 15:2). In other words, the gospel is both gift and responsibility.

In light of these observations, I should like to propose the following preliminary thesis concerning the relationship between justification, salvation, and last judgment, a thesis that of necessity will have to be amplified and clarified as we proceed: Paul affirms that the persons who have received the gospel of God's gracious mercy by faith and who have been justified through it will receive the final gift of salvation at the last judgment. This is purely an act of God's grace that the believers will receive if they remain obedient to the gift of God and his Spirit. For persons who have been justified but who then make a mockery of God's gift by their gross abuse and disobedience, such ones will not receive the gift of salvation at the last judgment; and they will suffer the wrath of God (Rom. 5:9f.). Thus the final criterion at the last judgment is, for Paul, not how many good works one has performed—this is irrelevant since it is the Spirit that enables man to do those deeds of love—but whether one has held fast and remained obedient to the new life in Christ. It is the criterion of the obedience of faith (Rom. 1:5 and 16:26) that will enable us to understand many of the Pauline last-judgment texts to which we now turn.

Last Judgment

The Pauline texts dealing with last judgment can be divided into four main categories:

1. texts describing the universal judgment of all people, including non-Christians;

2. texts describing the judgment of Christians who have remained obedient;

3. texts describing the judgment of the apostolic work of Christian missionaries;

4. texts describing the judgment of Christians who have not been obedient to the hope of the gospel.

Within the limitations of this chapter, our primary focus will be on categories three and four, with only brief remarks directed to categories one and two.

Category 1. *Universal Judgment of All People*

The fact that Paul expects a universal judgment for all persons can clearly be assumed from his doctrine of the righteousness of God and justification, particularly since those themes are derived from the Old Testament and apocalyptic Judaism. However, Paul does not leave us guessing in this matter of a universal last judgment: he explicitly describes such a judgment for us. Two texts, one from an early and one from a late Pauline letter must suffice. According to 2 Thessalonians 1:8-9,[18] when God appears at the last day he will inflict "vengeance upon those who do not know God and upon those who do not obey the gospel of our Lord Jesus. 9 They shall suffer the punishment of eternal destruction and exclusion from the presence of the Lord and from the glory of his might. . . ." This identical point is reiterated in Romans 2:5-6: "But by your hard and impenitent heart you are storing up wrath for yourself on the day of wrath when God's righteous judgment will be revealed. 6 For he will render to every man according to his works. . . ." This category of Pauline judgment texts can be summarized very briefly in the apostle's own language: "All . . . will be judged" (Rom. 2:12).

Category 2. *Judgment of Obedient Christians*

As we will hope to show, Paul expects a last judgment for Christians that can have one of two outcomes: it can be salvation for the Christian who has been obedient in faith or wrath for the one who has been disobedient to his calling in Christ. We turn now to the former of the two categories.

It is the intention of the gospel that the apostle proclaims to lead man to salvation (e.g., Rom. 1:16). While salvation begins already now in the present (2 Cor. 6:2), its final manifestation is still to be found in the future (Rom. 13:11; 1 Thess. 5:8–9). Justification can never be equated with salvation: justification is the beginning of the Christian life, salvation its consummation and fulfillment. How does one move from one to the other? One answer is given in 2 Thessalonians 2:13: ". . . God chose you from the beginning to be saved, through sanctification [*en hagiasmō*] by the Spirit and belief in the truth." Salvation is the natural and expected end result for the justified person through sanctification. Only through *eis hagiasmos* will one be pure and blameless on the day of Christ. To be pure and blameless on the day of Christ is an overriding concern of Paul for all his congregations (Phil. 1:10–11; 1 Cor. 1:8).

A concise summary of Paul's theology can be found in deutero-Pauline Colossians (deutero-Pauline refers to material written by Paul's disciples or co-workers after his death). In describing who will be found irreproachable on the last day, it presents the all-important Pauline conditions: "provided that you continue in the faith, stable and steadfast, not shifting from the hope of the gospel . . ." (1:23). It is the Christian who remains steadfast and firm,[19] in short, obedient to the hope of the gospel, who will receive the final gift of salvation. It is in this fact (namely that consummated salvation is still a future event) that the apostle's entire paraenesis (ethical exhortation) is anchored. Because the Christian must stand firm in sanctification, Paul warns his churches to be blameless (1 Cor. 1:8; Col. 1:22); faultless (1 Thess. 3:13; 5:23; Phil. 2:15); and sincere and unoffending (Phil. 1:10). In short, the Christian must work out his salvation in fear and trembling.

Even though Paul stresses that justification is purely an act of God's mercy and that sanctification is entirely the gift of God's Spirit, he is quick to warn his audience that these involve their active participation and obedience to God's continued goodness. Otherwise they will be like the men of Israel with whom God was not pleased; "for they were overthrown in the wilderness. 6 Now these things are warnings for us, not to desire evil as they did" (1 Cor. 10:5–6). And so, because Paul wants to present his bride pure and blameless on the last day (2 Cor. 11:2), he reminds his congregation of this last day in no uncertain terms. No man should transgress "because the Lord is an avenger in all these things . . ." (1 Thess. 4:6). We must be careful not to despise our brother because we must all appear "before the judgment seat of God" (Rom. 14:10) where "each one may receive good or evil, according to what he has done in the body" (2 Cor. 5:10). To simply dismiss these texts as relics from Paul's Jewish past is to fundamentally misunderstand the scope and richness of Pauline theology.

Category 3. *Judgment of Christian Apostolic Work*

There are at least two texts that, by the very nature of their context, must be placed in a separate category: 1 Corinthians 3:5–15 and 4:1–5. 1 Corinthians 3:15 ("If any man's work is burned up, he will suffer loss, though he himself will be saved, but only as through fire") can only be correctly interpreted if one understands the entire pericope in which it is found, since it must be questioned whether the common understanding that Paul is here discussing the sins of individual Christians is correct.[20]

The "introspective conscience of the West"[21] has tempted us to overlook both the missionary context of 1 Corinthians 3 as well as its apocalyptically conditioned language. We would contend that 1 Corinthians 3:5–15 has nothing to do with the sins of individual Christians nor with their consequent salvation in spite of their sins. In fact, we would even go so far as to argue that the verb *sōzō* (to save) in verse 15 has nothing to do with Christology and is used here in an entirely secular sense of "to rescue, to deliver from danger or harm."

The issue in 1 Corinthians 3 is party strife, namely whether in the minds of the Corinthians, Paul or Apollos is superior. Paul, in this entire section, addresses himself to the absurdity of such a competitive attitude. It is clear that some members of the Corinthian congregation are disputing the effectiveness of Paul's ministry and apostleship, as becomes evident in Paul's response in 1 Corinthians 4:3–5. He not only warns the Corinthians, filled with pride, against judging his stewardship prematurely, but also points out that on the last day[22] God will reveal all that now seems to be hidden in darkness—in this case, the trustworthiness of Paul's relationship to the Corinthians (1 Cor. 4:12). The apostle reminds this congregation that it is finally the Lord who will judge (4:4) the effectiveness of his laborer's work and it is finally the Lord who will either burn up the ineffective labor or reward the faithful work with his reward, a reward that Paul may view as similar to the one given to the good and faithful steward in Matthew 25, namely, the "well done" makarism.

1 Corinthians 3:10 and following is also a warning to those charged with the responsibility of caring for the Corinthian church to take care how they build on the foundation, since on the last day the quality of building materials will be revealed through fire. The good will survive and the remainder will be destroyed. That laborer who has built a house with cheap materials, that is, ministered to the Corinthians via short cuts, with worldly wisdom rather than the cross of Christ, that man will be pulled out of his rubble heap just in the nick of time.[23] The entire thrust of our argument has been that neither 1 Corinthians 3:15 nor 4:5 has anything to do with the good works of the individual Christian or with his or her personal salvation; both deal with a concrete situation in the life of the Corinthian congregation concerning the validity and effectiveness of apostolic ministry. Paul, on the one hand, uses a well-known apocalyptic illustration (Isa. 26:11; 31:9; 66:24; Dan. 7:9ff.) to warn the Corinthians about premature judgment; on the other hand, he employs the argument that all apostolic work, good or bad, is known to God and will be judged by him on the last day.

Category 4. *Judgment of Disobedient Christians*

Thus far we have reviewed last judgment texts in Paul that deal with universal judgment, with the gift of salvation for obedient Christians at the last judgment, and with God's scrutiny of apostolic work on the last day. We now turn to those texts that postulate a negative outcome for disobedient Christians on the last day. In proposing such a fourth category of Pauline judgment texts we stand in direct opposition to such scholars as Kühl[24] who hold that once the believer has been justified, salvation will result in an irrevocable manner.

There are several texts that indicate that Paul not only warns Christians about a possible rejection by God if they abandon the hope of the gospel, but that also flatly state that God can and will reject disobedient Christians. Such warning is explicitly found in 1 Corinthians 10 and 1 Corinthians 11:27 and following, and implied in Galatians 6:7, the text dealing with sowing and reaping. Less clear is 2 Thessalonians 1:8, where it is stated that vengeance will be inflicted "upon those who do not know God and upon those who do not obey the gospel of our Lord Jesus," and 1 Corinthians 6:9, where the rhetorical question is raised, "Do you not know that the unrighteous will not inherit the kingdom of God?" It is unlikely that the 2 Thessalonians passage refers to Christians; the text in 1 Corinthians is more difficult to interpret. Ambiguity also surrounds the understanding of Galatians 5:21b, "I warn you, as I warned you before, that those who do such things shall not inherit the kingdom of God." We are, however, inclined to see both the 1 Corinthian and the Galatian texts as referring to Christians, since both are found in paraenetic contexts addressed to Christians.

These preliminary references bring us to the single most important passage in this category of judgment texts: 1 Corinthians 5:1–8. It is one of the most troublesome Pauline judgment texts and the one most frequently used as a support for the argument that the baptized Christian is guaranteed salvation, especially verse 5. Those who interpret verse 5 in this way are all dependent on what has become the widely accepted translation of the Greek text, typified by the Revised Standard Version: ". . . You are to deliver this man to Satan for the destruction of the flesh, that his spirit may be saved in the day of the Lord Jesus." But where in the Greek text does one find any *autou* (his) which would permit us to translate "his spirit" rather than "the spirit"? It does not exist. Is there any other contextual warrant for translating *pneuma* (spirit) as the condemned man's spirit, other than the exegetical bias of "the introspective conscience of the West"? Much to be preferred is the more literal translation of the King James Version: "To deliver such a one into Satan for the destruction of the flesh, that the spirit may be saved in the day of the Lord Jesus."

While this translation may be the more literal, does it assist us in understanding Paul's intention in these verses? It does, for by taking seriously the fact that Paul refers to "the Spirit" rather than "his spirit," one is forced to rethink the whole matter. My suggestion is, quite simply, that Paul is not at all referring to the offender's spirit, but God's Spirit present in the Corinthian congregation. He is telling the Corinthians to cast out the works of the flesh and to return them to their proper authority, Satan, so that God's Spirit may continue to be present and thus preserve the congregation for the last day (cf. 1 Cor. 1:7–8). This understanding stands parallel to the succeeding verses that speak of the old and the new lump, and coheres very well with 1 Corinthians 3:16–17: "Do you not know that you are God's temple and that God's Spirit dwells in you? 17 If any one destroys God's temple, God will destroy him. For God's temple is holy, and that temple you are." In fact, this understanding coheres with much of the exhortation present in 1 Corinthians, namely, that the presence of God's Spirit in the Corinthian church by no means leads to guaranteed assurances about their status before God (e.g., see 1 Cor. 10:5–6, 12). Thus, the focus of Paul's concern in 1 Corinthians 5 is not primarily that of one man's sin, but the arrogance of a congregation that would tolerate this behavior and fail to realize that the presence of such "fleshly" actions jeopardizes the entire church's standing before God. His mandate is clear: rid yourselves of all corruption so that God's Spirit may be saved, that is, may continue to dwell in your midst (1 Cor. 3:16).[25] Commenting on the function of the Spirit in this verse, Conzelmann remarks: "But for Paul the Spirit is not a habitual possession, but a gift, and moreover a gift to the community."[26]

This interpretation of the Spirit's function within the life of the Corinthian congregation found in 1 Corinthians 5:5 is similar to other statements made by Paul. In 1 Corinthians itself, in addition to 3:16, one should note the relevant discussion about the Spirit and the flesh in 2:10–3:4, which serves as the substructure of the practical implication and actions taken in chapter 5. Also, Paul's comment in Galatians 5:5 is helpful for an understanding of 1 Corinthians 5: "For through the Spirit, by faith, we wait for the hope of righteousness." Since it is only through the Spirit that one hopes for the final gift on the last day, it is critical for the congregation, by faith, to permit God's Spirit to dwell in its midst. It is for this reason that Paul must outline so carefully the radical difference between the desire of the flesh and the Spirit in Galatians 5:16–26, and must categorically state in 5:21b: "I warn you, as I warned you before, that those who do such things shall not inherit the kingdom of God." Paul is quite explicit that the gift of the Spirit at baptism (1 Cor. 12:12–13) does not grant an indelible mark that automatically leads to salvation; rather, the Christian is only obedient and in the process of salvation as he participates in the Spirit (Phil. 2:1). Even the deutero-Pauline Ephesians (4:30) recognizes that it is possible to "grieve the Holy Spirit."[27] Apparently the Corinthians and the Galatians were in danger of confusing the gift of the Spirit with the full payment, rather than recognizing it to be only the first installment (*arrabōn*) of that which is yet to come if the Christian continues to participate in the Spirit. Finally, Paul's words in 1 Thessalonians 4:6 and following, that the Lord is an avenger to everyone who disregards the Holy Spirit given by God, further support our interpretation of 1 Corinthians 5:5.

While Paul's primary concern in this pericope is the Christian community, his comments concerning the sinner do have important implications for the overall theme concerning the relationship between justification and last judgment. Paul's point with regard to this offender appears to be clear and consistent; anyone who is baptized, justified, and a member of the church, but who is not obedient to the gift and possibility of his new existence will not be tolerated. He who is disobedient lives in the realm of Satan, in the realm of the flesh, and thus corrupts the body of Christ. Both in his formula of exclusion in 1 Corinthians 5:5 and in his citation of Deuteronomy 17:7 in 1 Corinthians 5:13, "Drive out the wicked person from among you," Paul is very consistent: the church member who is flagrantly disobedient no longer belongs to the realm of those who are being saved, but to the realm of those who are perishing (1 Cor. 1:18). The apostle urges his congregation to acknowledge the obvious for the sake of the Spirit.

Relevant to the specific discussion just completed as well as to the overall theme of this chapter are Käsemann's remarks with regard to 1 Corinthians 11:26 and following: "The self-manifestation of Christ calls men to obedience and this means that, at the same time it calls them to account before the final Judge who is already today acting within his community as he will act towards the world on the Last Day—he bestows salvation by setting men within his lordship and, if they spurn this lordship, they then experience this act of rejection as a self-incurred sentence of death."[28]

3. Developments after Paul

The influence of Paul continues in heightened fashion after his death. Interestingly, he influenced groups who interpreted his theology in different, even contradictory, ways. Thus, one can trace two divergent paths of development (often referred to as "trajectories")[1] influenced by Pauline thought in early Christianity: one leading toward second-century gnosticism and one leading toward, for want of a more accurate term, orthodox Christianity.[2]

Pauline theology is rich and dialectical in nature. When it loses its tension by being simplified and taken out of its original context, it can be distorted most easily. Elaine Pagels and others have shown us how such "partial" Pauline theology was used extensively as a theological basis by the second-century Gnostics.[3] The Pauline concept of a future physical resurrection was often reduced to a present (or past) spiritual resurrection. The Pauline dialectic of faith that is active in love or of justification that bears good works, is given up for an easy view of faith that places no demands and seeks no responsibility or obedience from the believer. The ethical rigor of Pauline Christianity is virtually eliminated.

One post-Pauline trajectory that eventually leads to Christian gnosticism has its beginnings in what are frequently referred to as the deutero-Pauline epistles, Colossians and Ephesians. These were in all probability written by disciples or co-workers of Paul after his death.[4] Frequent discussion between Paul and his colleagues, as described, for example, in Acts 19:9 ("He withdrew . . . taking the disciples with him, and argued daily in the hall of Tyrannus"), undoubtedly gave them insight into a good deal of

Paul's theology. But as happens even today, students may misunderstand and even a slight change of nuance can lead to disastrous future interpretations. A case in point is Colossians 3:1. The text reads: "If then you have been raised with Christ, seek the things that are above, where Christ is, seated at the right hand of God." Because of its close connection with this verse, we should also look at Colossians 2:12: ". . . You were buried with him in baptism, in which you were also raised with him through faith in the working of God, who raised him from the dead." We have already had occasion to note how careful and precise Paul is in his use of verbal tenses. How then are we to explain the fact that here in Colossians we have a reference to the believer's resurrection in the past tense, "You have been raised," while elsewhere Paul is so insistent in referring to the futurity of the believer's resurrection?[5] Since these passages dealing with a future resurrection are significant for our understanding of Paul, we should look more closely at two or three of them, in addition to the references in 1 Corinthians 15 that we have already discussed.

Particularly relevant are two verses in Romans 6, the first being in verse 4: "We were buried therefore with him by baptism into death, so that as Christ was raised from the dead by the glory of the Father, we too might walk in newness of life." The reference to death in the past tense agrees with what we have found in Colossians. But note that Paul in Romans does not say, "You have been raised with Christ." Rather, as a consequence of Christ's death and resurrection, he concludes that the Christian "might walk in newness of life." Paul is even more precise in verse 5: "For if we have been united with him in a death like his, we shall certainly be united with him in a resurrection like his." Certainly the reference is to the futurity of the believer's resurrection. This same use of the future is evident in verse 8, once again underlining Paul's intentionality in such references: "But if we have died with Christ, we believe that we shall also live with him." The unlikelihood that Colossians is a faithful reflection of Pauline theology is further strengthened by the reference in Philippians 3:10–11: "That I may know him [Christ] and the power of his resurrection, and may share his sufferings, becoming like him in his death, 11 that if possible I may attain the resurrection from the dead." Once again, resurrection is a future hope, not a present or past fact.

In and of itself, the confusion of a verbal tense is not a tragic error. What the Pauline followers did was to eliminate the eschatological tension of the "already/not yet" present in Paul's theology; yet one should not overlook that this eschatological tension is preserved in other parts of Colossians (e.g., 3:4). But these students of Paul clearly did make it easier for gnostically oriented Christians to lift Colossians 2:11 and 3:1 out of context and give them their own interpretation. This is exactly what occurs in the document attributed by some to the gnostic writer Valentinus, *Epistle to Rheginus,* which is an essay on the resurrection.[6] What we find here is much closer to Colossians than to Paul: "we suffered with him, and we arose with him, and we went to heaven with him."[7] Is the tendency already begun in Colossians, which may be behind the warning in 2 Timothy 2:18 when it refers to those "who have swerved from the truth by holding that the resurrection is past already," further developed in *Rheginus?* Many scholars would answer affirmatively.

The intention of the Pauline school[8] was to apply and actualize the teachings of Paul to the problems and situations of their age. In so actualizing Paul we have seen that it is fully possible, inadvertently to be sure, to shift the nuances and structures of Paul's theology. We have seen this in the area of resurrection language; I will now suggest how this happened in another area of Pauline thought—justification and salvation.

As was the case with resurrection language, so also here Paul is very careful in his use of verbs. We have seen this with particular clarity in Romans 5:9–10: "Since, therefore, we are now justified by his blood, much more shall we be saved by him from the wrath of God. 10 For if while we were enemies we were reconciled to God by the death of his Son, much more, now that we are reconciled, shall we be saved by his life." Quite clearly, justification is a past event with continuing importance and salvation, while already initiated in the life of the Christian, is only to be consummated in the future. We have already reviewed this in some detail earlier and can, therefore, move directly to the point that has to be made as we compare Paul with the deutero-Pauline writers. Ephesians, like Colossians written by a follower of Paul, uses the verb "to save" in a non-Pauline way. In Ephesians 2:5 we read: "By grace you have been saved." In the authentic Pauline writings, salvation is always described as a future event and it is so characterized by use of the future tense, a subjunctive or a participle. In those two rare instances where Paul does use a past tense of the verb "to save" it is modified by a clear future orientation in the immediate context as, for example, in Romans 8:24, "For in this hope we were saved." Once again what may have appeared as a minor, almost incidental change in Ephesians, is to play into the hands of the Gnostics in a ominous way. They claimed that they in fact "had been saved," resulting in a perfectionism, elitism, and arrogance that forced mainstream Christian thinkers to actively resist and refute this movement.

We have just reviewed the beginnings of a trajectory that eventually leads to a major distortion of Paul's theology. Since Paul was such an influential figure one can easily imagine that attempts to distort his theology such as those of the Gnostics were quickly and vigorously resisted. Although this tendency to defend Paul is already at work in the pastoral letters (1 and 2 Timothy and Titus) we will limit our examination to James and Acts.

Although there has been much discussion about the authorship and purpose of James, there appears to be a consensus among biblical scholars that it was written in the second half of the first century by a pseudonymous Christian author intending to give concrete ethical exhortations to his congregation and perhaps to a wider group as well.[9] Since some of the language and theological concepts seem to contradict those used by Paul, the question arises whether it was written intentionally in opposition to Paul. This certainly would be one option. Such a sentiment coupled with what he thought was an inadequate testimony to Jesus Christ, led Martin Luther to give this book a very low evaluation.[10] I do not, however, accept this option as being the most likely, and prefer rather the view that it is written in the post-Pauline period and that it is written with an eye to correct those persons who are distorting Pauline theology. Rather than being anti-Pauline, it is pro-Pauline; James is attempting to defend Paul. Of course, as a member of the post-Pauline generation it is quite possible that the author of James is somewhat less than precise in his use of language and may also reduce the tension characteristic of Pauline eschatology. But such occasional lack of precision does not necessarily indicate a position in opposition to the apostle.

The New Testament itself refers to the fact that Paul was being misinterpreted and that this situation required defense and refutation. Particularly illuminating is 2 Peter 3:15b–17, a text that comes from the early second century: "So also our beloved brother Paul wrote to you according to the wisdom given him, 16 speaking of this as he does in all his letters. There are some things in them hard to understand, which the ignorant and unstable twist to their own destruction, as they do the other scriptures. 17 You therefore, beloved, knowing this beforehand, beware lest you be carried away with the error of lawless men and lose your own stability." In this instance someone writing in the name of Peter attempts to come to Paul's defense.[11]

The author of James, while living in the midst of the theological confusion of the post-Pauline age, attempts to transcend and correct it. We have already had occasion to note Paul's careful and precise use of present and future verbs and his distinction in the meaning of the verbs "to justify" and "to save." This distinction is totally overlooked in James 2:24: "You see that a man is justified by works and not by faith alone." The author of James is obviously living in an environment where not only the distinction between "to justify" and "to save" has become quite blurred, but faith is looked at so spiritually and abstractly that the dimension of ethical imperative is not stressed or even found to be necessary. It is this that he attempts to refute. Even though in this instance James misuses Pauline language and even employs the quotation about Abraham from Genesis 15:6 in a different way,[12] his essential understanding of Pauline theology is correct. He attempts to bring Paul's thought to bear on an ecclesiastical situation in which that theology had not only become confused, but also perverted by a type of Christian who cried "faith, faith" but never fully realized what that meant in terms of day-to-day behavior.

One of the major themes in James is well summarized in 1:22: "But be doers of the word, and not hearers only, deceiving yourselves"; further, it is urged that the Christian should not be a "hearer that forgets but a doer that acts . . ." (1:25). This specific point is then elaborated in 2:14–17:

What does it profit, my brethren, if a man says he has faith but has not works? Can his faith save him? 15 If a brother or sister is ill-clad and in lack of daily food, 16 and one of you says to them, "Go in peace, be warmed and filled," without giving them the things needed for the body, what does it profit? 17 So faith by itself, if it has no works, is dead.

Is not this, as well as the further discussion of this theme in 2:18 and following, precisely what Paul is suggesting with his formula in Galatians 5:6 of "faith working through love"? Is not this what Paul means in his statement that if "we live by the Spirit, let us also walk by the Spirit"? (Gal. 5:25). Is it not precisely to underline the theme that faith without works is useless that every Pauline letter has a paraenetic section? Although Paul does not use this identical language, such as faith being completed by works, the underlying pattern is quite similar.

In view of this discussion, the phrase in James 2:24 ("You see that a man is justified by works and not by faith alone") is not as alien to Paul as it may appear at first glance. Granting the confusion between justification and salvation, James appears to be stating that the Christian life is not acceptable to God unless deeds and works of love are carried out. Faith alone, faith not consummated by acts of love toward others, is empty. It is because a similar concept operates in Paul that he can assert in 1 Corinthians 13:13, "So faith, hope, love abide, these three; but the greatest of these is love," and in 2 Corinthians 5:10, "For we must all appear before the judgment seat of Christ, so that each one may receive good or evil, according to what he has done in the body."

In short, some in the early church take the theology of Paul out of its context of eschatological tension and thereby distort and pervert it. One of Paul's defenders against this tendency in the post-Pauline church is James. We now turn to the portrait of Paul in the Acts of the Apostles.

It has long been recognized that the portrait of Paul given by Luke in the Acts of the Apostles differs from the one we find in Paul's own letters. Professors John Knox[13] and Philipp Vielhauer[14] have, along with others, outlined some of these chronological and theological differences. The discrepancies between Paul's own theology and that presented by Luke can be accounted for by either assuming partial ignorance of some of the facts on Luke's part or by assuming that Luke consciously tried to present a certain image of Paul to his audience. As we shall see, most of the evidence favors the latter alternative and the central question we shall have to ask is for what reasons Luke was compelled to present Paul in a light different from the authentic Paul.[15]

A clue to the Lucan motivation in presenting Paul may be found in Acts 21:20–21. According to this account Paul has just arrived in Jerusalem and is in conversation with James and the elders. They address Paul as follows: " 'You see, brother, how many thousands there are among the Jews of those who have believed; they are all zealous for the law, 21 and they have been told about you that you teach all the Jews who are among the Gentiles to forsake Moses, telling them not to circumcise their children or observe the customs.' " In other words, Paul is gaining the precarious reputation of being a radical in certain Jewish-Christian circles. Paul's understanding of faith and justification, and statements such as "Christ is the end of the law" (Rom. 10:4), especially if they are not understood in their proper context, could make many Jewish Christians very uneasy and have them view Paul not only as a threat to their understanding of Christianity but as one who was undermining their theological perspective.

If Luke's audience contains a Jewish-Christian element[16] that is upset by Paul's alleged radicalism, it becomes conceivable that Luke would play down key elements of Pauline theology and why he could highlight the apostle's conservatism and faithfulness to the Jewish tradition. In fact, the portrait of Paul in Acts is that of a good Jew. Let us illustrate this point with a few examples.

In Acts 16:3 we read: "Paul wanted Timothy to accompany him; and he took him and circumcised him because of the Jews that were in those places, for they all knew that his father was a Greek." Paul, according to this account not only advocates circumcision for one of his co-workers, he actually performs this ritual act himself. The only way one can make sense out of this text is to view it as a way to appease Jewish Christians, since Paul's own testimony is in flagrant contradiction to this account.[17] In Galatians 5:2–4 Paul writes to the Galatians that if "you receive circumcision, Christ will be of no advantage to you. 3 I testify again to every man who receives circumcision that he is bound to keep the whole law. 4 You are severed from Christ, you who would be justified by the law; you have fallen away from grace." In a similar vain Paul writes to the Corinthians: "Was any one at the time of his call uncircumcised? Let him not seek circumcision. 19 For neither circumcision counts for anything nor uncircumcision, but keeping the commandments of God" (1 Cor. 7:18b–19). In addition, Acts 16:3 is contradicted by the fact that Paul refused to have Titus circumcised in Jerusalem: "But even Titus, who was with me, was not compelled to be circumcised, though he was a Greek" (Gal. 2:3).

There is fairly consistent evidence in the Pauline letters that leads one to the conclusion that Acts 16:3 is not an accurate portrayal of an event in which the historical Paul was involved.

But would not Paul's missionary strategy outlined in 1 Corinthians 9:19–23 contradict this conclusion?

For though I am free from all men, I have made myself a slave to all, that I might win the more. 20 To the Jews I became as a Jew, in order to win Jews; to those under the law I became as one under the law—though not being myself under the law—that I might win those under the law. 21 To those outside the law I became as one outside the law—not being without law toward God but under the law of Christ—that I might win those outside the law. 22 To the weak I became weak, that I might win the weak. I have become all things to all men, that I might by all means save some. 23 I do it all for the sake of the gospel, that I may share in its blessings.

Of particular importance is the statement that to "the Jews I became as a Jew, in order to win Jews; to those under the law I became as one under the law—though not being myself under the law—that I might win those under the law" (v. 20). Would Paul's missionary tactics toward the Jews have been so flexible as to include the circumcision of Timothy either as an act of piety or to reduce tensions with the Jews? The eminent New Testament scholar Günther Bornkamm would answer this question with an emphatic no.[18] There are, Bornkamm suggests, limits to Paul's missionary freedom and flexibility and one of these limits is the matter of circumcision; everything we have examined in Paul would support this position. But then, asks Bornkamm, what would be an example of Paul's becoming a Jew in order to win Jews? The answer is his participation in the act of purification in the Jerusalem temple as recorded in Acts 21:23–26. Concerning this act, Bornkamm comments: "He [Paul] did not thereby compromise himself in the least. For participation in this private ceremony undertaken only for his own person, certainly could not call into question the fact that the law was abolished as a way to salvation."[19]

With regard to the circumcision of Timothy as recorded in Acts 16:3 we would conclude that this was an impossible action for

Paul to have undertaken and the situation is altered by Luke for the sake of defending Paul against charges that he was a radical heretic. In defending Paul, Luke presents a very orthodox, conservative Paul; perhaps for Luke the only way to maintain a sense of balance was to let the pendulum swing fully to the right. This tendency in Luke can also be seen in his virtual ignoring or minimizing such controversial Pauline themes as justification, the theology of the cross, law, and eschatology. Further, the important matter of the collection from the Pauline churches to the Jerusalem church, a fact that underscores the Jewish Christian–Gentile Christian tension of the first century, is passed over without mention.

We have been suggesting that this conservative theological profile of Paul as found in Acts is another example of dynamic actualization; Paul must be portrayed to this largely conservative Jewish-Christian audience in such a way that they will see him as a valid representative of the faith and not as one whom they can simply dismiss as a heretic. Luke's actualization of Paul, his defense of Paul, may be one of the contributing reasons why the Pauline letters stand in the canon of Scripture today.

Is Luke's actualization of Paul not simply a distortion for the sake of convenience? Some today might even ask if such an approach is not inherently dishonest. This is an important issue and at least some brief resolution must be attempted. In the first place, we must be very clear that the modern mind and the ancient mind operate in very different contexts. Consistency, precision, and narrow definitions of truth and falsehood are not part of the "community of characteristics"[20] shared by the ancient writer. Samuel Sandmel in his illuminating article "The Ancient Mind and Ours" proposes that the "toleration of diversity by the ancient mind suggests an elasticity which we moderns do not possess . . . [and] they did not elevate consistency as the highest achievement of mankind."[21]

Once this fundamental distinction has been understood, one must ask in what way Luke belongs within the framework of ancient historiography and the ancient biographical tradition. If

Charles Talbert is correct that the closest literary parallel to Acts
is that of cultic biography, important new insights are achieved
with regard to understanding the style and purpose of Acts.[22]
Helpful also is the observation of D. R. Stuart that Aristoxenus'
life of Pythagoras consisted of "preachments in which he sought
to glorify the master and the ideals for which the master stood,
and to correct the vulgar errors according to which popular belief
had deformed the Pythagorean way of life. Thus, his treatment
. . . had much of the color of a saint's life."[23] Talbert adds that
this type of biography "functioned defensively. It had its *Sitz im
Leben* in the debates within the philosophical schools. It was
specifically designed to take sides in a debate."[24] Finally, one
should also remember that contemporary discussions of persons
in public life are not presented in a vacuum. If Mr. Reagan were
to accuse Mr. Carter of being fiscally irresponsible, it is more than
likely that Mr. Mondale would emphasize precisely those policies
of Mr. Carter that would refute that characterization. If Mr.
Carter were to portray Mr. Reagan as naive in regard to foreign
policy, it would be natural for Mr. Bush to provide evidence that
would make the *opposite* position credible. Although analogies are
never fully accurate, is it not possible that some conservatives
were attacking Paul as radical, anti-Jewish, and libertine, and that
Luke, the defender of Paul, chose to stress characteristics about
Paul that would allow for a more balanced understanding of the
apostle?

II. THE SYNOPTIC GOSPELS

4. The Gospel of Mark: A Word about Suffering

There is no precise parallel in the Graeco-Roman or Jewish religious world to the literary genre known as "gospel"; it is unique. The very fact that the gospel of Mark was written is testimony, therefore, to the dynamic character of early Christianity. Why else would someone have created this entirely new literary genre, unless to interpret the significance of the Word, the Christ event, for an entirely new situation?[1]

As we begin our examination of Mark, we must begin with two dates: the death of Jesus in the late twenties of the first century A.D. and the final composition of Mark in the late sixties.[2] What prompted someone to write a gospel some forty years after the death of Jesus? What factors were present in Mark's situation that necessitated that the traditions of Jesus, transmitted by the early Christian communities, be interpreted and put into another form? One of the major concerns we have, then, is to discover the situation of Mark's audience—what needs they had and what possible problems were present that Mark had to address.[3] To investigate this matter for Mark's gospel is more difficult than for the other gospels since New Testament scholars have determined that Mark was the first gospel written and that both Matthew and Luke use Mark as they write their gospels.[4] Consequently, there is considerably less comparative material for Mark's gospel and as a result all suggestions concerning this gospel must be more tentative than for the others. The advantage we have when we get to Matthew's gospel, for example, is that we can not only arrive at certain conclusions from evidence internal to the gospel (as we

can with Mark), but we can also make specific comparisons between Matthew and Mark and Matthew and Luke. Even though
we do not have such an advantage with Mark, contemporary
scholarship has found enough definite traces of Mark's hand in
the gospel so that we can receive a fairly firm impression of both
Mark's congregation and his intention in writing the gospel.[5]

One of the initial things that strikes the careful reader of Mark
is the frequency with which the term "gospel" is used.[6] First,
Mark is the only one of the four canonical gospels that defines
itself as a gospel: "The beginning of the gospel of Jesus Christ,
the Son of God" (1:1). Second, Mark exhibits frequent and direct
use of the word "gospel" that is either eliminated or modified by
Matthew and Luke. In Mark 8:35 one reads: "For whoever would
save his life will lose it; and whoever loses his life for my sake and
the gospel's will save it." The parallels to this verse in Luke 9:24
and Matthew 16:25 both omit "and the gospel's." Similar alterations can also be found in Mark 10:29 and parallels, and in Mark
13:10 and parallels.

Why does Mark contain this unique emphasis on "gospel"? In
order to answer this we must say a few things about the use of
the term "gospel" in the first century. Important to keep in mind
is that the term was widely used in the imperial Roman cult where
it functioned to communicate the benefits that members of the
empire enjoyed through the gracious authority of Caesar who
was, of course, viewed as the divinely appointed ruler of Rome.
Additionally, "gospel" in the non-Christian world signaled victory in battle and the birth or enthronement of a Roman ruler.
Martin also cites the calendar inscription from Priene in Asia
Minor (9 B.C.), in which the emperor Augustus' birthday is hailed
as "joyful news [*euaggelion*] for the world."[7] Early Christians,
most notably Mark and Paul, take up this secular term and trans-
form it by giving its contents a new subject, Jesus Christ. In early
Christian usage, then, "the gospel" announces the saving benefits wrought by God's action in Jesus Christ.[8]

In early Christianity the term "gospel" originally meant precisely such an oral proclamation of God's new action in the death

and resurrection of Jesus. Alongside this oral proclamation, the term was also applied to certain written documents that eventually came to be known as gospels, namely Matthew, Mark, Luke and John. Yet only one of these gospels, Mark, actually refers to itself as a gospel. Matthew, in the opening verse of his gospel, uses the term "book" and although it is used in a limited sense, it is indeed an accurate description of his work as a whole as can be seen by the frequent description of this gospel by contemporary scholars as a "catechetical handbook."[9] It does have many similarities to a teaching handbook. Luke refers to his two-volume work as a narrative (1:1).[10] It is a historical, theological, and travel narrative including the Jewish backgrounds of the gospel, the ministry of Jesus, and the advance of the church in the Graeco-Roman world. While John does not give any self-descriptive terminology at the outset, the placement of the magnificent hymn confessing Jesus as the Word at the beginning of his gospel gives a clear indication of the profound theological concerns throughout the fourth gospel.[11] Matthew, Luke, and John are very much "gospels" in the secondary, later sense of the term. But what about Mark? While Mark is clearly a gospel in this same literary sense of the term, he very much preserves the original sense of the word as oral proclamation not only in those texts just noted, but also in his overall intention. I very much share Professor Marxsen's perspective that *"the 'gospel' which Mark writes is his commentary on the term 'gospel' which Paul leaves (for the most part) unexplained.* Commentary, however, does not mean 'explanation.' Exegesis is, rather, *the* form of primitive Christian preaching. Just for this reason, we may not think first of the 'Book' which Mark writes. Rather, we should think of the proclamation which represents that which, or better, the one who is proclaimed. Insofar as Jesus is the content of the tradition, he is also the content of the gospel. Insofar as he sets in motion this proclamation as Risen Lord, he is himself the gospel. This means that he proclaims himself. This in turn corroborates our earlier statement . . . that Mark writes *a* sermon which is gospel."[12]

Let us return to the opening verse of Mark's gospel: "The

beginning of the gospel of Jesus Christ, the Son of God."[13] The
uniqueness of Jesus is described by two titles that were apparently in use in Mark's congregation, Christ and Son of God. Let
us begin with the latter term. It is found also in 3:11, a close
approximation may be noted in 5:7 ("Son of the Most High
God"), and for the third and final time only in 15:39. In 1:1 the
term is in a relatively neutral context. The context in which it is
located in 3:7–12 is most illuminating. These verses are a Marcan
summary of the healing activities of Jesus. It concludes in this
way: " 10 for he had healed many, so that all who had diseases
pressed upon him to touch him. 11 And whenever the unclean
spirits beheld him, they fell down before him and cried out, 'You
are the Son of God.' 12 And he strictly ordered them not to make
him known." The "secrecy motif" that emerges here plays a
significant role in the theology of this gospel as we will see
shortly. In 5:7 it also is an unclean spirit that addresses Jesus as
"Son of the Most High God."

How was this term "Son of God" comprehended in Mark's
congregation? First, it must be mentioned that all titles in the
New Testament such as Son of God, Christ, Son of David, and
Lord are ways in which the early church attempted to describe the
uniqueness of the Christ event.[14] Furthermore, all of these titles
had functioned in other contexts prior to their use as descriptions
and theological appellations for Jesus. Although, the term "Son
of God" did have a Jewish background it appears to have been
heavily influenced by Hellenistic religious thought, especially by
the concept of a divine man who was known and worshipped for
his miracle-working abilities.[15] These characteristics were also
present in the emperor who was understood to be the divinely
appointed ruler of Rome. Professor Gerhard Friedrich comments
that the "ruler is divine by nature. His power extends to men, to
animals, to the earth and to the sea. Nature belongs to him; the
wind and the waves are subject to him. He works miracles and
heals men. He is the savior of the world who also redeems individuals from their difficulties."[16] This definition parallels remarkably many of the presentations of Jesus in Mark's gospel.

When Mark's audience used the term "Son of God" or heard it with reference to Jesus they tended to understand Jesus primarily as a miracle-working divine man.[17] While Mark in no way wanted to underestimate the powerful acts performed by Jesus, he wished rather to demonstrate that the key to the uniqueness of Jesus lies not in his miracle-working, but in his suffering and death. Herein lies both his uniqueness and, as Paul would say, his scandal in the sense of being a stumbling block.

Beginning with Mark 8:31, but foreshadowed already in the earlier conflict stories between Jesus and the Jewish leaders and the account of the death of John the Baptist, there is an enormous stress on the suffering and death of Jesus. In fact, this stress is so great that it led one scholar in the early twentieth century to describe Mark's gospel as a passion narrative with a long introduction.[18] That description, in fact, is not far from the truth. Mark communicates this emphasis primarily by using an alternate christological title, Son of man. In 8:31 we read: "And he began to teach them that the Son of man must suffer many things, and be rejected by the elders and the chief priests and the scribes, and be killed, and after three days rise again." Particularly significant is the statement in the next verse: "And he said this plainly." This is quite the opposite to the previous exhortations to secrecy. What is it that can now be said plainly? That Jesus, as Son of man, must suffer and be killed and then rise again. This identical theme is repeated in 9:31–32 and in 10:33–34. The reader is then invited to follow this Son of man who "came not to be served but to serve, and to give his life as a ransom for many" (10:45). As in the story that immediately follows, the reader is invited to follow Jesus on the way to the passion in the same way as does the blind man who has received his sight. The remainder of the gospel of Mark is filled with references to the passion of Jesus and an ethical perspective for Mark's congregation derived therefrom.

Now at last we are able to turn our attention to the final reference to the term "Son of God" in Mark 15:39. To fully understand the intention of Mark we must ponder verses 33–39 as a unit:

> And when the sixth hour had come, there was a darkness over the whole land until the ninth hour. 34 And at the ninth hour Jesus cried with a loud voice, "Elo-i, Elo-i, lama sabach-thani?" which means, "My God, my God, why hast thou forsaken me?" 35 And some of the bystanders hearing it said, "Behold, he is calling Elijah." 36 And one ran and, filling a sponge full of vinegar, put it on a reed and gave it to him to drink, saying, "Wait, let us see whether Elijah will come to take him down." 37 And Jesus uttered a loud cry, and breathed his last. 38 And the curtain of the temple was torn in two, from top to bottom. 39 And when the centurion, who stood facing him, saw that he thus breathed his last, he said, "Truly this man was the Son of God!"

It is the Roman centurion, the one who shares in a culture entertaining the divine man ideology, who points to the crucified Jesus as the Son of God. Clearly we see Mark's purpose: the centurion's confession that Jesus is the Son of God only as the suffering and crucified one is to serve as a model for the Marcan congregation.

From this perspective of the true identity of the Son of God, Mark cogently presents ethical implications to his audience. This Jesus who is announced "plainly" beginning in 8:31 as the one who must suffer and die issues a call to those who would follow him on a similar path: "If any man would come after me, let him deny himself and take up his cross and follow me. 35 For whoever would save his life will lose it; and whoever loses his life for my sake and the gospel's will save it" (8:34–35). This lifestyle is essentially characterized by humility, a humility anchored in the cross. This is made clear in 9:35: "And he sat down and called the twelve; and he said to them, "If any one would be first, he must be last of all and servant of all.'" This identical point is made in chapter 10 to counter the disciples misunderstanding as they request of Jesus to sit "one at your right hand and one at your left, in your glory" (v. 37). After indicating the impossibility of granting such a request, the pericope concludes in this way: "And Jesus called them to him and said to them, 'You know that those who are supposed to rule over the Gentiles lord it over them, and their great men exercise authority over them. 43 But it shall not be so among you; but whoever would be great among you must be your servant, 44 and whoever would be first among you must be slave of all. 45 For the Son of man also came not to be served but to serve, and to give his life as a ransom for many' " (vv. 42–45).

We have seen how Mark tries to clarify for his congregation what it means to confess Jesus as Son of God by reinterpreting this christological title by means of another, Son of man. There is a lengthy and controversial scholarly discussion concerning both the prehistory of the phrase "Son of man" and its meaning in early Christianity.[19] However that may be decided, this much is clear: for Mark the title "Son of man" either was understood already or was still sufficiently fluid so that it could be understood as a title referring both to the humiliation (suffering, death, cross) and to the exaltation of Jesus as judge on the last day (as for example in 8:38, "For whoever is ashamed of me and of my words in this adulterous and sinful generation, of him will the Son of man also be ashamed, when he comes in the glory of his Father with the holy angels.").

We must now return to the opening of the gospel and examine the other title used to describe Jesus, namely, Christ. It is rather striking that after this initial introductory reference the title does not appear again until 8:29 and then in such a way that it is essentially rejected. In order to better understand the inner dynamic surrounding the use of this title in Mark's gospel, a few words must be said about the prehistory of the term "Christ."[20] The Greek term *christos* is a translation of the Hebrew word *mašîah*, which means "anointed," and is found in connection with the anointing of the king of Israel and of the priest. In such Old Testament passages as 1 Samuel 10:10 and following and 16:13, which refer to the anointing of Saul and David, we observe that anointing implies a sacred act that brings the spirit of Yahweh upon the person and it also has the implications of implying a successor. The Old Testament term is found in a wide variety of different conceptual frameworks and it is important to realize that messianic expectations were quite diverse in the Judaism of the New Testament period. Probably the dominant expectation in the period of Jesus was of a political figure, a new king like David, who would usher in the kingdom by removing the Roman occupation armies from what was in fact God's land. Other expectations of the messiah in this period included the image of a new Moses, or a miracle-working prophet like Elijah, or simply one of the great prophets of old. The fact that Jesus died on a cross, humiliated, was both paradoxical and scandalous to first-century Jews since it so totally shattered all Jewish messianic expectations. And yet early on Christians used the title "Christ" freely, but in a radically altered sense. A study of Mark 8 suggests that this transformation of meaning did not come easily.

The pericope containing Peter's confession that Jesus is the Christ stands at the mid-point of the gospel (8:27–30). In fact this passage is so central to the structure of Mark's gospel that one can describe it as the turning point in the gospel. The text reads as follows:

And Jesus went on with his disciples, to the villages of Caesarea Philippi; and on the way he asked his disciples, "Who do men say that I am?" 28 And they told him, "John the Baptist; and others say, Elijah; and others one of the prophets." 29 And he asked them, "But who do you say that I am?" Peter answered him, "You are the Christ." 30 And he charged them to tell no one about him.

In light of our previous discussion it should no longer come as a surprise that some responded to the question of Jesus' identity by suggesting that he was "Elijah" or "one of the prophets." What is surprising is that Peter's presumably correct confession that Jesus is the Christ is not enthusiastically acclaimed or hailed. Rather, it is veiled in silence! "And he charged them to tell no one about him." Even more dramatically, Peter is then rebuked by Jesus in verse 33: "But turning and seeing his disciples, he rebuked Peter, and said, 'Get behind me, Satan! For you are not on the side of God, but of men.' " What is it according to the account in Mark that provoked such a sharp response from Jesus toward Peter? According to Mark's description it was Peter's prior rebuttal of the statement in verse 31 that the "Son of man must suffer many things, and be rejected by the elders and the chief priests and the scribes and be killed, and after three days rise again." It becomes clear that Peter's perception of Jesus is quite other than that of a humiliated and suffering messiah. That Mark is intent on highlighting the conflicting concepts of messiahship is also evident in his contrasting use of the motifs of veiling and openness. What Peter confesses must be kept silent; the description of Jesus as the humiliated and suffering one is said "plainly" (v. 32), in the sense of boldness and openness.

In light of Peter's serious misunderstanding, what view of the title "Christ" did he have, assuming that there is some valid historical tradition reflected in this scene? Unfortunately, it seems that Peter's conception did not have room for a Jesus who would be rejected and who would suffer and die; on the other hand, it is likely that Peter stood close to that strand in first-century Judaism that expected a triumphant political hero as the messiah. Even if this is true, it still does not answer for us why Mark would be interested in relating this story to his audience some forty years later and why he places it in such a pivotal position in the structure of his gospel. Would Mark have any interest at all around the year A.D. 70 in combatting a notion of Jesus as a political leader in the image of David? That is not very likely, but are there other possibilities? In fact, the gospel of Mark itself suggests that the term "Christ" could be understood in another way at the time it was written. In 13:21–22 we find the following warning: "And then if any one says to you, 'Look, here is the Christ!' or 'Look, there he is!' do not believe it. 22 False Christs and false prophets will arise and show signs and wonders, to lead astray, if possible, the elect." Apparently there is a concept of a messiah sufficiently prevalent for Mark to urge his congregation that it is false. Mark also makes clear that at least one major dimension of this false Christology is related to a misuse of "signs and wonders," a frequent New Testament expression for those things more commonly, but not quite as accurately, referred to as "miracles."[21] In view of this association of Christ with "miracle-working" and in view of the fact that a "veiling" of identity similar to what we have just seen in 8:30 is also found after several miracle cycles and miracle-working summaries in Mark's gospel (3:12; 5:43; 7:36) makes it quite likely that some in Mark's congregation were misunderstanding the title "Christ" in the direction of giving priority to this dimension of Jesus' activity, a problem not altogether unrelated to our previous discussion about the title "Son of God." Mark certainly does not want to deny that Jesus performed "signs and wonders," but he does want to stress that that activity is not his claim to uniqueness. Certainly we have much comparative material to suggest that miracle workers abounded. The uniqueness of Mark's miracle-working Jesus lies precisely in his suffering and death (8:31). This theme is the interpretative key that dominates the gospel. In the first half of the gospel it lies below the surface structure; in the second half it is repeated in 9:31 and following and 10:33 and following, and it is then amplified dramatically in the passion narrative.

Moving on from this insight we realize that the collection of all the miracle stories in the first half of the gospel, with the important exception of two, is done intentionally. Repeatedly they are shrouded in secrecy. Mark appears to be suggesting that the miracles can only be properly interpreted in light of the cross. It is only when one gets to 8:31 and following, the theme of the suffering Jesus, that matters can be spoken about plainly. The two miracle stories that occur in the second half of the gospel can only be understood from this perspective; in fact their position in the gospel may be programmatic in terms of understanding Mark's intention with regard to all the miracles. In 9:14–29 one finds the healing miracle of the epileptic boy. Just prior to this healing narrative one reads of Jesus in verse 12b "that he should suffer many things and be treated with contempt." The miracle story itself concludes with the definite stress that there is no inherent automatic or magical power residing in the disciples that allows them to heal. In response to the disciples question in 9:28 as to why they could not cast out the dumb and deaf spirit, Jesus emphatically responds that this "kind cannot be driven out by anything but prayer." The power of the Father rather than the miracle-working ability of the disciples is the critical factor, a point that should be clear from Mark's reference to prayer in 11:22 and following: "Have faith in God. . . . 24 Therefore I tell you, whatever you ask in prayer, believe that you have received it, and it will be yours." Immediately following this conclusion to the healing account of the epileptic boy, it is stated once again that the "Son of man will be delivered into the hands of men, and they will kill him" (9:31). Quite clearly, the healing activity of Jesus can only be properly understood in light of his death.

The only other miracle account that occurs in the second half of the gospel occurs in a section structurally similar to the one we just reviewed. In a context where the ethical implications of the cross are stressed, we find the following comments just prior to the miracle story about the blind man: ". . . Whoever would be great among you must be your servant, 44 and whoever would be first among you must be slave of all. 45 For the Son of man also came not to be served but to serve, and to give his life as a ransom for many" (10:43b–45). This identical stress on humility follows immediately after the healing story in 11:1 and following, Jesus comes to Jerusalem showered with such acclamations as "Hosanna! Blessed is he who comes in the name of the Lord! 10 Blessed is the kingdom of our father David that is coming! Hosanna in the highest!" But notice in what manner he enters— on a colt, as a dramatic symbol of humility. A contradiction similar to that between Peter's misunderstanding of what it meant to be Christ and Mark's stress on suffering and humility is recapitulated in this scene.

This particular miracle story, together with the epileptic healing, is not only of interest because of its paradigmatic significance, for the way by which all miracles are to be understood in this gospel, but also because of its very probable symbolic meaning at another level. For example, what is the significance of the fact that this is the second time a healing is recounted about a blind man receiving sight? Once again we appear to have structural parallelism at work. The first healing of a blind man in 8:22–26 stands just before the main announcement that the Son of man must suffer and die; 10:46–52 stands just before the entrance to Jerusalem and the account of the actual suffering and death of Jesus. Mark seems to be suggesting that to finally see, to finally understand Jesus is to recognize him as the humble, suffering one. And only when such healing takes place, where such insight is given, can one truly follow him on the path of discipleship, which is a path marked by humility and the possibility of suffering. Is not this the point that Mark intends to make in the closing verse of the second account of the healing of the blind man: "And Jesus said to him, 'Go your way; your faith has made you well.' And immediately he received his sight and followed him on the way." The way to be followed is quite clearly the way of humility and suffering—in short, the way of the cross.

5. The Gospel of Matthew: A Word about Righteousness

Of the many rich insights that have been made with regard to Matthew's gospel, the suggestion that it was intended, at least partially, to be a catechetical handbook has proven especially useful.[1] Catechetical, which comes from the Greek term "catechesis," refers to instruction. In this sense one of the primary functions of Matthew's gospel is to instruct its community in the fundamentals of living the life of Christian discipleship.

Because of its teaching purpose Matthew's gospel is organized in a way that makes it easy to master. While other possible divisions in the gospel are not to be excluded,[2] it does appear as if the central organizing principle revolves around the five major teaching narratives.[3] The evangelist has taken *Jesus material* and *church tradition* and fashioned them into theologically coherent units. The hand of Matthew is visible not only in his theological emphasis, but also by the literary device "when Jesus had finished . . . ," which concludes each of the five teaching narratives. The five major sections are:

1. Matthew 5–7, the Sermon on the Mount. It concludes in Matthew 7:28–29, *"And when Jesus finished* these sayings, the crowds were astonished at his teaching, 29 for he taught them as one who had authority, and not as their scribes."

2. Matthew 10, instructions to the disciples. It concludes in Matthew 11:1, *"And when Jesus had finished* instructing his twelve disciples, he went on from there to teach and preach in their cities."

3. Matthew 13, eschatological parables. These conclude in
   Matthew 13:53, *"And when Jesus had finished* these parables,
   he went away from there. . . ."

4. Matthew 18, teachings on mercy, discipline, and forgiveness. This section concludes in Matthew 19:1, *"Now when
   Jesus had finished* these sayings, he went away. . . ."

5. Matthew 23–25, instructions and warnings concerning the
   last day of judgment. These final exhortations conclude in
   Matthew 26:1, *"When Jesus had finished* all these sayings, he
   said to his disciples. . . ."

These five teaching narratives do not comprise the entire gospel. In addition to the fact that these teaching sections are followed frequently by miracle stories emphasizing that Jesus is the
messiah of word *and* deed, these sections are placed after Jesus'
birth and temptation at the beginning and before his death and
resurrection at the end. In the opening (Matt. 1–2) and closing
parts of his gospel (Matt. 26–28) Matthew shares with his congregation some profound insights about the uniqueness of this Jesus
whom they confess as Christ, aspects of which we shall examine
shortly.

As with every document in the New Testament, we must ask
about Matthew's audience—for whom and to whom was this gospel addressed? Significant advances have been made in answering this question and we are much indebted to the research of W.
D. Davies.[4] Davies's essential suggestion is that the formation of
Matthew's gospel must be placed in the context of Judaism after
A.D. 70. After the destruction of the temple and Jerusalem in A.D.
70 by the Romans, Judaism was in shambles. In fact, so fierce was
this destructive blow that only one of the several first-century
Jewish groups survived, the Pharisees. This post-destruction pe-
riod, which coincides with the last quarter of the first-century
A.D., is a period of reconstruction and codification, a phenome-
non that eventually develops into what is referred to as Rabbinic
Judaism. This post-destruction Judaism is defensive and vies with
Christianity as a competitor. According to Davies, both Judaism

and Matthew's community interact and influence each other in negative ways. The essential point is that one will not adequately understand Matthew's setting unless one keeps in mind its relationship with the synagogue across the street as well as the stance of that synagogue toward Matthew's congregation.

To define more closely the evangelist's background and that of the congregation is somewhat more difficult and since we only have a paucity of information all such conjectures are bound to be speculative. However, I have always been impressed with Stendahl's suggestion that the evangelist may have been a converted Jewish rabbi who worked closely with other such associates in the composition and writing of his gospel.[5] I would go somewhat beyond Stendahl in urging that one recognize the singular creativity of Matthew himself: committees can work on documents, to use a modern analogy, but finally only one person can give it coherent and consistent shape.[6]

With regard to the composition of Matthew's congregation, we are inclined to see it as Jewish Christian in origin, but with a goodly number of Gentile Christians at the time of composition. For the most part Matthew's gospel is quite intelligible when viewed as an attempt to assist former Jews in understanding the newness of the commitment they have made to Jesus as the Christ. There is perhaps a tendency to see this commitment as entailing a less rigorous understanding and application of the religious life than they had previously experienced. Matthew unilaterally rejects such a perspective. Rather he argues to the Christian converts, "unless your righteousness exceeds that of the scribes and Pharisees, you will never enter the kingdom of heaven" (5:20). This verse, as I shall hope to demonstrate, will be a key to understanding the entire gospel.

If Matthew 5:20 may prove to be the central theme of the gospel, this theme is applied to the structure of the gospel by use of the categories "ethics and eschatology."[7] By *ethics* is meant that new lifestyle that is now possible to the disciple because of God's entry into history through Jesus Christ; by *eschatology* is meant the complex of events dealing with the end-time: the last judgment, death, resurrection, and the consummation of history. Not only are these categories prominent throughout the gospel, they actually shape the composition of it. The first teaching narrative stresses the theme of ethics, the constitution of the kingdom of God, and the final teaching section in Matthew 23–25 stresses the theme of eschatology with symbolic portrayals of God's judgment on the last day. While each of these opening and closing discourses has a specific focus, it always includes both themes. Matthew 5–7 stresses ethics, but not ethics understood abstractly; ethics are understood in light of eschatology, which is the main stress at the end of the Sermon on the Mount. Similarly, while Matthew 23–25 is concerned primarily about eschatology, God's judgment on the last day is clearly dependent upon obedience to his will. Further, not only are the categories of ethics and eschatology intertwined in the first and last discourses, but throughout the gospel as well. All of these interrelationships flow from the key verse of Matthew 5:20, "For I tell you, unless your righteousness exceeds that of the scribes and Pharisees, you will never enter the kingdom of heaven." Righteousness is specifically related to entrance into the kingdom, or put another way, ethics is the basis for eschatological judgment. This point can be seen in Matthew 7:13–23:

"Enter by the narrow gate; for the gate is wide and the way is easy, that leads to destruction, and those who enter by it are many. 14 For the gate is narrow and the way is hard, that leads to life, and those who find it are few.

"15 Beware of false prophets, who come to you in sheep's clothing but inwardly are ravenous wolves. 16 You will know them by their fruits. Are grapes gathered from thorns, or figs from thistles? 17 So, every sound tree bears good fruit, but the bad tree bears evil fruit. 18 A sound tree cannot bear evil fruit, nor can a bad tree bear good fruit. 19 Every tree that does not bear good fruit is cut down and thrown into the fire. 20 Thus you will know them by their fruits.

"21 Not every one who says to me, 'Lord, Lord,' shall enter the kingdom of heaven, but he who does the will of my Father who is in heaven. 22 On that day many will say to me, 'Lord, Lord, did we not prophesy in your name, and cast out demons in your name, and do many mighty works in your name?' 23 And then will I declare to them, 'I never knew you; depart from me, you evildoers.' "

Verses 13–14 are a summary of the previous ethical instructions beginning in chapter 5. The life of discipleship is difficult and entrance into the kingdom is via a narrow gate. The phrase "the gate is narrow, and the way is hard" is characteristic of Matthew's portrayal of discipleship throughout his gospel. Verses 15–20 warn that there will be false prophets who come in the name of Jesus, a theme found elsewhere in the New Testament as well. The criterion laid down for testing whether prophets are true or false is by their fruits, that is, by their works. Even this criterion is seen in light of eschatology: "Every tree that does not bear good fruit is cut down and thrown into the fire. Thus you will know them by their fruits" (vv. 19–20).

Perhaps the clearest example of the close interconnection between the themes of ethics and eschatology as well as sections one and five, is to be seen in verses 21–23. Here again the concern is with entering the kingdom which is the final eschatological goal of the Christian. It is not simply lip service, abstract confession, saying "Lord, Lord," but it is doing "the will of my Father who is in heaven" that will be the decisive issue. The following verse makes quite clear that it is finally not frenetic activity in the name of Jesus, but doing the will of the Father that is the decisive matter. To underline the seriousness of this, verse 23 is an out-and-out rejection of those who have substituted misguided activity for faithfulness to the will of the Father: "And then will I declare to them, 'I never knew you; depart from me, you evildoers.' " The interconnections between this theme and Matthew 25 are striking. At the end of the allegory of the ten virgins in Matthew 25:11–12 one reads: " 'Lord, Lord, open to us.' 12 But he replied, 'Truly, I say to you, I do not know you.' " Two phrases just encountered in Matthew 7 recur: "Lord, Lord" and "I do not know you." Matthew is consciously binding the first and last teaching narratives together. They are both concerned with ethics and eschatology, the essential difference being that Matthew 25 puts the major stress on eschatology, viewing ethics in light of that stress. But since we will spend more time on this further on, let us return to Matthew 5–7.

The first thing that must be said about the Sermon on the Mount is that in its present form it is a composition of Matthew. As is characteristic of Matthew's gospel throughout, Matthew collects Jesus material and church interpretation and places them in the context of his own theological perspective. In the Sermon on the Mount, Matthew assembles disparate words of Jesus and puts them into a unified whole. This observation can be tested by looking at Matthew 5–7 in the gospel parallels. One will find that much of the material found at this point in Matthew is found also in Luke, but in the third gospel it is scattered throughout. We of course know from redaction criticism that it is Matthew's technique to bring to unified expression materials originally found in different locations. But even common sense would suggest to us that it is more likely for an author to bring together that which is scattered rather than to scatter throughout one's gospel that which has been already unified.

The Sermon on the Mount begins this way: "Seeing the crowds, he went up on the mountain, and when he sat down his disciples came to him." The setting places Jesus on the mountain to give ethical instruction to his disciples. Other than the frequent Old Testament reference to the mountain as a place of revelation, it is also the place where Moses goes to receive ethical instruction. As Professor Davies outlines for us, there are striking analogies, if not conscious typologies between the structure and content of Matthew's gospel and the Old Testament.[8] One need only think of the fact that Matthew has five teaching narratives and that the Pentateuch is comprised of five books. Is this purely coincidental? Hardly. With regard to this opening verse two additional points should be noted: (1) Jesus sits down, in good rabbinic fashion, to give instruction. (2) Instruction is given to the disciples. This is not an ethic intended for everyone to follow, but for those who have responded to the call of discipleship. If one views the kingdom of God as a phrase involving political rhetoric, then the kingdom has a king—the Father, a constitution —the will of the Father, and it is comprised of a people—disciples. What follows is the "constitution" of the kingdom for its constituency.

The Sermon on the Mount begins with a section frequently referred to as "the beatitudes," a term taken from the opening word of the central verses, *makarioi,* from which the English word "makarism" is derived. The translation of *makarios* as "blessed" is not especially helpful, however, since for most Americans it is not a precise term. More helpful is the suggested translation by W. F. Albright, "fortunate are those . . ."[9] Fortunate does capture the sense of the eschatological, which is central to these beatitudes. Those who participate in the lifestyle outlined in the beatitudes are fortunate for they shall "enter," they shall receive the joys of the kingdom on the last day. The practice that leads to entrance in the kingdom is here detailed in general terms that will be made even more concrete in the remainder of this first teaching section. One should note, however, that according to verses 3 and 10, there is already now a participation, however partial, in the kingdom. The second half of these verses is not in the future, but in the present. "Blessed are the poor in spirit, for theirs *is* the kingdom of heaven." Those who are humble already now participate in that kingdom which has been inaugurated in the coming of Jesus of Nazareth. Likewise, verse 10: "Blessed are those who are persecuted for righteousness' sake, for theirs *is* the kingdom of heaven." One sign of participation in the kingdom is that one runs the high risk of persecution. This is a reality now for the disciple as certainly as it will bring its reward in the consummation of the kingdom on the last day (vv. 11, 12).

The beatitudes provide for us a fascinating example of how Matthew actualizes the gospel tradition for the needs of his congregation as he perceives them. The beatitudes in Matthew are considerably amplified beyond what we find in Luke and therefore beyond what we find in their common source, Q.[10] Leaving aside the obvious parallel to Matthew 5:11 (the persecution makarism) in Luke 6:22, the beatitudes as found in Luke 6 are unusually brief and read as follows:

> 20 "Blessed are you poor,
> for yours is the kingdom of God.
> 21 "Blessed are you that hunger now,
> for you shall be satisfied.
> "Blessed are you that weep now,
> for you shall laugh."

Not only has Matthew expanded these verses by adding additional beatitudes, but he has altered and expanded what one finds in the Lucan parallel. Throughout Matthew shifts from the second person "you" to a generalized third person. More significantly one should note how Matthew alters "Blessed are you poor" into "Blessed are the poor in spirit." As can be seen from the remainder of Matthew's gospel, he certainly is not unconcerned about the poor. Rather, at this point in his gospel Matthew is concerned with the necessity of humility as an essential criterion of the disciples life. Thus he changes the Q source by adding "in spirit" since this was a major concern he was addressing in his congregation. One should also note that Matthew's alteration of "kingdom of God" to "kingdom of heaven," a change he frequently, but not always, makes throughout his gospel, probably reflects his Jewish background and his reluctance to use the divine name.

Before we proceed, it may be useful to say a further word about alterations and additions to the gospel traditions by the authors of the gospels. First, what motivates such changes to the traditions? For Matthew and the primitive church, Jesus is the Risen Lord present in their midst, compelling them always to make his Word a dynamic Word. Second, as we discuss certain changes in the beatitudes, we must be clear that Matthew is not fabricating this material *de novo.* It is not a creation *ex nihilo,* out of nothing.

Rather Matthew—and this is paralleled by the other evangelists as well—is formulating, shaping, and interpreting certain elements already part of the Christ event and placing them in their present context so as to emphasize and actualize them for the present needs of his audience.

In Matthew 5:6, we observe how the words of the first evangelist once again differ from the Lucan version of 6:21: "Blessed are you that hunger now, for you shall be satisfied." Matthew adds a term of central theological importance to him, "righteousness." Matthew 5:6 reads: "Blessed are those who hunger and thirst for *righteousness,* for they shall be satisfied." In making this change we must once again stress that Matthew is not in any way downplaying the need for concern with those who are hungry, as he makes abundantly clear in Matthew 25. Rather, he is stressing to his congregation that righteousness, that is, doing the will of the Father, is not *adiaphora,* optional, but an essential ingredient for entrance into the kingdom on the last day. This term "righteousness" recurs again in verse 10 (also a Matthean addition) and, of course, again in that key verse, 5:20.

Matthew's ethical rigorism is stressed in a rather similar way at another point in the Sermon on the Mount, the Lord's Prayer.[11] This prayer is only found in Matthew and Luke, suggesting that it comes from the Q source, which both had in common. At the point in Matthew 6:10/Luke 11:2 where the original prayer reads, "Thy kingdom come," the first evangelist adds, "Thy will be done, on earth as it is in heaven." Once again, through these very significant alterations one can recognize concerns of great magnitude that Matthew believes are vital to his audience.

To return to the opening of this first teaching section we have seen how Matthew stresses that the disciple of Jesus has been enabled to participate in a lifestyle characterized by such gifts as humility, righteousness, and peacemaking. Disciples who faithfully participate in that type of life will inherit the kingdom on the last day. To outline with clarity this lifestyle of discipleship as well as its rigor is the purpose of the Sermon on the Mount.

The newness of the life of discipleship is stressed in 5:13–16. Disciples are to be "salt" and "light" in a world that is both "flat" and "dark." Not only does the disciple add a new ingredient to the human situation, he does so in an actively visible way: "You are the light of the world. A city set on a hill cannot be hid. 15 Nor do men light a lamp and put it under a bushel, but on a stand, and it gives light to all in the house. 16 Let your light so shine before men, that they may see your good works and give glory to your Father who is in heaven" (5:14–16). The disciple is to bear fruit, he is to do good works not as an act of self-glory, but as an act of glory to his Father in heaven.

It is fully possible that some in Matthew's congregation had come to believe that the life of Christian discipleship is easier, less rigorous, than their previous participation in Judaism. This would appear clear from the next few verses we will examine, but also from the conclusion to the Sermon on the Mount. We have already noted 7:15 concerning the false prophets. Just before that one reads: "Enter by the narrow gate; for the gate is wide and the way is easy, that leads to destruction, and those who enter by it are many. 14 For the gate is narrow and the way is hard, that leads to life, and those who find it are few" (7:13–14). This theme echoes throughout Matthew especially in the familiar words "many are called but few are chosen" (22:14).

To emphasize that the Christian life is involved in costly rather than cheap grace,[12] Matthew speaks sharply against those in his congregation who would think that the Christian church is involved in a blanket dismissal of the law or of the Old Testament itself. This point is made in a brief introduction to a section commonly referred to as the antitheses found in 5:21–48. The title for this section derives from the formulaic expression, "You have heard that it was said to the men of old . . . but I say to you that. . . ." It is in the introduction to these antitheses that we read: "Think not that I have come to abolish the law and the prophets; I have come not to abolish them but to fulfill them." The next verse underscores the importance of keeping the commandments and immediately thereafter we find the verse we have argued is the key to the entire gospel: "For I tell you, unless your righteousness exceeds that of the scribes and Pharisees, you will never enter the kingdom of heaven."

The immediate questions that come to mind relate to the meaning of the word "fulfill" and the meaning of a righteousness which must "exceed" that of the scribes and Pharisees. That the term "fulfill" in all likelihood means "to bring something to its essential or root meaning" is suggested by the antitheses that follow. The first antithesis makes this point quite clearly.

"You have heard that it was said to the men of old, 'You shall not kill; and whoever kills shall be liable to judgment.' 22 But I say to you that every one who is angry with his brother shall be liable to judgment; whoever insults his brother shall be liable to the council, and whoever says, 'You fool!' shall be liable to the hell of fire." (5:21–22)

Jesus according to Matthew clearly does not in any way abolish the commandment "You shall not kill." Rather, he brings it to its root meaning. What is it finally that leads to the external act of murder? Anger. Therefore this antithesis radicalizes the commandment to the point of including anger as well. Jesus breaks through any possible formal, external, or legal understanding of this commandment so as to deal with its very cause. This same pattern can be seen in the second antithesis:

"You have heard that it was said, 'You shall not commit adultery.' 28 But I say to you that every one who looks at a woman lustfully has already committed adultery with her in his heart. 29 If your right eye causes you to sin, pluck it out and throw it away; it is better that you lose one of your members than that your whole body be thrown into hell." (5:27–29)

It is not only the external act of adultery that is condemned, but the cause of it as well—lust. It is, to give a contemporary analogy, not only going to bed with someone else's spouse that is rejected, but also lusting over the centerfold of a pornographic magazine. It is precisely in this matter of intensification of the Old Testament commandments that the righteousness of the Christian disciple is to exceed that of the scribes and Pharisees.

Matthew 6 initiates a series of concerns dealing with the practice of the religious life and begins with this warning: "Beware of practicing your piety before men in order to be seen by them; for then you will have no reward from your Father who is in heaven." One of the basic concerns is with hypocrisy, an act of pretending by the use of certain external actions that do not coincide with one's inner attitude. This credibility gap is offensive to Matthew whether it appears among Christians or Pharisees (cf. Matthew 23) and he repeatedly warns his congregation against it. The disciple receives his approval from God on the last day and not from human judges in the present. All religious practice has as its motivation the praise of God and not one's own praise. And so Matthew stresses in these opening verses that acts of charity and prayer are things that are carried out secretly "and your Father who sees in secret will reward you" (vv. 4 and 6). Such acts of almsgiving are to be carried out so naturally and simply that the left hand does not know what the right hand is doing. The point is that a gift for the sake of others should not always be accompanied by a bronze plaque designating in bold letters the name of the donor. One of the most vivid illustrations of this theme in contemporary life that immediately comes to mind is the story of a marvelous retired physician who, upon becoming chronically ill, was rejected by his family and placed in what was called at the time New York's Welfare Island. In that somewhat depressing institution he was placed in a six-man ward. Whenever the others in his ward had needs, they would be miraculously taken care of by means of gifts from this gentleman through a volunteer. His ward-mates never knew where their gifts came from. Certainly we have here a classic example of the right hand not knowing what the left hand is doing.

The remainder of the Sermon on the Mount continues to give advice and instruction concerning the life of discipleship. We shall examine one final example from this first teaching narrative in Matthew's gospel, the Lord's Prayer. Insofar as it follows directly upon the sections dealing with praying and giving alms in secret, it continues in giving practical advice as to the method of prayer. Here the issue is not that of praying in secret, but of the brevity of prayer: "And in praying do not heap up empty phrases as the Gentiles do; for they think that they will be heard for their many words" (6:7). The Lord's Prayer that follows is, of course, a model of brevity and conciseness. Yet it must be remembered that this prayer deals with far more than the methodology of prayer—it is a summary of the essence of the teaching of Jesus. At the moment we can only give brief indications of this here and expand upon it when we discuss in greater detail the teaching of Jesus.

As particularly Professor Jeremias has pointed out, the use of "Father" as a direct address to God was apparently not customary in Judaism at the time of Jesus. For many Jews the political situation from the time of the exile had so deteriorated that God appeared enormously distant and life filled with despair. Given this situation it is in fact rather radical for Jesus to address God as Father. It is precisely this degree of intimacy and trust that is characteristic of Jesus' attitude to God and it is precisely this dimension of God that is being revealed through the ministry of Jesus. This God who is loving, caring, and embracing is illustrated in the parable of the prodigal son in Luke 15. "Hallowed be thy name" is characteristic of the daily Jewish prayer and is taken over by Jesus the Jew. God and his name are most holy and sacred. It may be for this reason, to repeat our previous observation, that Matthew so often uses the more Jewish phrase "kingdom of heaven" rather than "kingdom of God"; it is a sign of awe and respect for the divine name.

"Thy kingdom come." As we shall see further on, the category "kingdom of God" is absolutely central to the teaching of Jesus and many of his parables deal with fleshing out the content and ethic of this kingdom of God. As shall become evident, it is in and through his ministry that the kingdom breaks into the human situation in a new way. While this kingdom is already breaking in, it is not yet completely fulfilled. Because of this "not yet" dimension, because of this "eschatological reservation," the disciples are taught to pray "thy kingdom come." Into this strictly eschatological context, Matthew adds, "Thy will be done, on earth as it is in heaven," a phrase that clearly breaks the original connection between verses 9 and 11. As we have already observed, Matthew adds verse 10, because it is so terribly important to his actualization of the gospel to his congregation. They need to be reminded of the necessity of ethical rigorism.

Verse 11 is translated by the Revised Standard Version in this way: "Give us this day our daily bread." An alternative translation appears in a footnote of the Revised Standard Version: "Give us our bread for the morrow." Without question this is one of the most difficult verses to translate in the New Testament, because of the unintelligibility of the Greek. Sometime ago, Professor Jeremias indicated that the unintelligibility of the Greek may be due to the fact that someone translated an Aramaic (the language of Jesus) phrase literally, rather than idiomatically, into the Greek. As many of us are aware, translation of any foreign language is only successful if one presents not a word-for-word literal translation, but one that expresses the original thought in the idiom, the common phraseology of the native language involved. Therefore, Professor Jeremias suggests that a "backwards" translation from the Greek sentence as we now find it back into Aramaic might be revealing. And revealing it is. Jeremias proposes that originally Jesus prayed, "Give us tomorrow's bread today."[13] The request would then be that the bread, the heavenly manna, that comes from the kingdom beyond, from that kingdom that has broken in but is not yet fulfilled, be given to his disciples as they live in the midst of their frail, sinful, and broken world. The prayer would be that God's work, God's food, which is a transcendent gift, be made available today and everyday to those disciples who ask for it. These themes, as we shall see, find echoes throughout the gospel. This is also the case with verse 12: "And forgive us our debts, as we also have forgiven our debtors," which is amplified and illustrated in the parable of the unforgiving servant in 18:23–25. As God freely forgives, so must the forgiven disciple forgive the brothers and sisters. The final verse of the Lord's Prayer is verse 13, which Jeremias translates as "protect us from the Evil One."[14] Here the reality factor of the presence of demonic forces is stressed, but with the assurance of the Father's protecting hand against such forces.

We have looked at several dimensions of the Sermon on the Mount, the first teaching narrative in Matthew's gospel, and have noted its overriding concerns with illustrating the ethic of the kingdom in light of that last judgment awaiting every disciple at the end of time. In other words, ethics are discussed in light of eschatology. Let us now turn to the fifth and last teaching narrative in this gospel where the emphasis is reversed and where eschatology is discussed in light of ethics.

This final narrative section opens in Matthew 23 and this chapter especially can only be properly understood as reflecting the current situation in Matthew's congregation with regard to post-70 Judaism. It begins on a strongly ethical note that dominates all of Matthew 23. The chapter begins in this way: "Then said Jesus to the crowds and to his disciples, 2 'The scribes and the Pharisees sit on Moses' seat; 3 so practice and observe whatever they tell you, but not what they do; for they preach, but do not practice.'" Here we note the essence of Jesus' concern as Matthew presents it—hypocrisy—illustrated by the criticism that the Pharisees preach, but do not practice. The teaching of the Pharisees is not the problem, it is their failure to act upon their teaching. It is this lack of credibility, this hypocrisy that is refuted in an almost liturgically repetitive way in verses 13, 16, 23, 25, 27, and 29. Typical of these "woes" is the pericope found in verses 23–24:

"Woe to you, scribes and Pharisees, hypocrites! for you tithe mint and dill and cummin, and have neglected the weightier matters of the law, justice and mercy and faith; these you ought to have done, without neglecting the others. 24 You blind guides, straining out a gnat and swallowing a camel!" (23:23–24)

Not only must one adhere to an ethical position, one must act it out. One cannot just say "Lord, Lord," one must do the will of the Father. This initial chapter undoubtedly serves not only as a criticism of that Judaism contemporary with Matthew's congregation, but also as a warning to the congregation itself that it not fall into this same type of hypocrisy.

Having stressed essentially ethics in chapter 23, Matthew now shifts to a strongly eschatological perspective in chapters 24 and 25. Typical of the flavor of these chapters is 24:44: "Therefore you also must be ready; for the Son of man is coming at an hour you do not expect."

The stress on eschatology, especially that of meeting the Lord on the last day, is intentional in this first gospel. One of the problems that confronted the Christian communities at the end of the first century is referred to by scholars as "the delay of the parousia." Parousia in the Greek New Testament is used frequently to mean "coming" or "advent," especially in the sense of the final messianic advent. The earliest Christians were understandably enthusiastic and excited in the period following the resurrection of Jesus. This together with lines of influence from apocalyptic Judaism led many of these Christians to believe that the messianic age that Jesus had inaugurated would be fulfilled at any moment, and certainly within their lifetimes. When this expectation remained unfulfilled after several decades, an understandable disappointment set in. Often this disappointment led to a slackening in the seriousness with which the Christian life was led. One result was that "most men's love will grow cold" (24:12). Therefore Matthew quickly adds in the next verse, "But he who endures to the end will be saved."

The "delay of the parousia" theme moves center stage at the end of Matthew 24 and occupies much of chapter 25. The concern is well expressed in 24:45–51:

"Who then is the faithful and wise servant, whom his master has set over his household, to give them their food at the proper time? 46 Blessed is that servant whom his master when he comes will find so doing. 47 Truly, I say to you, he will set him over all his possessions. 48 But if that wicked servant says to himself, 'My master is delayed,' 49 and begins to beat his fellow servants, and eats and drinks with the drunken, 50 the master of that servant will come on a day when he does not expect him and at an hour he does not know, 51 and will punish him, and put him with the hypocrites; there men will weep and gnash their teeth." (24:45-51)

Note how centrally the concern is expressed: "My master is delayed." If this delay leads a disciple to not be faithful to the will of the Father, then that servant will be punished on the last day and God will "put him with the hypocrites." Why with the hypocrites? Presumably because he said, "Lord, Lord," but did not practice faithfully his confession with regard to his fellow servants. Matthew is most concerned to point out to his audience that one must be ready, one must be prepared and faithful "for the Son of man is coming at an hour you do not expect" (24:44). The so-called delay of parousia dare not become an excuse in the practice of discipleship.

The delay of the parousia motif also plays a prominent part in the allegory of the ten virgins in 25:1-13. As Matthew deals with this issue he skillfully summarizes major aspects of his theology as well in this story, and therefore it is a most important pericope for our examination.

"Then the kingdom of heaven shall be compared to ten maidens who took their lamps and went to meet the bridegroom. 2 Five of them were foolish, and five were wise. 3 For when the foolish took their lamps, they took no oil with them; 4 but the wise took flasks of oil with their lamps. 5 As the bridegroom was delayed, they all slumbered and slept. 6 But at midnight there was a cry, 'Behold, the bridegroom! Come out to meet him.' 7 Then all those maidens rose and trimmed their lamps. 8 And the foolish said to the wise, 'Give us some of your oil, for our lamps are going out.' 9 But the wise replied, 'Perhaps there will not be enough for us and for you; go rather to the dealers and buy for yourselves.' 10 And while they went to buy, the bridegroom came, and those who were ready went in with him to the marriage feast; and the door was shut. 11 Afterward the other maidens came also, saying, 'Lord, lord, open to us.' 12 But he replied, 'Truly, I say to you, I do not know you.' 13 Watch therefore, for you know neither the day nor the hour."

This story is trying to illumine and illustrate what "the kingdom of heaven" *shall* be like: it shall be like ten virgins who took their lamps as they were going to meet the bridegroom. It is on the basis of sufficient or insufficient oil that some are and some are not admitted to the marriage feast with the bridegroom. The central point is that possession of sufficient oil is the basic criterion for admission to the marriage feast. This comparison of "the kingdom of heaven" with the virgins achieves meaning only if the term "oil" is intelligible to Matthew's congregation; but the immediate context indicates only that the "oil" is used as fuel for lamps.

Furthermore, the text does not describe normal Jewish nuptial practice, nor is any description given of the "virgins," of the "bridegroom," of the "marriage feast," or even of the more minor details in the story.[15] These problems push us beyond these thirteen verses for some more intelligible understanding, since it is not reasonable to assume that Matthew would have devoted more than half the story to the lamp/oil motif unless it had some intelligible significance to himself and his audience.

Since the story does not allow us to discover its meaning or intention within itself, due primarily to the ambiguity of the symbolic language employed, it is more likely an allegory. Various elements in 25:1–13 cohere not with each other but with a theological framework outside the story itself. Crossan distinguishes between two general categories of metaphors: "There are metaphors in which information precedes participation so that the function of metaphor is to illustrate information about the metaphor's referent; but there are also metaphors in which participation precedes information so that the function of metaphor is to create participation in the metaphor's referent."[16] The first type of metaphor is represented in the allegory; the second, in the parable.

Via suggests that "the structure, shape, and interconnections of an allegory are determined by something outside itself—by its meaning or referent. . . . An allegory, then, communicates to a person what he already knows, though it communicates it in symbolic and altered fashion."[17] What is it that readers of the allegory of the ten virgins know that is here being communicated to them in symbolic and altered fashion?

In attempting to shed light upon 25:1–13 in view of the context in Matthew 23–25, it is important to observe that this entire discourse is concerned with practicing and keeping what has been commanded by Jesus. Both beginning (23:3–4) and conclusion (25:45–46) stress the motif that only by doing the deeds inherent in the Christian life will one be found acceptable at the final judgment. Unless Matthew is somehow inconsistent, there is a strong probability that the allegory of the ten virgins is somehow related to this same overall emphasis of the fifth discourse.

A number of themes found in the allegory of the ten virgins are paralleled in Matthew's fifth discourse. The division motif is found not only in 25:2 (five and five), but also in 24:40–41 (one and one). Also the parable of the talents in 25:14–30 speaks more sharply of a separation between those who have multiplied their talents and the one who has buried it than does Q. In the virgin allegory the separation is between those who are foolish and those who are wise, whereas in the talents story the separation is between the "good and faithful servant" (25:21) and the "wicked and slothful servant" (25:26). In 24:45 it is between the "faithful and wise servant" and the one who is not faithful and wise.

Throughout the fifth discourse the wise and faithful ones are the ones who are active in doing good deeds. It is thus likely that the separation between the five foolish virgins and the five wise virgins is related to this overall theme of practicing, observing, and doing (23:3; 24:46; 25:40, 45). It is also probable that the allegory of the virgins is related to the warning not to be like the hypocrites who are condemned in 23:27–28.

The themes of the coming of the master and of eschatological judgment are found throughout (24:30–31, 36–37, 50–51; 25: 19–21, 31–33). The coming of the end had been delayed (24:34, 48; 25:5), so Matthew urged the Christians in his congregation not to lessen their performance of good deeds. One central point in the exhortation is that "he who endures to the end [in the performance of love] will be saved" (24:13).

Matthew deals with the delay of the parousia from at least two different angles: the warning to *watchfulness* and the warning about *preparedness.* The allegory of the ten virgins may be intended to deal with the second area of concern. Those who go to sleep (die) prepared will be like the five wise virgins who had enough oil for their lamps, and not like those foolish virgins who had lamps but an insufficient supply of oil. Oil has a critical significance for the story and, given our understanding of the intentions of the fifth discourse, it probably serves as a symbol for the good deeds mentioned throughout and highlighted and brought to culmination in 25:31–46.

Because of the close connection between Matthew's first and fifth discourses, we now examine the Sermon on the Mount, particularly 7:13–27, where parallels to this pericope abound. Although 7:24–27 is taken from Q, Matthean redaction is easy to detect. First, Matthew adds the distinction between the "wise" and the "foolish." Second, he alters Q's account of the second house. In Matthew the second man builds his house upon a foundation of sand. The foolish man is like a tree that does not bear fruit (7:17–19) or the person who says "Lord, Lord" (7:21 and 25:11) but does not do the will of the Father; he is, in fact, very similar to the foolish virgins who do not have sufficient oil.

In addition, the Sermon on the Mount shares an almost identical phrase with the allegory of the virgins. In 7:23 we read, "I never knew you," and in 25:12, "Truly, I say to you, I do not know you." The wording at 25:12 is identical with Luke 13: 26–27. It may well be that this Q logion served as a basic element in Matthew's construction of the allegory of the ten virgins and that in 7:23, owing to its probable polemic against a formative and threatening post-70 Judaism, Matthew is purposely giving a literal translation of a Jewish *Bannformel,* "formula of exclusion."

In Matthew 25, "I do not know you" serves as a formula of rejection for those who are not properly and adequately prepared; in Matthew 7, for those who hear the words but do not obey them. Those rejected in both places come with certain credentials; they are not rejected because these actions are wrong, but because they are inadequate. If there is any relationship between Matthew 25 and 7, then the likelihood is increased that the oil is another of several symbolic expressions employed by Matthew for the concept "doing the will of the Father."

The "door" theme is an important one for Matthew. On the eschatological day, Jesus will stand at the door (24:33) and will admit those properly prepared (25:10; 7:21). That entrance through the door is not easy is vividly stressed in 7:13: "Enter by the narrow gate. . . ."

The lamp/oil symbol is of critical importance in Matthew 25. There are several significant references to lamps and light that are compatible with our suggestion that the "oil" in Matthew 25 refers to nothing other than "good deeds." Central among these references is 5:14–16: "You are the light of the world. . . . 15 Nor do men light a lamp and put it under a bushel, but on a stand, and it gives light [*lampei*] to all in the house. 16 Let your light so shine [*lampsato*] before men, that they may see your good works and give glory to your Father who is in heaven." Why does one light a lamp? So that one's good works will give glory to the Father. Similarly the ten virgins lit up their lamps before the bridegroom, but in the case of the five foolish virgins, their oil, their good deeds, was not sufficient. When the real test of their oil arrived, the result was similar to the house built on a sandy foundation: it was found to be inadequate.

Now we can discuss the terms "bridegroom" and "marriage feast" in Matthew. In 9:15 we have not only a connection between the bridegroom and the wedding guests but the explicit identification of Jesus as the bridegroom. The theme of the wedding feast is elaborately presented in 22:1–14, a Q pericope redactionally enhanced by Matthew, particularly verses 11–14. One guest had no "wedding garment," so was cast into the outer darkness. The wedding garment in Matthew "symbolizes the ethical quality expected in the church."[18]

The delay in the parousia is a nuanced, yet characteristic Matthean concern (cf. 24:48; 25:19). And in all those places where Matthew uses the verb *egeirō* independently of his sources he is referring to a real rising from physical death (9:25; 10:8; 16:21, and 17:9). It is likely he intends it to be so understood in 25:7, but then *katheudō* in 13:25 and 25:5 can only mean "death."

The symbolic language of 25:5–7, then, refers to the death and resurrection of the virgins. Even if some will die before the delayed parousia comes, they had better not let that factor lead them to believe that the final entrance criteria into the kingdom had become less rigorous.

In the wider New Testament witness, "oil" is used in a variety of ways, but nowhere else with the suggestion of good deeds as implied above. But the term "virgins" is illuminated. As Jesus is the bridegroom for Matthew, so the church is the virgin who meets her bridegroom at the wedding banquet. The primary support for this comes from Paul in 2 Corinthians 11:2: "I betrothed you to Christ to present you as a pure bride to her one husband." So virgin in Matthew 25 probably refers to all Christians in the interval before the marriage that will occur when Christ returns at the parousia.

The "oil" of the virgins has still not been identified from its immediate context, from Matthew's gospel, or from the entire New Testament. In the *Midrash Rabbah* to Numbers (Num R. xiii 15, 16), referring to the phrase "mingled with oil" in Numbers 7:19, the midrash comments that this alludes "to the Torah, the study of which must be mingled with *good deeds,* in accordance with that which we have learned." We find here an explicit identification of "oil" with "good deeds." This usage of oil is identical to what we have suggested the symbol "oil" means in 25:3, 4, and 8. It is then clear why there can be no transfer of "oil" or "good deeds" or "obedience" from one person to the other, and it is equally absurd to purchase good deeds from the dealers (25:9).

The fact that 25:1–13 could not be understood on its own terms supports those scholars who have viewed it as an allegory. This factor, coupled with such later concerns as the delay of the parousia, suggests that it does not stem from the historical Jesus level (Stage 1) but was created by Matthew on the basis of certain traditions he had received. By focusing primarily on the smaller and larger Matthean contexts, we have discovered not only Matthew's intention in creating the allegory of the ten virgins but also that this allegory summarizes much that is central to the theology of Matthew.

We have observed that the theme of "delay" is expressed as a major concern in 24:24 and in 25:5. It is also central to 25:14–30, the parable of the talents. "For it [the kingdom of heaven] will be as when a man going on a journey called his servants and entrusted to them his property. . . . 19 *Now after a long time* the master of those servants came and settled accounts with them" (25:14, 19). The entire action of the parable is concerned with an interval period that will continue for a "long time" and it recounts the lives of these persons each of whom had received different amounts of money.

The servants who had received the five and the two talents, or let us say $5,000 and $2,000, put these gifts immediately to active use. On the last day after the return of the master, the five-talent servant responds: " 'Master, you delivered to me five talents; here I have made five talents more.' 21 His master said to him, 'Well done, good and faithful servant; you have been faithful over a little, I will set you over much; enter into the joy of your master' " (vv. 20–21). The scene at the last judgment with the two-talent servant is identical. The major concern in this story is with the one-talent servant and it is evident that Matthew is primarily concerned with him as a example of what the Christian disciple ought not to do. Upon receiving his one talent, or in our currency about $1,000, he went and "dug in the ground and hid his master's money" (v. 18). Contrary to the active use to which the other two put their gifts, this servant's action is striking for its inactivity. As a result of this nonuse of the gift, there is quite a different scene on the last day and one should pay careful attention that about one-half of the entire parable is consumed in this dialogue. The setting is the same: ". . . After a long time the master of those servants came and settled accounts with them" (v. 19). This final servant responds: " 'Master, I knew you to be a hard man, reaping where you did not sow, and gathering where you did not winnow; 25 so I was afraid, and I went and hid your talent in the ground. Here you have what is yours' " (vv. 24–25). Immediately striking is the inconsistency between the servant's confession about God and the consequences he draws from that in terms of his practice. He recognizes that God is both demanding and unusually creative in bringing about results out of nothing. Instead of trusting in this God whom he has just confessed, he is afraid and takes God's talent and puts it in the ground. By putting it in the ground it escapes both God's discipline as well as his creative intention. The master's answer is stinging: "You wicked and slothful servant! You knew that I reap where I have not sowed, and gather where I have not yet winnowed? 27 Then you ought to have invested my money with the bankers, and at my coming I should have received what was my own with interest. . . . 30 And cast the worthless servant into the outer darkness; there men will weep and gnash their teeth' " (vv. 26–30). Rather than receiving the commendation "Well done, good and faithful servant," this one-talent servant is greeted with a rejection, "You wicked and slothful servant." The negative attribute "wicked and slothful" is important. Not only has this servant done wrong, he had not done what he ought to have done, that is, to use the talent in a creative way commensurate with his theological confession. It is also evident from this scene that the final encounter of the disciple with God is not automatically positive, but may well contain rejection. One is instantly reminded of such Matthean themes as "Not every one who says to me, 'Lord, Lord,' shall enter the kingdom of heaven, but he who does the will of my Father who is in heaven" (7:21) or "Many are called, but few are chosen" (22:14).

What is Matthew's point in recounting this particular story in his final eschatological teaching narrative? He is making an analogy between the talents and the life of the Christian disciple, which is to be a life actively using God's gifts in accordance with his will for the glory of God. This dimension of actively bearing fruit for the other in the marketplace is what leads to the commendation of the five- and two-talent servants and the rejection of the one-talent servant. Why, one might ask, is the one-talent servant singled out? Perhaps because the majority of disciples are one-, rather than five-talent people and because it is the ordinary person who might feel that his abilities are not significant in God's eyes. To this Matthew responds that it is God who is the giver and that it is he who is the creative force behind the gift. Therefore precisely the one-talent servant should risk his life in the hands of the faithful and creative God who both gave the gift and who on the last day will ask for an account of how that gift was used. Matthew's image of God as hard and creative, which so dominates Matthew 25, is remarkably similar to Paul's statement in Romans 11:22 that God is a God of severity and kindness.

The consummation of Matthew's eschatological perspective is to be found in the last part of Matthew 25, verses 31–46. It is an encouragement to ethical intensity from the perspective of the enthroned Son of man on the last day. While many elements in this pericope are debated among scholars, it is clear that Matthew wishes to stress that "bearing fruit," "doing the will of the Father" involves concrete actions to "the least of these my brethren," and that Jesus identifies himself precisely with these.[19] To worship Jesus is not an involvement in abstract spirituality, but service to those who are hungry, thirsty, strangers, naked, sick, or in prison. On the last day of judgment the exalted Son of man will exercise his role as judge and will separate the sheep from the goats, the faithful from the unfaithful, not on the basis of whether they have simply confessed "Lord, Lord," but whether they also have done the will of the Father in serving the needs of those at the periphery of society as just illustrated.

We have now looked at the first and last of Matthew's five teaching narratives and we have noted that the themes of ethics and eschatology are important themes in Matthew's actualization of the gospel to the needs of his congregation. In our detailed analysis of the close interconnections between Matthew 5–7 and 23–25, we have already seen a major foundation of Matthew's overall structure as well as some of his greatest theological concerns. In light of this background we will make very quick references to the remaining three teaching narratives in order to detect other ways in which Matthew attempts to apply the good news of Jesus Christ in a dynamic and relevant way to his congregation at the end of the first century.

Matthew 10, the second of the teaching sections, contains the commissioning and instruction of the twelve disciples. There are two passages that are especially difficult to understand, verses 5–6 and verse 23. We read as follows:

These twelve Jesus sent out, charging them, "Go nowhere among the Gentiles, and enter no town of the Samaritans, 6 but go rather to the lost sheep of the house of Israel." (vv. 5–6)

When they persecute you in one town, flee to the next; for truly, I say to you, you will not have gone through all the towns of Israel, before the Son of man comes. (v. 23)

They both contain a narrow perspective of Jesus' mission both geographically and chronologically. Is this Jesus' perspective? If this is the case how does one understand an account such as that of the Syrophoenician woman (Mark 7:24–30) or of the Canaanite woman (Matt 15:21–28), in other words a gentile woman, whose daughter is healed by Jesus? If it is unlikely that the rigidness of this perspective is to be traced back to the historical Jesus, it is equally unlikely that Matthew himself would have created these verses since they would be in obvious conflict with his congregation's mission to the gentiles as inaugurated by the Risen Lord: "And Jesus came and said to them, 'All authority in heaven and earth has been given to me. 19 Go therefore and make disciples of all nations, baptizing them in the name of the Father and of the Son and of the Holy Spirit, 20 teaching them to observe all that I have commanded you; and lo, I am with you always, to the close of the age" (Matt. 28:18–20). If these verses in their present form do not, in all probability, derive from Jesus or Matthew, is there another option?

Very attractive is the suggestion that Matthew originally had before him verses 5–6 and 23b as a single unit: "Go nowhere among the Gentiles, and enter no town of the Samaritans; for

... you will not have gone through the towns of Israel before the Son of man comes." These words would have come from a conservative Jewish Christianity. This was presumably part of the treasury of Matthew's church, yet Matthew was somewhat at odds with it. According to Professor Green, Matthew "has neutralized the original force of the saying, which he could hardly have assimilated, by using the two halves to endorse a missionary programme with a limited historical scope."[20] This thesis makes eminently good sense and neatly illustrates how Matthew not only actualizes the words and deeds of the historical Jesus to the situation of his church, but also as in this case, the earliest traditions of the Matthean community.

The third Matthean teaching section is appropriately referred to as "eschatological parables." There are a series of discussions in the form of parables that reflect on the present nature of the kingdom in light of the final consummation. Especially characteristic is Matthew 13:47–50:

"Again, the kingdom of heaven is like a net which was thrown into the sea and gathered fish of every kind; 48 when it was full, men drew it ashore and sat down and sorted the good into vessels but threw away the bad. 49 So it will be at the close of the age. The angels will come out and separate the evil from the righteous, 50 and throw them into the furnace of fire; there men will weep and gnash their teeth."

There is the very realistic perception that the church present before Matthew is, to use a phrase of Augustine, a *"corpus mixtum."*[21] It contains good and bad now and at the last day there will be a separation and a judgment. That which is fully expressed in Matthew 25 is anticipated in this chapter. From these verses above it becomes apparent that the first evangelist is attempting to communicate to his audience that in the present the church is not yet perfect, is not one hundred percent pure, and that it is not up to the disciples to "clean house" in the sense of reaching such a level of total spirituality. That is an impossible goal in the earthly manifestation of the kingdom. This perspective is confirmed in the parable of the weeds in the wheat (vv. 24–30) and its allegorical interpretation in verses 36–43 to which we now turn.

The parable and its interpretation appear in Matthew 13 as follows:

Another parable he put before them, saying, "The kingdom of heaven may be compared to a man who sowed good seed in his field; 25 but while men were sleeping, his enemy came and sowed weeds among the wheat, and went away. 26 So when the plants came up and bore grain, then the weeds appeared also. 27 And the servants of the householder came and said to him, 'Sir, did you not sow good seed in your field? How then has it weeds?' 28 He said to them, 'An enemy has done this.' The servants said to him, 'Then do you want us to go and gather them?' 29 But he said, 'No; lest in gathering the weeds you root up the wheat along with them. 30 Let both grow together until the harvest; and at harvest time I will tell the reapers, Gather the weeds first and bind them in bundles to be burned, but gather the wheat into my barn.' "

. . . 36 Then he left the crowds and went into the house. And his disciples came to him, saying, "Explain to us the parable of the weeds of the field." 37 He answered, "He who sows the good seed is the Son of man; 38 the field is the world, and the good seed means the sons of the kingdom; the weeds are the sons of the evil one, 39 and the enemy who sowed them is the devil; the harvest is the close of the age, and the reapers are angels. 40 Just as the weeds are gathered and burned with fire, so will it be at the close of the age. 41 The Son of man will send his angels, and they will gather out of his kingdom all causes of sin and all evildoers, 42 and throw them into the furnace of fire; there men will weep and gnash their teeth. 43 Then the righteous will shine like the sun in the kingdom of their Father. He who has ears, let him hear."

Many scholars have come to the conclusion that neither the allegorical interpretation nor the parable derive from Jesus and that their origin lies either in the Matthean church or with Matthew himself.[22] The focus of both, and certainly the allegory, deals with a church situation in which it is clear that there are "false prophets," those who have made a confession, but do not carry it out in obedience to their heavenly Father. In short, the problem of hypocrisy is present. Shall their vow be a campaign in the congregation to rid itself of all the undesirable types? Should a new sect be set up so as to purify the corrupt church? The response is a firm negative: " 'No; lest in gathering the weeds you root up the wheat along with them. 30 Let both grow together until the harvest . . .' " (vv. 29–30). This verse is amplified in the interpretation: "Just as the weeds are gathered and burned with fire, so will it be at the close of the age. 41 The Son of man will send his angels, and they will gather out of his kingdom all causes of sin and all evildoers, 42 and throw them into the furnace of fire; there men will weep and gnash their teeth. 43 Then the righteous will shine like the sun in the kingdom of their Father. He who has ears, let him hear" (vv. 40–43). One notes here several characteristic Matthean emphases: (1) the sharp eschatological stress of what is to happen "at the close of the age"; (2) the separation motif on the last day that we have already noted through Matthew 24–25, but also in 22:11–14:

"But when the king came in to look at the guests, he saw there a man who had no wedding garment; 12 and he said to him, 'Friend, how did you get in here without a wedding garment?' And he was speechless. 13 Then the king said to the attendants, 'Bind him hand and foot, and cast him into the outer darkness; there men will weep and gnash their teeth.' 14 For many are called, but few are chosen."

and (3) the theme that "the righteous will shine like the sun in the kingdom of their Father," which is remarkably similar to the lamps burning in the allegory of the ten virgins and the several other parallels we noted in that context.

Matthew 13 appears in the middle of the gospel in general and it is also the middle one of the five teaching narratives. It serves to reinforce the teaching given previously and to stress the seriousness of the judgment to come. It serves as a major link between the beginning and the end of the first gospel in Matthew's effort to lift firmly before the eyes of his congregation the importance of and the interconnection between ethics and eschatology.

As we move to the fourth teaching discourse in Matthew 18 we will have to ask whether there is a contradiction between Matthew's warning against premature judgment in Matthew 13 and the firm exhortations about the necessity of discipline in this chapter. But before we engage in that discussion, we must give a few introductory words to Matthew 18. The primary concern Matthew is attempting to communicate to his audience is that he who would be a disciple must be humble and forgiving. This lifestyle of humility and forgiveness must be expressed especially toward "these little ones who believe in me" (v. 6; see also v. 10). It is in this context of taking effort so that none "of these little ones should perish" (v. 14) that one finds the pericope on discipline (18:15–20), a text found only in Matthew's gospel. Immediately preceding this pericope is the significant story of the sheep, with its tremendous stress on mercy, and immediately thereafter is the repeated stress on the necessity of unlimited forgiveness. Peter comes up to Jesus in verse 21 and asks him, "Lord, how often shall my brother sin against me, and I forgive him? As many as seven times?" Peter undoubtedly thought that he was being quite generous, yet there is still a certain limit beyond which he would not go. To this Jesus responds, "I do not say to you seven times, but seventy times seven" (v. 22). Clearly Jesus emphasizes that the ethic of the kingdom is not a calculating one, but one characterized by unlimited mercy and forgiveness. Sandwiched between these two texts one finds the pericope on discipline and ecclesiastical authority:

"If your brother sins against you, go and tell him his fault, between you and him alone. If he listens to you, you have gained your brother. 16 But if he does not listen, take one or two others along with you, that every word may be confirmed by the evidence of two or three witnesses. 17 If he refuses to listen to them, tell it to the church; and if he refuses to listen even to the church, let him be to you as a Gentile and a tax collector. 18 Truly, I say to you, whatever you bind on earth shall be bound in heaven, and whatever you loose on earth shall be loosed in heaven. 19 Again I say to you, if two of you agree on earth about anything they ask, it will be done for them by my Father in heaven. 20 For where two or three are gathered in my name, there am I in the midst of them." (18:15–20)

The major concern of this pericope is how one deals with the fellow disciple who "sins against you." This may strike us strange in an age of permissiveness where one is expected to tolerate all kinds of action and seldom to criticize or ridicule. In verse 15 the advice is explicit: if a brother sins against you such a situation cannot be left to solve itself; concrete action must be taken and three specific steps are outlined with increasing degrees of severity. The first step is to go to the brother alone, tell him his fault and if he listens to you "you have gained your brother" (v. 15). If this initiative fails, then the second course of action is to take one or two others along and to try again. If this second step is not successful, then the final positive step is to "tell it to the church . . ." (v. 17). If there is still at this point a refusal of the brother who sins against you to change his attitude and behavior and "he refuses to listen even to the church, let him be to you as a Gentile and a tax collector" (v. 17). In other words by his own action this brother has removed himself from the community; he has technically excommunicated himself by his refusal to listen.

Before we move further to the conclusion of the text we must raise the question whether this process of discipline just outlined stands in contradiction to Matthew 13. In all likelihood no such contradiction exists. The situation to which Matthew 13 reacts is probably a campaign to take everyone's spiritual temperature and then arbitrarily, from a human rather than divine perspective, separate those who do not reach a certain point on the thermometer. God who knows the secret of the heart will on the last day separate the weeds from the wheat. But to state such a position does not mean that "anything goes" in the Christian church. Quite the contrary; there must be discipline in the present so that none might perish on the last day. When there are flagrant, publicly visible denials of the Christian ethic, then those involved must be confronted both for the sake of themselves and of the community. The focuses in Matthew 13 and 18 are quite different and only as they are held together can life in the community be healthy. If Matthew 13 is advocated to an extreme then a laissez-faire attitude develops in which virtually no correction or discipline takes place; if Matthew 18 is advocated to an extreme then a legalistic rigorism sets in that is self-destructive.

How is it that Matthew can attribute such authority to the "church"? Before we can answer that we must recognize that Matthew's is the only gospel that uses the term "church" and that it is only used here and in Matthew 16:18. Why? The use of the term "church" *(ekklēsia)* marks a certain developmental point in the history of early Christianity. In Greek there are two virtually synonymous terms used to speak of an assembly of people, usually in the sense of political gathering, *synagogē* (synagogue) and *ekklēsia* (church). Jews of the diaspora had selected the first term and early Christians also used it with little difficulty. This is especially attested in the gospel of John. Only as the break with Judaism develops to the point of rupture is it no longer possible for Christians to use the term *synagogē* and they then select the alternate term *ekklēsia*. [23] Matthew is the first and only gospel to testify to this state of affairs that is so frequent elsewhere in the New Testament.

From Matthew's perspective at the end of the first century, his church stands in need of ethical teaching and ecclesiastical structure. Both are commanded by Jesus. In our present context, 18:18 is of critical importance: "Truly, I say to you, whatever you bind on earth shall be bound in heaven, and whatever you loose on earth shall be loosed in heaven." When one examines this verse carefully, the church is truly given a staggering responsibility. Finally, it is the Risen Lord who stands behind this responsibility and it is his authority that makes the church and its teaching and structures authoritative. "All authority in heaven and on earth has been given to me" (28:18). Specifically, in 18:18 the church is given the authority to bind and loose. This is a Jewish idiom that can either mean the communication of authoritative teaching or the exercise of discipline. The former meaning, as we shall see, is appropriate to the usage of this phrase in Matthew 16 and the later meaning is appropriate to our present context. It is the responsibility of the church to both instruct the converts and to dismiss the flagrant sinner who is unrepentant.

Our pericope on ecclesiastical discipline concludes in this way: "Again I say to you, if two of you agree on earth about anything they ask, it will be done for them by my Father in heaven. 20 For where two or three are gathered in my name, there I am in the midst of them" (18:19–20). What should be stressed here is that the reference to two or three is not in the first instance where two or three are gathered together for prayer or for worship but where two or three are gathered together for the process of disciplining one of the brethren. It is in the midst of that action that the Father is present in their midst.

There are two other elements in Matthew's gospel we need to review: the commission to Peter in Matthew 16 and the infancy narratives in Matthew 1 and 2. Our movement to study the first of these, Matthew 16, is an easy transition since we have just observed that two of the elements in Matthew 18, the themes of "church" and "loosing/binding" also occur in Matthew 16.

The critical section of Matthew 16 involves verses 13–20:

Now when Jesus came into the district of Caesarea Philippi, he asked his disciples, "Who do men say that the Son of man is?" 14 And they said, "Some say John the Baptist, others say Elijah, and others Jeremiah or one of the prophets." 15 He said to them, "But who do you say that I am?" 16 Simon Peter replied, "You are the Christ, the son of the living God." 17 And Jesus answered him, "Blessed are you, Simon Bar-Jona! For flesh and blood has not revealed this to you, but my Father who is in heaven. 18 And I tell you, you are Peter, and on this rock I will build my church, and the powers of death shall not prevail against it. 19 I will give you the keys of the kingdom of heaven, and whatever you bind on earth shall be bound in heaven, and whatever you loose on earth shall be loosed in heaven." 20 Then he strictly charged the disciples to tell no one that he was the Christ.

One of the reasons this pericope has invited such lively discussion is that from verse 16b through verse 19 there is no parallel in any of the other gospels. Why? This question becomes even more acute when one realizes the importance that especially verse 18, "And I tell you, you are Peter, and on this rock I will build my church, and the powers of death shall not prevail against it," has had in the development of the papacy. Because of its strategic importance in the history of the papacy many Protestants have been inclined to question its authenticity or to argue that the term "rock" could not possibly refer to Peter himself but rather to his confession of faith. Recent New Testament scholarship has moved us beyond these limited options and has opened for us a whole new perspective.[24]

The starting point for this new perspective is verse 16: "Simon Peter replied, 'You are the Christ, the Son of the living God.'" Matthew goes beyond the text of Mark before him by adding the phrase "the Son of the living God." One knows from elsewhere in the New Testament that such a confession is usually made about the Risen Christ rather than the earthly Jesus. We immediately receive a clue that we may be dealing with a post-resurrectional setting. This is further suggested by the phrase "flesh and blood." In Galatians 1:15–16 Paul writes to those churches in these words: "But when he who had set me apart before I was born, and had called me through his grace, 16 was pleased to reveal his Son to me, in order that I might preach him among the Gentiles, I did not confer with flesh and blood. . . ." Paul makes clear to the churches of Galatia that the gospel he proclaims was communicated to him by the Risen Lord and not through the agency of man.

At this point it is important that we set aside possible twentieth-century prejudices. Whether you as the reader find the fact of appearances of Jesus after his resurrection comprehensible or not is for the moment irrelevant; to understand the minds of early Christians it is essential to grasp this phenomenon of post-resurrection appearances. They believed not only in the suffering death and resurrection of Jesus, but also that this Risen Jesus appeared to certain of his disciples after his resurrection. There are many references to this in the New Testament, perhaps the clearest of which is in 1 Corinthians 15. Here Paul is recounting the gospel he had preached to these Corinthians. He begins with this summary: "For I delivered to you as of first importance what I also received, that Christ died for our sins in accordance with the scriptures" (v. 3). If we simply stopped at this point we would first of all not be faithful to Paul but we would be short-circuiting the mind-set of early Christianity. Paul's description of the gospel continues as follows: ". . . and that he appeared to Cephas, then to the twelve. 6 Then he appeared to more than five hundred brethren at one time, most of whom are still alive, though some have fallen asleep. 7 Then he appeared to James, then to all the apostles" (vv. 5–7). The entire thrust of vv. 5–7 is the fact of the appearance of the Risen One, and here as elsewhere the first of these appearances is always to Peter.

Without attempting to be facetious, we must ask whether anything more transpired between the Risen Lord and Peter than a swift, passing "Hi, Pete!" In other words, was there some point, some content to the appearance of the Risen One to Peter? In *Peter in the New Testament* we suggest that there definitely was content and intentionality in this appearance and we refer to it as a "church-founding" appearance.[25] It was at this moment, through the agency of Peter, that the church came into existence, and in all likelihood the remembrance of that tradition is contained in Matthew 16:18–19 with a variation of this tradition in John 21:15–17.

In view of this discussion we must take a closer look at verse 18: "And I tell you, you are Peter, and on this rock I will build my church, and the powers of death shall not prevail against it." Unfortunately, the English translation blurs the fascinating play on words that takes place in the Greek text and in the underlying Aramaic, the language Jesus spoke. If we reconstruct the Aramaic text it reads like this: "And I tell you, you are *Kephā'* and on this *kephā'* I will build my church. . . ." Simon, son of Jona, is receiving a new name, presumably to describe a new function. Simon receives the additional appellation of "rock." You are "rock" (or in colloquial English would the rough equivalent be "Rocky"?) and on this "rock" (that is, on you, Simon) I will build my church. This identity of "Peter" and "rock" in the Aramaic is without question and this same relationship is maintained in the Greek text as well: "You are *Petros* and on this *petra* I will build my church." Here again is the identity between "Peter" and "rock" with the exception that in Greek the word as a man's name has to be changed into the masculine form *Petros,* since rock in Greek, *petra,* is a feminine form.

Through the human agency of Peter, frail and whimsical as he is, the church has its beginning. This dimension of "beginning" is confirmed by verse 18b and its use of the future tense, "I *will* build my church." The church is possible only because of Christ's resurrection and the church-founding appearance of the Risen Lord. In addition to these dramatic divine events, one should not overlook the "miraculous" nature of Peter's selection, this man who at various times was fickle, weak, and denied his Lord. The miracle, if you will, is that God works through the most ordinary of human beings and human circumstances. In a very obvious way this is what the incarnation (God becoming flesh) is all about —using the most ordinary means of God's creation for his glory.

There are a few additional items we must examine in this critical section of Matthew's gospel. In verse 18 we note the only other use of *ekklēsia* (church) in Matthew's gospel, a fact that certainly makes clear that the present formulation of this word is Matthean. The promise is given that this church which is being built and will continue to be built in the future shall be protected from all assaults from the demonic forces operative in the world. The church, and not the "gates of hell," shall prevail. Verse 19 with its reference to "the keys of the kingdom," strongly influenced by Isaiah 22:15–25, originally referred to permitting persons to enter and to leave the church. John 20:23 provides a helpful parallel: "If you forgive the sins of any, they are forgiven; if you retain the sins of any, they are retained." This early formulation "keys of the kingdom" is expanded in Matthew's church by the addition of the rabbinic formula of "binding–loosing." In the first place, this addition in Matthew's gospel is addressed in the singular to Peter alone. This is different from its context in Matthew 18 where the "you" is a plural form addressed to the wider group of the disciples. We also noted that in Matthew 18 the concept of binding and loosing was used in a disciplinary sense.

While it may possibly be used in this sense in Matthew 16, it is fully possible that it is used in the teaching authority in the sense of "permitting" or "forbidding" certain actions. This later interpretation gathers support from the verses just preceding the pericope under discussion. In 16:11b–12 we read: " 'Beware of the leaven of the Pharisees and Sadducees. 12 Then they understood that he did not tell them to beware of the leaven of bread, but of the teaching of the Pharisees and Sadducees." In this situation of post-70 Judaism there is tension between Christianity and Judaism at a number of points, not least of which in the area of authoritative teaching. It may well be that in such a situation Matthew must reinforce Peter's position as authoritative teacher in the church. This understanding is strengthened at several points in Matthew's gospel where it is Peter who is uniquely the spokesman for the twelve and the communicator of authoritative teaching and interpretation. We have already noticed that it is only in Matthew's gospel that the name "Peter" is inserted as the person who raises the question about forgiveness (18:21). Another clear example of this tendency to elevate Peter as an authoritative interpretator is in 17:24–27. The passage begins in this way: "When they came to Capernaum, the collectors of the half-shekel tax went up to Peter and said, 'Does not your teacher pay the tax?' " After a small dialogue between Peter and Jesus, Matthew has Jesus give this response: "Then the sons are free. 27 However, not to give offense to them, go to the sea and cast a hook, and take the first fish that comes up, and when you open its mouth you will find a shekel; take that and give it to them for me and for yourself." It is Peter who questions, facilitates, and interprets matters pressing in the life of this church and Matthew reinforces this position in 16:19. Clearly Peter serves as a model of discipleship and receives a prominence unequaled in the other gospels. Why does Matthew do this? Is he faithful to the gospel tradition?

The simplest way to explain what Matthew is doing is to go back to our previous observations about the post-resurrectional character of certain elements in 16:17–19. What Matthew is doing is taking a post-resurrectional church-founding appearance and retrojecting it back into the historical ministry of Jesus. In other words, the change of name, or the addition of the name Cephas to Simon, as well as the makarism to Peter, is something that takes place at the moment of the appearance of the Risen Lord to Peter and for the purposes of actualizing his gospel message in the midst of a conflict situation with post-70 Judaism, Matthew "retrojects" it back to a much earlier point in his gospel so as to give Peter a prominence that was important for the existential and theological position of his congregation.

Finally, before we leave this passage in Matthew 16 we must point out its multi-dimensionality. It is one of the striking examples of the dynamic, creative impulse of early Christianity. In this passage we find words and scenes from the historical Jesus (e.g., the question to Peter about his identity), traditions from the early church (e.g., "binding and loosing") and elements revealing Matthew's own theological perspective (e.g., the editorial and compositional work as a whole as well as the addition of specific items themselves, such as the addition of the name "Jeremiah" in verse 14). While an uniformed reader might normally categorize post-resurrectional appearances as a merely peripheral element from early Christianity, it should be highlighted in a special way since it is so terribly important for our context. Specifically the post-resurrectional appearance to Peter serves as the substructure for the entire pericope. Once again we have seen how neatly Matthew weaves and molds together many originally disparate elements for the sake of actualizing the gospel for the needs of his congregation.

There is one final area of Matthew's gospel that is very important for us to explore because it too gives us enormous insight into the contextual situation of Matthew's congregation and the evangelist's response to it. This first area for exploration is Matthew 1 and 2, sometimes referred to as the infancy narratives, chapters that have some degree of parallel in the opening chapters of Luke. Although any attempt to concisely describe these chapters is likely to contain some imprecision, nevertheless the title of Krister Stendahl's article *"Quis et Unde?"* (Who and from Where?) gives us, at the very least, a starting perspective.[26] The first part of his title, *"Quis,"* suggests that Matthew 1 is concerned with "who" Jesus is, that is, with the question of his identification; the second part of the title, *"Unde,"* deals with the question of his geographic origins, from where, whence does he come.

Matthew 1 is certainly concerned about Jesus' identity. Verse 1 of that chapter, translated literally, opens in this way: "The book of the beginning [*genesis*] of Jesus Christ, the son of David, the son of Abraham." It is concerned about the origins of this Jesus, and the genealogy that follows is quite obviously interested in affirming the link between Jesus and David and Jesus and Abraham. The genealogy itself goes all the way back to Abraham and the fact that Joseph, Jesus' father, is a son of David is repeated at several points.

All of chapter 1, and for that matter chapter 2 as well, can only be understood as a response to a polemical situation, in all likelihood a situation of tension between the emerging church and post-70 Judaism. The Jewish synagogue "across the street" is denying certain central things about this Jesus so as to make invalid the claim that he is the messiah. The first two chapters of Matthew can be viewed as responding to such criticisms. In other words, we are not dealing with abstract theological statements, but with theological reflection addressed to a very specific and concrete situation in the Matthean church.

Let us gain access to Matthew 1 via verse 18a: "Now the birth of Jesus Christ took place in this way. When his mother Mary . . ." At this point the English translation has a tendency to be somewhat imprecise. The same word appears in Greek here as in verse 1: *genesis,* beginning. The repetition of this key word and the name Jesus Christ, as well as the awkward word order, all point to the preceding verses. In fact, without detailed attention to the preceding part of the chapter, verses 18–25 will never become finally intelligible. When one begins to look more closely at verses 1–17 one notes that Mary is not the first woman, but the fifth, to appear in this genealogy.

What is highly unusual for a Jewish genealogy is the reference to women and these references are not, for example, found in Luke 3. It is logical to assume that the appearance of four women prior to Mary would suggest that in some way they are important for Matthew's theological presentation. First, let us list them. There is Tamar in verse 3, Rahab and Ruth in verse 5, and the wife of Uriah, Bathsheba, in verse 6.

Let us look more carefully at each of these women to see how they function in the Old Testament. The story of Tamar is found in Genesis 38. According to this account Tamar was a widow who had not born any children. One day "she put off her widow's garments, and put on a veil, wrapping herself up" (v. 14). When Judah, her father-in-law, saw her "he thought her to be a harlot" (v. 15). The story continues: " 'Come, let me come in to you' . . . and she conceived by him" (vv. 16 and 18). What interests us most is the biblical description of Tamar in verse 24, "Tamar your daughter-in-law has played the harlot; and moreover she is with child by harlotry," and the fact that the geneology in Matthew is continued precisely by this act of harlotry in the birth of Perez and Zerah.

Rahab is referred to in Joshua 2:1–21 and 6:17–21 and the account is straightforward and simple: she is a harlot who hid the spies of Jericho in her home and she and her household were spared death when the Israelites conquered the city. The description of Bathsheba is also straightforward and also has sexual connotations. The account in 2 Samuel 11:2–5 is as follows:

It happened, late one afternoon, when David arose from his couch and was walking upon the roof of the king's house, that he saw from the roof a woman bathing; and the woman was very beautiful. 3 And David sent and inquired about the woman. And one said, "Is not this Bathsheba, the daughter of Eliam, the wife of Uriah the Hittite?" 4 So David sent messengers, and took her; and she came to him, and he lay with her. (Now she was purifying herself from her uncleanness.) Then she returned to her house. 5 And the woman conceived; and she sent and told David, "I am with child."

Rather important to note is that Solomon, the great king of Israel, is the second child born to David and Bathsheba.

Why Matthew makes specific reference to Ruth and what theological purpose he has in mind is less clear. Of the many suggestions made, one of the more popular is that her non-Israelite background was central. This may be. Yet one should be sensitive that in the case of the other three women as well as in the case of Mary, there are definite sexual connotations. One does not have to look very far in the book of Ruth to find this dimension. Let us look at Ruth 3:1–5:

Then Naomi her mother-in-law said to her, "My daughter, should I not seek a home for you, that it may be well with you? 2 Now is not Boaz our kinsman, with whose maidens you were? See, he is winnowing barley tonight at the threshing floor. 3 Wash therefore and anoint yourself, and put on your best clothes and go down to the threshing floor; but do not make yourself known to the man until he has finished eating and drinking. 4 But when he lies down, observe the place where he lies; then, go and uncover his feet and lie down; and he will tell you what to do." 5 And she replied, "All that you say I will do."

This is nothing other than an account of Ruth's seduction of Boaz. The Hebrew of verse 4, *wegillít margelótāw*, can either be translated "and uncover his legs" or as in the Revised Standard Version, "and uncover his feet." *Margelótāw* is related to *regal*, "foot," which according to Campbell "can serve as a euphemism for the penis or the vulva, either as sexual organs or as the urinary opening. . . . The question is whether the storyteller meant to be ambiguous and hence provocative. It seems to me that he did. . . ."[27]

When we turn to Matthew 1:18–25 it becomes clear that there is something unusual about Jesus' birth and Matthew attempts to explain the phenomenon as an action of the Holy Spirit and he uses a text from Isaiah 7 to assist in his explanation. Why is this necessary? I would suggest that here some, in their attempt to deny that Jesus was messiah, argued in the heat of polemical confrontation that Jesus was born illegitimately, and we do have texts from a slightly later period in Jewish history that witness to such accusations. Not irrelevant to this consideration is a passage toward the end of Matthew's gospel in a scene following the burial of Jesus:

Next day, that is, after the day of Preparation, the chief priests and the Pharisees gathered before Pilate 63 and said, "Sir, we remember how the impostor said, while he was still alive, 'After three days I will rise again.' 64 Therefore order the sepulchre to be made secure until the third day, lest his disciples go and steal him away, and tell the people, 'He has risen from the dead,' and the last fraud will be worse than the first." 65 Pilate said to them, "You have a guard of soldiers; go, make it as secure as you can." 66 So they went and made the sepulchre secure by sealing the stone and setting a guard (27:62–66).

The only way this passage can be understood is in light of Matthew's negative tension with post-70 Judaism, a fact strongly supported by the observation that this pericope only occurs in Matthew's gospel. In essence the first evangelist is reporting what must have been a common Jewish position and shows, through the agency of Pilate, how it was and should continue to be refuted. Thus, the end of the gospel evidences Matthew's strong concern with Jewish propaganda. If this is the case explicitly at the end of the gospel, do we find a similar phenomenon at the beginning? In this connection one must pay careful attention to verse 64: "Therefore order the sepulchre to be made secure until the third day, lest his disciples go and steal him away, and tell the people, 'He has risen from the dead,' and the last fraud will be worse than the first.' " What is the first "fraud," this first "error" *(plana)* in comparison to which this last will be worse? The commentaries are amazingly silent at this point. A possible suggestion would be that the first "fraud" that the Jews are referring to is that of Jesus' virginal conception. If this is in fact the situation, then a very interesting parallelism can be detected: as the Jews try to undermine the validity of resurrection in chapter 27 and Matthew refutes the argument by answering that a guard of soldiers was present to prevent theft of the body, so in Matthew 1 as the Jews try to make slanderous comments about the birth of Jesus, Matthew responds by arguing that Jesus' conception was not illegitimate, but virginal.

As we now return to Matthew 1, we can now see that the chapter is complex and that Matthew may have had several purposes in mind. If aspersions were being cast on the birth of Jesus, as we believe is probable, then Matthew's response is two pronged: (1) a positive description of how Jesus was born in verses 18–25, which we shall look at momentarily, and (2) a review of Jewish history to point out to his critics that their own past was not above criticism and that despite irregularities and even human sinfulness God faithfully carries out his divine plan.

With this background we can see the force of verse 18: "Now the birth of Jesus Christ took place in this way." The description that follows is written both with regard to the past just reviewed and with regard to various slanderous comments circulating in the vicinity of the Matthean community. Matthew continues: "When his mother Mary had been betrothed to Joseph, before they came together she was found to be with child of the Holy Spirit; 19 and her husband Joseph, being a just man and unwilling to put her to shame, resolved to divorce her quietly." Marriage in the Jewish culture of this time, as best we can reconstruct it, involved two stages, betrothal and marriage. At the point of betrothal the woman legally belonged to the man even though she would continue to live with her family for about a year. Joseph's dilemma is that during this betrothal period, before the marriage was consummated, Mary was found to be pregnant. Upon learning this his decision was "to divorce her quietly." Matthew has already suggested that Mary was "found to be with child of the Holy Spirit." Through the frequent literary device "Behold, an angel of the Lord appeared to him in a dream," Joseph is instructed that "that which is conceived in her is of the Holy Spirit.. . ." It is further announced to Joseph that Mary "will bear a son, and you shall call his name Jesus, for he will save his people from their sins." We note that Matthew is concerned not only to discuss the virginal conception but also who Jesus is, that is, "He will save his people from their sins." It is because of this double concern that Matthew finds so appropriate the reference in Isaiah 7:14 which he quotes: "Behold, a virgin shall conceive and bear a son, and his name shall be called Emmanuel." Immediately following the word "Emmanuel" in verse 23 Matthew adds "which means, God with us." Perhaps that is the unique witness of the New Testament—that God has become human in the person of Jesus. That is exactly what Christians over the centuries have meant by "incarnation"—"enfleshment," "taking on human form." One could even go further and state that the major focus of the New Testament is on the humanity of God— that God the soverign creator and Lord of history has entered into the midst of his world in Jesus of Nazareth.

Some have disputed that Matthew really means "virgin" in the strict sense as he quotes Isaiah 7. The argument usually assumes that Matthew is using a Hebrew text and that the Hebrew word *'almâ* usually means "maiden" or "young woman." While this translation of *'almâ* is correct, this argument overlooks the fact that Matthew is dependent on the Greek translation of the Old Testament, that the Greek word he is translating is *parthenos,* and that elsewhere in the Greek translation of the Old Testament this word predominantly means "virgin." In short, Matthew means "virgin" quite literally and this is one reason that Isaiah 7:14 in its Greek form was so attractive to him. As we have argued in *Mary in the New Testament,* there is enough similarity between the virginal conception in Matthew and Luke that in all probability both evangelists were dependent on a prior tradition about the virginal conception.[28]

Let us return for a moment to Matthew's genealogy, especially the last verse: "and Jacob the father of Joseph the husband of Mary, of whom Jesus was born, who is called Christ" (v. 16). We have already observed that verses 18–25 are really an extended footnote to this chapter. But is there not a contradiction between the text, verse 16, and the footnote? If Jesus was virginally conceived how can Joseph be his father? Even though Joseph was not the physical father, he is according to Jewish custom the legal father and in this sense Jesus is a son of David as is Joseph.

We have seen, then, that Matthew 1 is a very complex chapter that can only be properly understood in the context of Matthew's audience. With the broadest of strokes we have learned that central to Matthew's concern is the question of the identity of Jesus and the manner of his birth. In Matthew 2 the evangelist now turns to the question of the geographical origin of Jesus and in his response there is once again a substantial use of the Old Testament.

Before we move into a more detailed investigation of Matthew 2, let us pause for a moment and discuss a text from the gospel of John that may be quite helpful to us in our present reflections. The verses we will consider are taken from John 7:40–43 and we find here a discussion among Jews concerning the identity of Jesus. The scene as depicted by the fourth evangelist comes considerably after Jesus has spoken during the feast of Tabernacles.

When they heard these words, some of the people said, "This is really the prophet." 41 Others said, "This is the Christ." But some said, "Is the Christ to come from Galilee? 42 Has not the scripture said that the Christ is descended from David, and comes from Bethlehem, the village where David was?" 43 So there was a division among the people over him.

Verse 40 reveals to us a fact that is prominent not only in John's gospel but throughout the New Testament period we are studying—that there were divided opinions concerning the identity of Jesus. Some were willing to admit, "This is really the prophet," and others were willing to make precisely that identification which the gospel itself discusses, "This is the Christ." John concisely comments upon this situation: "So there was a division among the people over him" (v. 43). As part of this dialogue that went on, two elements stand out according to verse 42: the issue of his relation to David and the issue of whether he comes from Bethlehem. The first of these Matthew dealt with in his first chapter and the second of these elements he deals with in his second chapter. The Bethlehem matter is an interesting as well as a perplexing one since the name of the city only occurs in Matthew 2, Luke 2, and John 7. Further complicating the matter is that Matthew and Luke in an effort to locate the birth of Jesus in Bethlehem get him there in radically different ways. Why does Bethlehem become an issue? Let us look at John 7:41–42. Some have confessed that Jesus is the Christ. Those who refute this position, knowing that Jesus is from Galilee and that most of his activity took place in that northern part of Palestine, raise the question whether Scripture does not testify to the fact that the Christ is to come from Bethlehem, obviously expecting a positive answer. The very way by which the question is put would suggest that it was not widely known or shared that the messiah was to come from Bethlehem. In fact there is only one Old Testament allusion to this matter, Micah 5:2, and it plays no prominence in the varieties of Judaism of the first century. The Micah text is worded in the following way:

> But you, O Bethlehem Ephrathah,
>> who are little to be among the clans of Judah,
> from you shall come forth for me
>> one who is to be ruler in Israel,
> whose origin is from of old,
>> from ancient days.

One possible explanation of these various phenomena is to begin with the fact that Micah 5:2 was relatively unimportant in the first century. As the discussion, dialogue and tension intensified between those Jews who believed that Jesus was the Christ and those who did not, those Jews who did not so believe used every possible argument from Scripture and elsewhere in their refutation. Knowing that Jesus came from Galilee someone found, so they thought, the perfect text to undermine the claim that Jesus was the messiah, Micah 5:2, and this increasingly plays a significant part in future discussion. John does not go into the issue any further and Mark either does not know about it or believes it to be irrelevant; only Matthew and Luke take up the matter in a significant way and independently of one another.

While Matthew's treatment of geography in chapter 2 deals with a number of important motifs we cannot elaborate in this context, the major thrust is straightforward and concise; it consists of a movement from Bethlehem in Judea to Nazareth in Galilee. The chapter opens with the assertion "Now when Jesus was born in Bethlehem of Judea in the days of Herod the king . . ." (v. 1). After some brief references to Herod, the Bethlehem reference is supported by the full quotation from Micah 5:2 referred to above. The movement from Bethlehem to Nazareth is moved forward step by step in this Matthean narrative by use of the literary device of a "dream" which we first encountered in Matthew 1:20. This literary technique appears in 2:12 and in 2:13 following: ". . . Behold, an angel of the Lord appeared to Joseph in a dream and said, 'Rise, take the child and his mother, and flee to Egypt, and remain there till I tell you; for Herod is about to search for the child, to destroy him.' 14 And he rose and took the child and his mother by night, and departed to Egypt, 15 and remained there until the death of Herod. This was to fulfill what the Lord had spoken by the prophet, 'Out of Egypt have I called my son' " (vv. 13–15).

Matthew is the only New Testament book that indicates that the baby Jesus was taken to Egypt and via Egypt to Nazareth. With all the Old Testament parallelism already noted in this gospel, the suggestion lies close at hand that Matthew wishes strongly to suggest that as Moses saved his people out of Egypt so now the redemption of God's people once again has its origin in Egypt. This possibility is strongly underscored by Matthew's quotation from Hosea 11:1, "Out of Egypt have I called my son." One should also note how Matthew uses Old Testament quotations throughout this chapter as a way of substantiating from Scripture the movement from Bethlehem to Nazareth.

The dream technique is used twice more, in verses 19–20 and verse 22. The content of the first dream is this: "But when Herod died, behold, an angel of the Lord appeared in a dream to Joseph in Egypt, saying, 20 'Rise, take the child and his mother, and go to the land of Israel, for those who sought the child's life are dead.' " This dream gives the authorization to leave Egypt and the final one in verse 22 gives the authorization to enter Galilee and Jesus "went and dwelt in a city called Nazareth . . ." (v. 23).

We have now completed our discussion of Matthew. I hope we have caught some of his theological sophistication and dynamic creativity as he attempts to apply the gospel to the complex situation of his audience and of his environment. For Matthew to simply have repeated the gospel of Mark would have forced him to ignore some of the burning issues with which his congregation was confronted. Under the guidance of the Risen Lord, Matthew takes the gospel tradition and creatively allows it to speak to the uniqueness of his situation. It is to that kind of a dynamic rather than static theological process that the entire New Testament invites and challenges the contemporary church.

6. The Gospel of Luke: A Word about Mercy

To examine the gospel of Luke from the perspective of dynamic actualization is an exciting venture for at least two reasons. First, Luke's gospel and his second volume, the Acts of the Apostles, are a rich demonstration of this process both in their totality and in their manifold individual examples. Second, the process of actualization can be easily demonstrated in Luke's gospel by comparison with the gospel of Mark, which he uses and alters, and with the gospel of Matthew. Additionally, and we have already had occasion to give some illustrations of this earlier, Luke's second volume can at many points be compared with Paul's own account of his ministry in his letters. Just one further word before we proceed. Precisely because the resources of Luke and Acts are so rich and broad—these two volumes contain approximately twenty-five percent of the entire New Testament—there will be an element of frustration in our presentation simply because we can only select a handful of passages and themes from these two volumes.

Why did Luke write these two volumes?[1] His own answer is given at the outset of the gospel:

Inasmuch as many have undertaken to compile a narrative of the things which have been accomplished among us, 2 just as they were delivered to us by those who from the beginning were eyewitnesses and ministers of the word, 3 it seemed good to me also, having followed all things closely for some time past, to write an orderly account for you, most excellent Theophilus, 4 that you may know the truth concerning the things of which you have been informed. (1:1–4)

Contrary to Mark and Matthew, Luke does not describe his work primarily as a gospel or a book but as an "orderly account" of the Christian past so that Theophilus "may know the truth concerning the things of which he had been informed." An orderly account is exactly what Luke presents. Its movement from Jerusalem in Luke 1 to Rome in Acts 28 is majestic in its sweep and precision. The issue of presenting "the truth" is prominent throughout since Luke constantly is giving his perspective, which he obviously assumes is relatively accurate, on matters and events that are controversial in the first-century Christian church.

To determine the nature of Luke's audiences is not an easy task and it is a subject under very serious discussion at the present by many biblical scholars. One of the dominant views has been that Luke and Acts together are an apologetic work, apologetic being used in its early Christian sense of a literary "defense," specifically as a defense of the church over against the charges and incipient persecution of the Roman empire. The eminent scholar W. G. Kümmel is representative of this position when he asserts that "the aim of defending the Christians against the charge of enmity toward the state is unmistakeable."[2] While not all who share this position would argue that this is the only or sole purpose in Luke's writing, they would agree that it was a dominant purpose.

In a small but influential book dealing with Luke as historian, Professor C. K. Barrett raises the question whether one could properly assume that a Roman official would take seriously such an apologetic document and whether he would be willing to wade through so many apparent irrelevancies from his purely political perspective. Further, how should a Roman politician understand the frequent references to Israel and the Old Testament and the theological argumentation based on those references?[3] It remained, however, to the Norwegian scholar Jacob Jervell not only to agree with the substance of Barrett's concern but to go beyond it, to challenge the dominant perspective concerning the intention of Luke/Acts, and to offer an alternative interpretation.[4] Jervell suggests that the audience is not gentile Christian, as most have assumed, but that it is Jewish Christian and further that Luke is not essentially concerned with a political apology but with the question, "Why does the church carry on the gentile mission, and how has it come about?"

My own perspective of Luke/Acts has been significantly shaped by the suggestions of Professor Jervell, but in a variety of ways I go beyond his more limited suggestions so that I can apply them to a broader sweep of Lucan theology. With regard to Luke's audience, I am inclined to see it as a very conservative Jewish-Christian church that is rather narrow in its theological perspective. It is a church that does not understand that "there is a wideness in God's mercy," to use the words of a hymn sung in many churches today. Their narrowness is evidenced in their reluctance to accept gentile Christians into their midst. Luke must show them why inclusion of the gentiles is necessary both in light of God's promises in the Old Testament and in light of contemporary history. Further, this narrowness is also revealed by a rigidness internal to the congregation with regard to whom God's mercy and forgiveness is granted. At many points a narrow self-righteousness is apparent in this congregation that Luke is addressing. So many of the parables and teaching illustrations that Luke employs are intended to "blow open," to widen, to broaden this limited perspective, and one of the clearest examples of this is the story of the Pharisee and the tax collector which we will examine below.

Before we can review Luke's theological concerns there are a few other preliminary matters that would be helpful to discuss. Among these would be the question of Luke's identity. Is it accurate to assume that he was a physician and a colleague of Paul? Those who endorse this assumption generally refer to three New Testament passages: Colossians 4:14 ("Luke the beloved physician and Demas greet you"); 2 Timothy 4:11 ("Luke alone is with me") and Philemon 23 and following ("Epaphras, my fellow prisoner in Christ Jesus, sends greetings to you, 24 and so do Mark, Aristarchus, Demas, and Luke, my fellow workers"). The only one of these texts that stems from Paul's hand with any degree of certainty is Philemon 23–24; the other two come from the deutero-Pauline school, having been written in all probability by followers or disciples of the apostle. Without question a Luke is mentioned; but what allows us to conclude that this Luke is the same Luke we are now discussing? Because a certain Mary at Smith College has received an outstanding award can I without further checking assume that that is the same Mary whom I have in my class? In other words, there must be caution in making simple identification of common names.

Is the author of Luke/Acts a physician? That assumption has been made by the reference to the Colossian text just reviewed in which Luke is referred to as "the beloved physician." This identification is then further supported by its proponents by reference to the high frequency of medical terminology in Luke/Acts. The late Henry Cadbury, one of America's premier biblical scholars, wrote his doctoral dissertation on this question of whether the author of Luke/Acts was a physician.[5] If compared with other historians such as Josephus, Plutarch, or Lucian, does Luke use a significantly greater degree of medical language than the others? Cadbury's investigation indicated that Luke did not and that his use of medical terminology was quite natural for a historian whose account included reports and accounts of many healings. In light of this conclusion, the story began to circulate that "Cadbury received his doctorate by depriving Luke of his"!

All of this is not to categorically deny that Luke, the author of Luke/Acts, may have been an associate or traveling companion of Paul; in fact for reasons we cannot possibly explore in this context, I am rather open to and intrigued by this possibility. What I have been attempting to suggest is that the factors to be weighed in reaching any conclusion on this matter are complex and that we must, therefore, avoid simplistic conclusions.

A few words about the structure of the gospel. About one-half of Luke's gospel is without parallel in the other gospels; specifically, 548 out of the gospel's 1138 verses are unique to it. Of the remaining half, 235 verses are taken from Q and 350 are taken from Mark's total of 661 verses and, on the whole, the Marcan order is retained quite well. What these statistics suggest is that

Luke's focus should be reasonably easy to ascertain from his significant and extensive additions to the gospel of Mark which he had before him as he was writing his own gospel.

It is interesting to observe how Luke incorporates this significant bulk of non-Marcan material within the Marcan framework. Essentially he does this in two stages with two insertions, a smaller and a larger one, into the Marcan structure. Between Mark 3:19 and 3:20, Luke inserts material that is now found in Luke 6:20–8:3; between Mark 9:50 and 10:1 Luke inserts what is now Luke 9:51–18:14. Obviously this latter insertion marks a massive interruption between Mark 9 and 10.

Luke's gospel is probably the most difficult to outline and the following suggestion should at best be viewed as tentative. It is possible to detect three major parts to the gospel, all of which are geographically oriented.

   I. Jesus in Galilee (4:14–9:50)
  II. Journey to Jerusalem (9:51–19:27)
 III. Jesus in Jerusalem (19:28–23:49)

To this outline of the major sections, one should add a prologue and an epilogue. The prologue is really an introduction to the entire two volumes and consists of a preface (1:1–4), the infancy narratives (1:5–2:52), and a section dealing with the birth, baptism and temptation of Jesus (3:1–4:13). The epilogue consists of Luke 23:50–24:53 and essentially includes the appearance of the Risen Lord among his disciples on the way to Emmaus.

Just one final word about the section II of the proposed outline. One will note that it consists almost entirely of the materials that are unique to Luke's gospel and that Luke's setting for this material is that of Jesus teaching on the way to Jerusalem. That this is Luke's own setting for the narrative is evident from the fact that at several points (9:51; 13:22, 33) it is mentioned that Jesus and his disciples are on the way to Jerusalem—yet they never seem to reach their destination within the context of this section.

In short, we have already had a chance to observe the enormous creativity of Luke just at the structural and compositional level. We now turn to examine that same tendency in the theological presentation of Luke's gospel. Essentially, we wish to view Luke's theological emphasis by examining three dimensions of his emphasis: (1) God's love to the despised; (2) the issue of the political innocence of the Romans in the death of Jesus; and (3) God's plan of salvation history.

As we turn to the first category of Lucan theology, God's love to the despised, we will observe that this love is expressed to at least three specific groups of the despised: sinners, Samaritans, and women. Before we look at specific texts, there is one overarching text in Luke 4 that sets the stage not only for this theological category but for the gospel as a whole, and therefore it is essential for us to study.

In Luke's gospel, the very first address of Jesus is given in the synagogue at Nazareth. The account is recorded in this way:

> And he came to Nazareth, where he had been brought up; and he went to the synagogue, as his custom was, on the sabbath day. And he stood up to read; 17 and there was given to him the book of the prophet Isaiah. He opened the book and found the place where it was written,
>
> 18 'The Spirit of the Lord is upon me,
> because he has anointed me to preach good news to the poor,
> He has sent me to proclaim release to the captives
> and recovering of sight to the blind,
> to set at liberty those who are oppressed,
> 19 to proclaim the acceptable year of the Lord.''
>
> 20 And he closed the book, and gave it back to the attendant, and sat down; and the eyes of all in the synagogue were fixed on him. 21 And he began to say to them, "Today this scripture has been fulfilled in your hearing."

Most striking is the intense concern for the poor in this quotation from Isaiah. As we have previously noted, this identical concern is manifested in Luke's version of the beatitudes. Jesus, according to Luke, is making quite clear to his audience to whom it is that he has been sent: the poor, the captives, the blind, and the oppressed. The "Spirit of the Lord" is not upon him to be "spiritual" in some abstract, pietistic way, but to be spiritual in the sense of concretely demonstrating God's love and mercy to those in greatest need. The uniqueness of Jesus according to this text is that that which had been promised to the prophet Isaiah is "today" present and fulfilled in Jesus of Nazareth. This genuine concern for the disenfranchised was just as offensive to some in Jesus' audience as it is in some quarters of the church today. The response to this message is portrayed in verses 28–30 of this fourth chapter:

> When they heard this, all in the synagogue were filled with wrath. 29 And they rose up and put him out of the city, and led him to the brow of the hill on which their city was built, that they might throw him down headlong. 30 But passing through the midst of them he went away.

This opening sermon is actualized throughout the gospel. We now turn our attention to three types of despised or disenfranchised in the third gospel, the first of which are the "sinners."

God's Love to the Disenfranchised

Sinners

The first text in this category is 5:1–11, the miraculous catch of fish, a story that in its present form has no parallel in the other gospels. Particularly important are verses 6–8:

> And when they had done this, they enclosed a great shoal of fish; and as their nets were breaking, 7 they beckoned to their partners in the other boat to come and help them. And they came and filled both the boats, so that they began to sink. 8 But when Simon Peter saw it, he fell down at Jesus' knees, saying, "Depart from me, for I am a sinful man, O Lord."

Luke portrays the chief of the apostles, Simon Peter, as confessing to Jesus, "Depart from me, for I am a sinful man, O Lord." Among other things we find here an example of humility that Luke wishes to convey to his rather "stuffy, arrogant" congregation, a theme that will repeat itself.

In 7:36–50 we read Luke's account of the story of the woman with ointment:

One of the Pharisees asked him to eat with him, and he went into the Pharisee's house, and took his place at table. 37 And behold, a woman of the city, who was a sinner, when she learned that he was sitting at table in the Pharisee's house, brought an alabaster flask of ointment, 38 and standing behind him at his feet, weeping, she began to wet his feet with her tears, and wiped them with the hair of her head, and kissed his feet, and anointed them with the ointment. 39 Now when the Pharisee who had invited him saw it, he said to himself, "If this man were a prophet, he would have known who and what sort of woman this is who is touching him, for she is a sinner." 40 And Jesus answering said to him, "Simon, I have something to say to you." And he answered, "What is it, Teacher?" 41 "A certain creditor had two debtors; one owed five hundred denarii, and the other fifty. 42 When they could not pay, he forgave them both. Now which of them will love him more?" 43 Simon answered, "The one, I suppose, to whom he forgave more." And he said to him, "You have judged rightly." 44 Then turning toward the woman he said to Simon, "Do you see this woman? I entered your house, you gave me no water for my feet, but she has wet my feet with her tears and wiped them with her hair. 45 You gave me no kiss, but from the time I came in she has not ceased to kiss my feet. 46 You did not anoint my head with oil, but she has anointed my feet with ointment. 47 Therefore I tell you, her sins, which are many, are forgiven, for she loved much; but he who is forgiven little, loves little." 48 And he said to her, "Your sins are forgiven." 49 Then those who were at table with him began to say among themselves, "Who is this, who even forgives sins?" 50 And he said to the woman, "Your faith has saved you; go in peace."

Note the emphasis on the description of this woman as a "sinner," in the sense of not conforming to the Pharisee's perception of religiosity. This is stressed in verse 37: ". . . a woman of the city, who was a sinner . . ."; in verse 39, "If this man were a prophet, he would have known who and what sort of a woman this is who is touching him, for she is a sinner"; and verse 47, "I tell you, her sins, which are many, are forgiven, for she loved much." The religious life according to this narrative is involved in actively loving and having mercy upon the other and not in some abstract, academic notion of what it means to be religious.

She whom most in Luke's congregation would place quite at the periphery becomes the hero, the example the others are to emulate.

The parable of the prodigal son in 15:11–32 also contains these twin themes of sin and mercy.[6]

And he said, "There was a man who had two sons; 12 and the younger of them said to his father, 'Father, give me the share of property that falls to me.' And he divided his living between them. 13 Not many days later, the younger son gathered all he had and took his journey into a far country, and there he squandered his property in loose living. 14 And when he had spent everything, a great famine arose in that country, and he began to be in want. 15 So he went and joined himself to one of the citizens of that country, who sent him into his fields to feed swine. 16 And he would gladly have fed on the pods that the swine ate; and no one gave him anything. 17 But when he came to himself he said, 'How many of my father's hired servants have bread enough and to spare, but I perish here with hunger.' 18 I will arise and go to my father, and I will say to him, 'Father, I have sinned against heaven and before you; 19 I am no longer worthy to be called your son; treat me as one of your hired servants.' 20 And he arose and came to his father. But while he was yet at a distance, his father saw him and had compassion, and ran and embraced him and kissed him. 21 And the son said to him, 'Father, I have sinned against heaven and before you; I am no longer worthy to be called your son.' 22 But the father said to his servants, 'Bring quickly the best robe, and put it on him; and put a ring on his hand, and shoes on his feet; 23 and bring the fatted calf and kill it, and let us eat and make merry; 24 for this my son was dead, and is alive again; he was lost, and is found.' And they began to make merry.

25 "Now his elder son was in the field; and as he came and drew near to the house, he heard music and dancing. 26 And he called one of the servants and asked what this meant. 27 And he said to him, 'Your brother has come, and your father has killed the fatted calf, because he has received him safe and sound.' 28 But he was angry and refused to go in. His father came out and entreated him, 29 but he answered his father, 'Lo, these many years I have served you, and I never disobeyed your command; yet you never gave me a kid, that I might make merry with my friends. 30 But when this son of yours came, who has devoured your living with harlots, you killed for him the fatted calf!' 31 And he said to him, 'Son, you are always with me, and all that is mine is yours.

32 It was fitting to make merry and be glad, for this your brother was dead, and is alive; he was lost, and is found.' "

One of the two sons goes to his father, as if he were already dead, and asks and receives his share of the inheritance. In a short period of time, he "blows" the entire share of the inheritance and is in desperate straights. He comes to the realization that life with his father is infinitely to be preferred even if he has to return and be placed in the status of a hired hand. He now formulates the approach to his father: "Father, I have sinned against heaven and before you; I am no longer worthy to be called your son, treat me as one of your hired servants." His self-description as "sinner" has an immediate consequence that he is no longer worthy to be called a son. The father's reaction is radically different than the son anticipates. Upon seeing him at a distance, the father, having compassion, runs, embraces, and kisses the son. The key to the action is once again an act of mercy, having compassion. Because this son who was dead is once again alive there is to be a big banquet in which there is great joy. Clearly in Luke's context this parable intends to inform the reader about God the Father, as one who is gracious, merciful, and loving even and precisely to his children who have strayed far away from him. As soon as they have the slightest inclination to return to him, he runs toward them and embraces them. Because only in this reconciliation between the Father and the son is there life, true life, is this moment to be celebrated.

But the story is not over. If the prodigal son is similar to the sinful woman in the previous story, then the elder son is quite similar to the Pharisee in that story. Both have very limited perceptions of God and the religious life. While believing that they are very religious, the irony is that they really have no intimate relationship to the Father. Their false perception of what it means to be religious prevents true fellowship with the Father. Here in Luke 15, when the elder son hears about the festivities surrounding his younger brother's reconciliation, "he was angry and refused to go in" (v. 28). He then responds negatively to his father's invitation to enter and celebrate by telling him how unfair this whole celebration is in light of all he had faithfully done for the father. The father answers the elder son, "Son, you are always with me, and all that is mine is yours" (v. 31). It is exactly here that we see the dilemma of the elder son and perhaps through him the dilemma of Luke's audience: the failure to realize the intimacy of relationship that has and continues to be open to them with their heavenly Father. But finally such a relationship can only be initiated by the embrace, by the mercy of the Father toward the child and not the other way around as is the case with the elder son. As in the previous story, only he or she who is forgiven much can love much. It is precisely in the recognition, not the denial, of our sinfulness that we can receive God's forgiveness and because of that forgiveness we are enabled to love the other. This is such an essential theological point that Luke does not tire in repeating it over and over again. Is not this exactly the theme we find in the parable of the Pharisee and the publican?

This parable is found in 18:9–14:

He also told this parable to some who trusted in themselves that they were righteous and despised others: 10 "Two men went up into the temple to pray, one a Pharisee and the other a tax collector. 11 The Pharisee stood and prayed thus with himself, 'God, I thank thee that I am not like other men, extortioners, unjust, adulterers, or even like this tax collector. 12 I fast twice a week, I give tithes of all that I get.' 13 But the tax collector, standing far off, would not even lift up his eyes to heaven, but beat his breast, saying, 'God, be merciful to me a sinner!' 14 I tell you, this man went down to his house justified rather than the other; for every one who exalts himself will be humbled, but he who humbles himself will be exalted."

This parable is explicitly addressed to those "who trusted in themselves that they were righteous and despised others" (v. 9). Clearly the Pharisee in Luke 7, the elder son in Luke 15, and now the Pharisee in Luke 18 fall into this category. In the story before us, two extremes on the religious spectrum of first-century Judaism are portrayed, the Pharisees who genuinely attempted to be religious persons and the tax collectors who were generally held in low esteem because as Jews they were collecting monies from their fellow Jews for the occupying force, the Romans. As the Pharisee prays in the temple he first differentiates himself from others by what he has not done and then describes himself positively by what he as a religious man does do: "I fast twice a week, I give tithes of all that I get" (v. 12). From this self-description it appears as if the religious life comprises certain external acts, rather than a state of being, a way of acting that involves the totality of the person.

The portrayal of the tax collector in this story is quite radically different. In an attitude of profound humility, he utters simply, "God, be merciful to me a sinner!" Luke's response is that this man, the tax collector, not the Pharisee, is the one who went away justified by God. God does not respond to persons outlining how good and deserving they are; he responds with grace, mercy, and forgiveness when one stands in his presence with humility and honesty, recognizing the human situation as sinful. In all likelihood the term "justified" functions very similarly to the way it does with Paul: it is the act of reconciliation initiated by God to those who recognize their sinfulness before him.

One final example we must include in this category of God's love toward sinners is the story of Zacchaeus in 19:1–10. As with all the other examples cited in this section, it is without parallel in the gospels and appears only in Luke.

He entered Jericho and was passing through. 2 And there was a man named Zacchaeus; he was a chief tax collector, and rich. 3 And he sought to see who Jesus was, but could not, on account of the crowd, because he was small of stature. 4 So he ran on ahead and climbed up into a sycamore tree to see him, for he was to pass that way. 5 And when Jesus came to the place, he looked up and said to him, "Zacchaeus, make haste and come down; for I must stay at your house today." 6 So he made haste and came down, and received him joyfully. 7 And when they saw it they all murmured, "He has gone in to be the guest of a man who is a sinner." 8 And Zacchaeus stood and said to the Lord, "Behold, Lord, the half of my goods I give to the poor; and if I have defrauded any one of anything,

I restore it fourfold." 9 And Jesus said to him, "Today salvation has come to this house, since he also is a son of Abraham. 10 For the Son of man came to seek and to save the lost."

Once again the central actor in the story is identified as a "sinner" (v. 7), undoubtedly referring to the previous description in verse 2 that he was a "chief tax collector and rich." The emphasis of the story is not only that this sinner received Jesus joyfully, but that he acts to rectify his previous wrongs. Zacchaeus says to the Lord, "Behold, Lord, the half of my goods I give to the poor and if I have defrauded any one of anything, I restore it fourfold." Immediately after this willingness to act, Jesus says to him, "Today salvation has come to this house . . ." (v. 9). Salvation is nothing that takes place in a vacuum, but a new relationship with the Father that allows the disciple to act in a totally new way. This theme of concrete action can already be found in Luke 3. Immediately after the scene where John the Baptist speaks with judgment and seeks repentance, the multitudes ask him, "What then shall we do?" (v. 12). What follows is advice that deals with a concrete turnabout in their lives:

And he answered them, "He who has two coats, let him share with him who has none; and he who has food, let him do likewise." 12 Tax collectors also came to be baptized, and said to him, "Teacher, what shall we do?" 13 And he said to them, "Collect no more than is appointed you." 14 Soldiers also asked him, "And we, what shall we do?" And he said to them, "Rob no one by violence or by false accusation, and be content with your wages."

Salvation, as the theme is developed by Luke, involves a total renunciation of one's past life and this change is expressed in concrete actions toward the other. As God's mercy reaches even to the sinner, so he expects even the sinner to relate to his fellow human beings in a new way.

Samaritans

God's love to the despised is also expressed in a concrete way to those persons known as Samaritans. This group shared a common history with the Jews, but a split occurred between them sometime in the third or fourth century B.C. While multiple factors were involved in this schism, one of the most prominent concerned the proper place to worship Yahweh.[7] The Jews held that it was Jerusalem and the Samaritans claimed that it was on Mt. Gerizim in the city of Shechem which is part of Samaria. This same controversy emerges in the gospel of John in the scene in which Jesus holds a conversation with a Samaritan woman. The woman comments, " 'Our fathers worshiped on this mountain [Mount Gerizim]; and you say that in Jerusalem is the place where men ought to worship.' 21 Jesus said to her, 'Woman, believe me, the hour is coming when neither on this mountain nor in Jerusalem will you worship the Father" (John 4:20–21). To fully understand the power of Luke's references to the Samaritans, we have to recognize the extreme tension and hatred that existed between the Jews and the Samaritans.

The first reference to a Samaritan we should examine is in the brief story of the healing of ten lepers. After the ten lepers had been cleansed, "one of them, when he saw that he was healed, turned back, praising God with a loud voice; 16 and he fell on his face at Jesus' feet, giving him thanks. Now he was a Samaritan" (Luke 17:15–16). It is a Samaritan who is singled out as illustrating what should be the proper attitude of thanksgiving and praise to God. If Luke's congregation was of a conservative Jewish-Christian type as we suggest, then it is likely that this example would have an irritating power to it. The story in Luke concludes in this way: "Then said Jesus, 'Were not ten cleansed? Where are the nine? 18 Was no one found to return and give praise to God except this foreigner?' 19 And he said to him, 'Rise and go your way; your faith has made you well' " (vv. 17–19). The despised Samaritan has become a model of faith for the Lucan congregation.

This motif is heightened in the parable of the good Samaritan. Since the dialogue between Jesus and the lawyer is critical for the setting of the parable in Luke, let us begin at that point.

And behold, a lawyer stood up to put him to the test, saying, "Teacher, what shall I do to inherit eternal life?" 26 He said to him, "What is written in the law? How do you read?" 27 And he answered, "You shall love the Lord your God with all your heart, and with all your soul, and with all your strength, and with all your mind; and your neighbor as yourself." 28 And he said to him, "You have answered right; do this, and you will live."

29 But he, desiring to justify himself, said to Jesus, "And who is my neighbor?" 30 Jesus replied, "A man was going down from Jerusalem to Jericho, and he fell among robbers, who stripped him and beat him, and departed, leaving him half dead. 31 Now by chance a priest was going down that road; and when he saw him he passed by on the other side. 32 So likewise a Levite, when he came to the place and saw him, passed by on the other side. 33 But a Samaritan, as he journeyed, came to where he was; and when he saw him, he had compassion, 34 and went to him and bound up his wounds, pouring on oil and wine; then he set him on his own beast and brought him to an inn, and took care of him. 35 And the next day he took out two denarii and gave them to the innkeeper, saying, 'Take care of him; and whatever more you spend, I will repay you when I come back.' 36 Which of these three, do you think, proved neighbor to the man who fell among the robbers?" 38 He said, "The one who showed mercy on him." And Jesus said to him, "Go and do likewise." (10:25–37)

The Lucan setting for this parable begins with a lawyer asking a very spiritual question, "Teacher, what shall I do to inherit eternal life?" (v. 25). The tone of the question is rather sarcastic and we are told that the lawyer was in fact trying to "test" Jesus. Jesus' first response is to ask the lawyer what the law says. The lawyer responds quite correctly, but he appears to rattle off his answer with superficial speed and without real understanding. Jesus answers curtly, "You have answered right; do this, and you will live" (v. 28). Realizing that he has been bettered in the discussion, he, out of desperation, or as Luke puts it "desiring to justify himself," asks Jesus who his neighbor is. Jesus continues not with a definition, but with a story—a story that deals not with spiritual life, but with the brokenness of human life to which the disciple is called to respond.

The road from Jerusalem to Jericho is almost as desolate today as it was in the first century; there is nothing but sandy hills and intense heat with no buildings from the outskirts of the one city to the other. Today as one travels in a slow moving bus the time is about an hour and a half and one sees a small building commemorating the location where the good Samaritan stopped to assist the injured man.

The setting of this parable is on this road going eastward from Jerusalem toward Jericho. A man traveling on that road is attacked and severely beaten by a group of thieves who rush down from the hills. They rob the man and leave him half dead on this desolate and sunbaked road. Two persons who ought to know well what the Torah teaches about loving one's neighbor, a priest and a Levite, passed by the severely injured man on the other side. However, a despised heretic, a Samaritan, becomes the hero of the story and it is he who becomes the example the Christian disciples are to follow. When the Samaritan saw the man, "he had compassion" (v. 33). The parable now spells out with great detail what it means to have compassion; in fact, the concern is so intense at this point, that almost forty percent of the parable is devoted to a detailed specification of what it means to have compassion. The Samaritan went to the injured man and "bound up his wounds, pouring on oil and wine; then he set him on his own beast and brought him to an inn, and took care of him. 35 And the next day he took out two denarii and gave them to the innkeeper, saying, 'Take care of him; and whatever more you spend, I will repay you when I come back' " (vv. 34–35). The depth of the Samaritan's compassion is expressed in his willingness to return to the inn to pay any additional expenses that may be necessary; this stands quite in contrast to the callousness of the Levite and priest who simply continue on their way. Love and compassion are not merely items included in a ritualistic recital of Torah, but dimensions of God's mercy that must be acted out concretely to the neighbor in need. For this reason Jesus instructs the lawyer to "Go and do likewise" (v. 37). Once again Luke selects a story in which the central figure is at the periphery of first-century Jewish society in the hope of shocking his audience into realizing that (1) faithfulness to God's will is not limited to a certain "in-group"; (2) that God's will of mercy and compassion must not only be recited and celebrated in liturgy, but most important of all, it must be acted out in daily life.

Women

God's love to the despised is also made real in Luke's gospel by the positive concentration on women, a group participating in a decidedly subordinate existence both in the general Graeco-Roman culture of the day and also within Judaism. Jesus' easy association with women and the seriousness with which he deals with them is indeed startling, if not radical.[8] The examples that follow are not dramatic in and of themselves, but they do underscore what has just been said about Jesus' attitude as portrayed by Luke.

In 7:11-17 we find the pericope dealing with the widow's son at Nain, a text found only in Luke's gospel.

Soon afterward he went to a city called Nain, and his disciples and a great crowd went with him. 12 As he drew near to the gate of the city, behold, a man who had died was being carried out, the only son of his mother, and she was a widow; and a large crowd from the city was with her. 13 And when the Lord saw her, he had compassion on her and said to her, "Do not weep." 14 And he came and touched the bier, and the bearers stood still. And he said, "Young man, I say to you, arise." 15 And the dead man sat up, and began to speak. And he gave him to his mother. 16 Fear seized them all; and they glorified God, saying, "A great prophet has arisen among us!" and "God has visited his people!" 17 And this report concerning him spread through the whole of Judea and all the surrounding country.

The central figure is certainly the mother. The young man is described as "the only son of his mother, and she was a widow" (v. 12). Jesus' attitude toward her is described as one of "compassion" and once again this compassion is not something abstract, but involves concrete action: he brings the mother's son to life and gives him to her.

Although we discussed the story of the woman with ointment (7:36-50) above under the category of sinner, it would fit equally well in our present discussion of women. It is a woman, indeed a sinful woman, whose faith serves as an example for all. Immediately after this text, Luke presents us with the account of the ministering women (8:1–3), again an account found only in his gospel:

Soon afterward he went on through cities and villages, preaching and bringing the good news of the kingdom of God. And the twelve were with him, 2 and also some women who had been healed of evil spirits and infirmities: Mary, called Magdalene, from whom seven demons had gone out, 3 and Joanna, the wife of Chuza, Herod's steward, and Susanna, and many others, who provided for them out of their means.

According to this text, Jesus travels with the twelve accompanied by "some women . . . who provided for them out of their means."

This same, easy association with women is demonstrated in the brief narrative about Mary and Martha in 10:38–42 and it is highlighted in Luke's passion narrative. Immediately following the description of Simon of Cyrene as the one who carried Jesus' cross, Luke adds: "And there followed him a great multitude of the people, and of women who bewailed and lamented him" (23:27). Both of these accounts are only found in Luke's gospel and it is a likely assumption that Luke has a special interest in highlighting Jesus' concern for women and that they equally share in God's mercy as revealed in the ministry of Jesus of Nazareth.

Political Innocence of the Romans in the Death of Jesus

We now come to the second major theological tendency in Luke's gospel that we have selected—the tendency to stress the political innocence of the Romans in the responsibility for the death of Jesus. In place of this is the stress that the Jews were heavily, if not completely, at fault with regard to the death of Jesus of Nazareth. The fact that Luke's presentation is unique is without doubt. The historical fact is clearly that the Romans bore the final responsibility in the death of Jesus; he died on a cross which is a Roman form of death.[9] More typically Jewish is stoning (cf. Acts 7), but that raises the question whether the Jews even had the juridical right to kill someone in a land occupied by Romans; in all likelihood they did not have permission and the stoning of Stephen in Acts 7 is an unauthorized crowd action. Further, Luke's unique presentation is evident from a comparison with the more balanced presentations of the other gospels. So the question is not whether Luke's portrayal is unique, but why it is. What issues is he trying to address that are of importance for his audience?

Let us first review the relevant texts in Luke's passion narrative and if it is at all possible for you to follow the discussion with a copy of the *Gospel Parallels*[10] before you, it would greatly assist you in the task of understanding. The first series of references will be those that stress the political innocence of the Romans.

Luke 23:4: "And Pilate said to the chief priests and the multitudes, 'I find no crime in this man.' " This explicit declaration of innocence is found only in Luke.

Luke 23:13–16:

Pilate then called together the chief priests and the rulers and the people, 14 and said to them, "You brought me this man as one who was perverting the people; and after examining him before you, behold, I did not find this man guilty of any of your charges against him; 15 neither did Herod, for he sent him back to us. Behold, nothing deserving death has been done by him; 16 I will therefore chastise him and release him."

According to this text, without parallel in the other gospels, both Pilate and Herod declare Jesus innocent of all charges made against him by the Jews.

Luke 23:20: "Pilate addressed them once more, desiring to release Jesus." Only Luke adds the phrase that Pilate desired to release Jesus. Mark 15:12 simply reads, "And Pilate again said to them . . ."

Luke 23:22 is a most interesting text because one can vividly see how Luke's interest led to the expansion of the Marcan text. Mark 15:14 states: "And Pilate said to them, 'Why, what evil has he done?" The Lucan text is expanded as follows: "A third time

he said to them, 'Why, what evil has he done? I have found in him
no crime deserving death; I will therefore chastise him and release him.' " Luke's addition is not only in terms of expanding
the verse so as to stress the innocence of Jesus, but also by
enumerating at the very outset of the verse that this is the third
time that Pilate has reached this conclusion.

Luke 23:47, perhaps more than any other verse, underscores
the critical importance of the historical-critical method and especially one dimension of that method, redaction criticism. For
without the insights received from that approach, an adequate
explanation of this verse is virtually impossible. To properly
grasp the significance of this text we must begin with the parallel
in Mark's gospel which Luke had before him. We read in Mark
15:39: "And when the centurion, who stood facing him, saw that
he thus breathed his last, he said, 'Truly this man was the Son of
God!' " Matthew who was also dependent on Mark at this point
renders almost the identical confession after having made some
alterations at the beginning of the verse. The Matthean version
(Matt. 27:54) is as follows: "When the centurion and those who
were with him, keeping watch over Jesus, saw the earthquake and
what took place, they were filled with awe, and said, 'Truly this
was the Son of God!' " As we now turn to the Lucan parallel we
see that a major alteration is made: "Now when the centurion saw
what had taken place, he praised God, and said, 'Certainly this
man was innocent!' "

The Marcan "Truly this man was the Son of God" has been
radically transformed by Luke into "Certainly this man was innocent!" We have already noted in our discussion of Mark how
critical the centurion's confession that Jesus is "the Son of God"
was for Mark's theological program. While this matter is not
unimportant for Luke, it is not his central concern at this moment. As a summary of his entire attempt to free the Romans of
involvement in the death of Jesus it would be quite beside the
point for the centurion to talk about "the Son of God"; the entire
force of his editorial activity and argumentation virtually compels
the centurion to shout out loudly and clearly only one thing:

"Certainly this man was innocent!" Luke's theology that addresses a concrete situation is the only explanation to this dramatic and forceful change from the Marcan text.

Thus far we have examined only those texts that put the Romans in a good light concerning the death of Jesus; we have yet to consider those texts that stress that it was the Jews who were at fault in this matter.

Luke 20:20: "So they watched him, and sent spies, who pretended to be sincere, that they might take hold of what he said, so as to deliver him up to the authority and jurisdiction of the governor." The parallel in Mark 12:13 does not intensify the dimension of hypocrisy as does the Lucan version. It reads simply: "And they sent to him some of the Pharisees and some of the Herodians, to entrap him in his talk."

Luke 20:26: "And they were not able in the presence of the people to catch him by what he said; but marveling at his answer they were silent." The "they" refers to the Jews. This same dimension of "trickery" we noted above is stressed once again.

Luke 23:2: "And they began to accuse him, saying, 'We found this man perverting our nation, and forbidding us to give tribute to Caesar, and saying that he himself is Christ a king.'" This verse, as is the case with most of the above, appears only in Luke. Here the Jews, according to Luke, are clearly attempting to make Jesus a political liability of the highest order, charges that surely would bring upon him the wrath of the Roman officials. Despite this effort, Pilate categorically states in verse 4, "I find no crime in this man." Upon hearing this the Jews in verse 5 insist even more vigorously that Jesus "stirs up the people, teaching throughout all Judea, from Galilee even to this place." The uniqueness of Luke's concern at this point is once again indicated by the absence of parallel verses in the other gospels.

Luke 23:18–19: "But they all cried out together, 'Away with this man, and release to us Barabbas'—19 a man who had been thrown into prison for an insurrection started in the city, and for murder." Note how Luke adds in verse 19 a description about Barabbas not found in the other gospels. The Jews by desiring to release Barabbas, a man accused of insurrection, are making evident that they view Jesus as even more a radical political traitor than Barabbas. In verse 25 this identical phenomenon appears, that is, a further negative characterization of Barabbas, and once again he is not only described as an insurrectionist, but as a murderer as well. "He released the man who had been thrown into prison for insurrection and murder, whom they asked for; but Jesus he delivered up to their will."

The critical question is why Luke shapes his passion narrative in the way he does. Here, of course, one's overall understanding of the purpose of Luke/Acts is determinative in answering this question. Those who stress the apologetic function of Luke/Acts will see Luke's desire to present the Roman government in a good light as especially influential in the shaping of this passion narrative. I, to the contrary, have a different understanding of the purpose of Luke/Acts, and understand Luke's shaping of passion narratives from a different perspective. Determinative for me is the gentile issue as a dominant one for Luke's audience. Luke is attempting to convince them that the extension of God's kingdom beyond the Jews to the gentiles is necessary not only because God promised their inclusion in the Old Testament, but also because many Jews rejected God's gift of his Son. This rejection made more urgent the movement to the gentiles. It is this later part of the gentile problem as just described that motivated Luke's emphasis in the passion narrative. In defending and explaining the necessity of the gentile mission to his conservative Jewish-Christian congregation, he exaggerates the Jewish involvement in the rejection and death of Jesus so as to underscore the perspective that the moment had arrived for God to fulfill his promise of gentile inclusion.

Two additional points need to be stressed. First, precisely because not all Jews rejected Jesus and a faithful remnant believed, was it possible for this group of believing Jews to be the messengers of the kingdom to the gentiles. The point is that there is not any unilateral rejection of Jesus by the Jews. Second, it should become apparent to us how easily Luke's gospel lends itself to serve as the basis for anti-Semitism. But this can only happen when Luke is read apart from its historical context. Redaction criticism has demonstrated to us forcefully that Luke is shaping the gospel tradition to address a very specific set of problems in his congregation. Luke overemphasizes certain dimensions of the tradition in order to correct distortions existing in the minds of his audience; if this fact has been lost sight of, one inevitably is led to misinterpret Luke.

Salvation History

The third and final dimension of Lucan theology which we have selected for review is the theme of salvation history, or to put it another way, Luke's understanding of history. Professor Hans Conzelmann[11] and others have alerted us to the fact that many in Luke's audience are downcast, because the parousia has not come yet; this problem is technically known as the delay of the parousia as we have discussed previously. In the midst of this disappointment that the end had not yet come some agitators appeared informing the congregation that the parousia, in fact, was at hand. That this is the situation in Luke's congregation can be observed in a comparison with Mark's gospel. Mark (13:6) reads: "Many will come in my name, saying, 'I am he!' and they will lead many astray." Now read Luke (21:8): "And he said, 'Take heed that you are not led astray; for many will come in my name, saying, 'I am he!' and, 'The time is at hand!' Do not go after them." For Luke those who will lead astray are not only messianic pretenders, but also those who say, "The time is at hand!"

In order to address this sense of disappointment and false expectation among some in his audience, Luke develops a theology of history, the first of its kind among Christians. History is divided into three periods: the period of Israel, the period of Jesus, and the period of the church. The period of Israel includes not only the Old Testament, but also Luke 1–2, and even Luke 3 if one accepts the view that John the Baptist belongs to the period of Israel. The period of Jesus, which for Luke is the center of history, includes Luke 4–24, and the period of the church includes the entire second volume, the book of Acts.

Luke's approach in dealing with this pastoral problem is to suggest that while Jesus is the center of history, his death, resurrection, and ascension have inaugurated a final stage in God's history, the church. Just as God's Spirit was present with Jesus so it is present in the church both directing and supporting its missionary activity. The delay of the parousia is not to be a disappointment because the Christian disciple is now participating in God's missionary advance to the entire gentile world. Luke summarizes this perspective quite succinctly in Acts 1:7–8: Jesus said to them, "It is not for you to know times or seasons which the Father has fixed by his own authority. 8 But you shall receive power when the Holy Spirit has come upon you; and you shall be my witnesses in Jerusalem and in all Judea and Samaria and to the end of the earth." All of Luke's second volume, Acts, is devoted to the activity of the church showing how under the guidance of the Spirit it advances from Jerusalem to the very capital of the gentile world, Rome.

This threefold view of history results in the fact that although the imminent expectation of the parousia is not totally given up, it certainly has been displaced from its controlling position and has lost its urgent character. Let me cite two examples. There are certain rough parallels between Luke 12:35–46 and the allegory of the ten virgins in Matthew 25. Luke 12:35–38 reads as follows:

"Let your loins be girded and your lamps buring, 36 and be like men who are waiting for their master to come home from the marriage feast, so that they may open to him at once when he comes and knocks. 37 Blessed are those servants whom the master finds awake when he comes; truly, I say to you, he will gird himself and have them sit at table, and he will come and serve them. 38 If he comes in the second watch, or in the third, and finds them so, blessed are those servants!"

The end is clearly not imminent: there is to be a second and a third watch. It is not the imminence of the end that is stressed, as in Matthew, but the fact of the delay, the fact that there will be a good stretch of time before the end arrives. Even when the end is used as a summons to moral activity it is not its nearness or imminence that is constitutive, but simply that it is inevitable, as a casual glance at Luke 14:7–14, a Lucan teaching section dealing with humility, indicates. The final two verses (vv. 13–14) suffice to illustrate the point: "But when you give a feast, invite the poor, the maimed, the lame, the blind, 14 and you will be blessed, because they cannot repay you. You will be repaid at the resurrection of the just." The moral exhortation is based simply on the fact of a future resurrection, certainly not because it is around the corner.

One might conclude our discussion about salvation history and eschatology in Luke in this manner. If the parousia is symbolized by midnight, then for the gospel of Mark it is 11:55 P.M., for Matthew it is 8:00 P.M. and for the gospel of Luke it is 4:00 in the afternoon. The parousia is clearly in sight, but the important work of the church to proclaim the kingdom of God to the ends of the earth has yet to be accomplished. Part of Luke's challenge is to convince this conservative Jewish-Christian audience of the urgency of that task and for it to comprehend the vastness of God's mercy. The life of Christian discipleship is not a closed imitation of the past but it is an open anticipation to the power of the Holy Spirit so as to actively be able to participate in God's future.[12]

III. THE JOHANNINE LITERATURE

7. The Gospel of John in the Johannine Community

The Johannine community is a fascinating object of study. Not only has this community produced a variety of literature, but we can see with much precision how new problems in the history of the community called forth new ways in which to actualize the message of Jesus Christ. What makes such study especially illuminating is that the Johannine documents cover almost three-quarters of the first century—in other words we can trace the transitions and growth of a given Christian community over a significant span of time. What we will attempt to do in this chapter is to trace the Johannine trajectory from its beginnings into the early second century.[1]

To proceed in this way reveals a basic presupposition that is shared by many, but not all, New Testament scholars—that there is a significant enough interrelationship between the five writings attributed to John that they can with reasonable accuracy be used to illuminate the development of the Johannine community. These writings include the gospel, 1, 2, and 3 John and the book of Revelation.[2] There is widespread consensus that the gospel and the three letters come from the same community; in fact, some scholars argue that all four documents were written by the same person, a position, however, I would not affirm. With regard to the relationship between the book of Revelation (also referred to as the Apocalypse) and the other four documents, the relationship is somewhat more tenuous. Nevertheless, the arguments of Professor R. H. Charles are sufficiently persuasive to suggest that Revelation stems from the same community as the others and that it stands in continuity with it.[3] In short, then, I will attempt to show that all five documents just mentioned stem from the Johannine community and with their help I will attempt to plot a Johannine trajectory.

Is it possible to locate this community geographically? Early church tradition as well as some contemporary scholars suggest Ephesus.[4] If Revelation is as closely connected with this community as I suggest, the area in the vicinity of Ephesus is further strengthened by the reference in Revelation 1:11, "Write what you see in a book and send it to the seven churches, to Ephesus and to Smyrna and to Pergamum and to Thyatira and to Sardis and to Philadelphia and to Laodicea." All of the cities mentioned form a cluster around Ephesus. Perhaps we are dealing with a mission field with Ephesus at its center.

Our analysis of the Johannine trajectory will begin with the gospel of John, which itself covers a number of moments in the history and development of the community with one of the most significant being in the year A.D. 85; then we will turn to the Johannine letters, probably written in the last decade of the first century; and finally we will complete our survey with the book of Revelation which was in all likelihood written at the turn of the century.

Professor Raymond E. Brown has effectively shown in his two-volume commentary on the fourth gospel that it was not written in its present form at one given point in the development of the Johannine community; rather the gospel as we have it before us today evolved over a good number of years.[5] Brown himself isolates six stages of development. How many stages one identifies is for the moment not important; what is important is to recognize that there are stages of development that evolved over a considerable period of time.

That moment which serves as a catalyst for the shaping of much of the tradition has been identified by Professor J. Louis Martyn in his excellent study, *History and Theology in the Fourth Gospel,* and much of my own analysis below is dependent upon the stimulation and suggestion offered by Martyn.[6] There are three texts that help us especially to isolate this moment: John 9:22, 12:42, and 16:2.

The first of these texts appears in chapter 9, which begins with a story about the healing of a blind man and this leads to a controversy concerning the identity of Jesus. In light of such a healing, how does one identify him? The Jews eventually involve the parents of the blind man into this discussion. In verse 19 they ask the parents, "Is this your son, who you say was born blind? How then does he now see?" The parents respond in this way:

His parents answered, "We know that this is our son, and that he was born blind; 21 but how he now sees we do not know, nor do we know who opened his eyes. Ask him; he is of age, he will speak for himself." 22 His parents said this because they feared the Jews, for the Jews had already agreed that if any one should confess him to be Christ, he was to be put out of the synagogue. (vv. 20–22)

The critical matter for our consideration is contained in verse 22: ". . . The Jews had already agreed that if any one should confess him to be Christ, he was to be put out of the synagogue." If this reference to excommunication from the synagogue appeared only once here, it would certainly peak our interest; in fact, there are two further, similar references.

Chapter 12, as we shall shortly see, concludes the first half of John's gospel, which deals with the public ministry of Jesus. In 12:42–43 we find these words: "Nevertheless many even of the authorities believed in him, but for fear of the Pharisees they did not confess it, lest they should be put out of the synagogue: 43 for they loved the praise of men more than the praise of God." Once again we notice a hesitancy on the part of certain Jews—this time they are not parents, but authorities—to confess openly that Jesus is the Christ for fear that they would be excommunicated from the synagogue. It becomes increasingly apparent that these references to excommunication from the synagogue are more than incidental; an internal problem within the congregation is being revealed. This assumption is further strengthened by the repetition of this same motif in John 16:2, a text that falls

into the second half of the gospel, that half containing the farewell discourses. Beginning in 16:1–2, we read: "I have said all this
to you to keep you from falling away. 2 They will put you out of
the synagogues; indeed, the hour is coming when whoever kills
you will think he is offering service to God." How can we best
understand the setting from which these texts arise?

The first thing we must do is to free ourselves from the notion
that Judaism and Christianity developed as two well defined and
opposing movements immediately after the death of Jesus. The
earliest believers in Jesus as the Christ were Jews and the gospel
of John testifies to the fact that it was fully possible for two types
of Jews—those who did and those who did not believe in Jesus
as the Christ—to coexist within the synagogue structure. In this
sense Christians were one of several first-century Jewish groups.
This situation of brotherly coexistence continued well into the
end of the first century. Why did it end? Probably for reasons
similar to those that lead to the tension between the Matthean
community and the synagogue. As Judaism was restructuring
itself, it had to tighten up and it consequently reduced its toleration for deviant beliefs, such as the confession that Jesus was the
Christ.

In what specific ways was this toleration reduced? Basic to all
synagogue worship is the recitation of a formal prayer called the
Eighteen Benedictions. Following a detailed discussion, Martyn
concludes that in the year A.D. 85 the twelfth of these Benedictions was revised so as to specifically exclude Christians. Martyn
renders this modified twelfth Benediction in the following way:[7]

> For the apostates let there be no hope
> And let the arrogant government
> be speedily uprooted in our days.
> Let the Nazarenes [Christians] and the Minim [heretics] be destroyed
>   in a moment
> And let them be blotted out of the Book of Life and not be inscribed
>   together with the righteous.
> Blessed art thou, O Lord, who humblest the proud!

In what practical ways does the Benediction affect the synagogue in which members of the Johannine community had participated? Martyn's incisive conclusion puts the matter this way: "Thus the Fourth Gospel affords us a picture of a Jewish community which has been (recently?) shaken by the introduction of a newly formulated means for detecting those Jews who want to hold a dual allegiance to Moses and to Jesus as Messiah. Even against the will of some of the synagogue leaders, the Heretic Benediction is now employed in order formally and irretrievably to separate the church from the synagogue."[8]

Not only does this event in A.D. 85 explain the setting of the excommunication verses in John 9:22, 12:42, and 16:2, but it also explains the basic twofold division of the gospel. For the most part John 1–12 deals with events prior to the break with the synagogue. There is a dialogue going on between those Jews who believe that Jesus is the Christ and those Jews who do not and there is obvious tension between the two. The second half of the gospel, John 13–20, deals with events after the break with the synagogue. The most important of these is the fact that a new Christian community exists that is in urgent need of support and guidance. Much of this second half could be referred to as a "support document" for this infant community, scarred by the break and living uncomfortably as a minority.

As we turn our attention to the first twelve chapters of the gospel of John we must first observe that there are at least four major stages in the development of this gospel that span a good deal of time. The first stage represents the transmission and early circulation of the Jesus material to Ephesus, if that in fact is the location of the community. The second stage, and we consider this the most important, is the shaping of the early Jesus material into coherent sections suitable for Jews in the synagogue so as to persuade them that Jesus is the Christ. We should not overlook that the intention of the gospel is unabashedly propagandistic. "Now Jesus did many other signs in the presence of the disciples, which are not written in this book; 31 but these are written that you may believe that Jesus is the Christ, the Son of God, and that

believing you may have life in his name" (20:30–31). Stage three
is the gathering of material, largely after chapter 13, that tries to
comfort, support, and advise the new community after the year
A.D. 85. Stage four marks the addition of materials throughout
the gospel that are anti-gnostic such as 6:51b–58 (notice the
constant repetition of the term "flesh")—the opening hymn in
John 1, the post-resurrectional chapter 21, and other elements as
well. Just from this very much simplified developmental sketch it
should be apparent how central the dialogue with the synagogue
and the subsequent split from it is in the formation of the fourth
gospel.

The dialogue with the synagogue is so dominant in the first half
of this gospel that if one does not understand how it functions
one is likely to miss an important dimension of the real-life situation of this community. Let us examine some passages prior to
A.D. 85 that reflect this dialogue between Jews who believe that
Jesus is the Christ and those who do not. John 5:36–47 is a
particularly important witness to this dialogue within the "Johannine" synagogue:

"But the testimony which I have is greater than that of John; for the
works which the Father has granted me to accomplish, these very works
which I am doing, bear me witness that the Father has sent me. 37 And
the Father who sent me has himself borne witness to me. His voice you
have never heard, his form you have never see; 38 and you do not have
his word abiding in you, for you do not believe him whom he has sent.
39 You search the scriptures, because you think that in them you have
eternal life; and it is they that bear witness to me; 40 yet you refuse to
come to me that you may have life. 41 I do not receive glory from men.
42 But I know that you have not the love of God within you. 43 I have
come in my Father's name, and you do not receive me; if another comes
in his own name, him you will receive. 44 How can you believe, who
receive glory from one another and do not seek the glory that comes
from the only God? 45 Do not think that I shall accuse you to the Father;
it is Moses who accuses you, on whom you set your hope. 46 If you
believed Moses, you would believe me, for he wrote of me. 47 But if you
do not believe his writings, how will you believe my words?"

The opening verses of the selection we have made speak about the relationship of the Father to Jesus and they do so in terms typical of the entire gospel. Jesus is the one who had been sent by the Father to do his will. Jesus acts only on behalf of his Father, and not on his own. Thus, in not accepting Jesus some Jews are not accepting the one divinely commissioned and sent by the Father. Rather than letting Abraham, Moses, and Scripture assist them in understanding God's intention with regard to Jesus, they use them against Jesus, as a way of proving his lack of credibility. Thus, much in the first half of the gospel centers on the relationship of Abraham, Moses, and Scripture (i.e., the Old Testament) to Jesus.

In the John 5 passage before us, two of these comparisons are made. The first one concerns Scripture. In verses 39–40 the gospel writer has Jesus speaking, "You search the scriptures, because you think that in them you have eternal life; and it is they that bear witness to me; 40 yet you refuse to come to me that you may have life." If the Jews truly understood their Scripture, they would understand that it points to Jesus as the source of eternal life; however, their idolatrous use of Scripture prevents them from recognizing that life, a key term for this gospel, is only available in Jesus.

These verses also have particular relevance to contemporary Christians for the temptation to use Scripture idolatrously today also exists. This gospel especially makes quite clear that Jesus Christ is God's Word to men and women and in that sense it is the Christ alone who is the Word of God. Scripture can never have this position of preeminence; Scripture, Old and New Testaments together, can faithfully witness to God's Word but it is never in itself God's Word in the primary sense of the term. To assert that is not only bad theology, it is also idolatrous.[9]

The relationship between Jesus and Scripture is developed further and made more precise in the succeeding verses. "Do not think that I shall accuse you to the Father; it is Moses who accuses you, on whom you set your hope. 46 If you believed Moses, you would believe me, for he wrote of me. 47 But if you do not believe his writings, how will you believe my words?" (vv. 45–47). The dialogue between the two partners proceeds in a most interesting way. It is obvious that the nonbelievers are pitting Moses over against Jesus. Jesus responds to this with the assertion that it will be their own hero, Moses, not Jesus, who will accuse them before the Father. Further, their pitting of Moses against Jesus stems from a basic misunderstanding of Moses, for Moses himself wrote about Jesus. They neither know or believe Moses, and if this is the case, it is hardly possible for them to believe in Jesus. Already from this brief selection we should have a sense of the intensity of the dialogue and discussion that was taking place in the synagogue in Ephesus among Jews about the person of Jesus.

This dialogue within the synagogue from which the Johannine church will emerge not only contrasts Jesus and Moses, but also Jesus and Abraham; much of John 8 is concerned with this comparison. Typical are verses 31–33: "Jesus then said to the Jews who had believed in him, 'If you continue in my word, you are truly my disciples, 32 and you will know the truth, and the truth will make you free.' 33 They answered him, 'We are descendants of Abraham, and have never been in bondage to any one. How is it that you say, "You will be made free"?' " Again it should become clear that their discussions make much more sense when we take seriously the original context in which they are found and it is precisely here that Martyn's thesis about the twelfth Benediction is so relevant.[10]

To fully understand the difference between the two Jewish groups in John's gospel one needs to know not only the original context, but the Old Testament as well, since this is the basic document used in the discussion. For example, the remainder of the Jesus–Abraham discussion in John 8 is a clear case in point, where both the original situation and the Old Testament must serve as essential background. Although the intensity of the Abraham–Jesus comparison continues in verse 34 let us concentrate particularly on verses 51–59:

"Truly, truly, I say to you, if any one keeps my word, he will never see death." 52 The Jews said to him, "Now we know that you have a demon. Abraham died, as did the prophets; and you say, 'If any one keeps my word, he will never taste death.' 53 Are you greater than our father Abraham, who died? And the prophets died! Who do you claim to be?" 54 Jesus answered, "If I glorify myself, my glory is nothing; it is my Father who glorifies me, of whom you say that he is your God. 55 But you have not known him; I know him. If I said, I do not know him, I should be a liar like you; but I do know him and I keep his word. 56 Your father Abraham rejoiced that he was to see my day; he saw it and was glad." 57 The Jews said to him, "You are not yet fifty years old, and have you seen Abraham?" 58 Jesus said to them, "Truly, truly, I say to you, before Abraham was, I am." 59 So they took up stones to throw at him; but Jesus hid himself, and went out of the temple.

Verse 56 is a crucial text: "Your father Abraham rejoiced that he was to see my day; he saw it and was glad." As the next verse underscores, the Jews are totally bewildered. Jesus, according to this gospel writer, then makes a response in verse 58 that so angered his audience that they took up stones to throw at him. What is it that is so irritating about the response, "Truly, truly, I say to you, before Abraham was, I am"? Here is where our knowledge of the Old Testament becomes critical.

In Exodus 3:13 and following we read:

Then Moses said to God, "If I come to the people of Israel and say to them, 'The God of your fathers has sent me to you,' and they ask me, 'What is his name?' what shall I say to them?" 14 God said to Moses, "I AM WHO I AM." And he said, "Say this to the people of Israel, 'I AM has sent me to you.' "

"I am who I am" is a translation of the Hebrew word *Yahweh,* the divine name. God is described by the verb "to be." He is a God of action who cannot be grasped or defined by static concepts. In all likelihood it is to this language and this concept that John has Jesus refer to in chapter 8 and the reference "before Abraham was, I am" is a very clear expression of Jesus' intimate relationship with the Father. This same relationship is expressed in quite different language in the magnificent opening hymn in

John 1: 1–3, "In the beginning was the Word, and the Word was with God, and the Word was God. 2 He was in the beginning with God; 3 all things were made through him, and without him was not anything made that was made." Here a Jewish-Hellenistic concept, *logos,* "Word," is used to describe Jesus and particularly the relationship between the Father and Jesus.[11] In short, then, it is Jesus' claim to share in the divinity of the Father that leads to the violent outburst among the Jews at the end of John 8.

The entire first half of the gospel, which has its setting in the public ministry of Jesus, is filled with hostility toward Jesus by many, and it reaches its climax in chapter 12 with the announcement of his impending death. This death is described symbolically by John as "the hour," a term first used in John 2 when Jesus, somewhat abruptly, tells his mother, "O woman, what have you to do with me? My hour has not yet come" (v. 4). John 7:25 summarizes the hostility evident throughout the first half of the gospel: "Some of the people of Jerusalem therefore said, 'Is not this the man whom they seek to kill?' " John 12 indicates that that moment has arrived: "And Jesus answered them, 'The hour has come for the Son of man to be glorified' " (v. 23). Then we read in verses 27 and following, "Now is my soul troubled. And what shall I say? 'Father save me from this hour'? No, for this purpose I have come to this hour. . . . 31 Now is the judgment of this world, now shall the ruler of this world be cast out; 32 and I, when I am lifted up from the earth, will draw all men to myself.' 33 He said this to show by what death he was to die."

It is significant that despite John's radically different context and his very different language structure, the theme of Jesus' death is so very prominent, a fact we have already observed in Pauline theology as well as in the Gospel of Mark. Not only does John share with them the fact of Jesus' death, but also the ethical implications of that death for the life of the believer. Just following the announcement that the hour of Jesus' death had arrived one finds words remarkably similar to those in Mark 8:34–37. John 12:25–26 reads: "He who loves his life loses it, and he who hates his life in this world will keep it for eternal life. 26 If any one serves me, he must follow me; and where I am, there shall my servant be also; if any one serves me, the Father will honor him." The further ethical implications of the suffering and death of Jesus are developed explicitly beginning in John 13, which marks the beginning of the second half of the gospel.

The opening verse of the second half of the gospel, 13:1, gives us some important clues concerning the setting of these final chapters: "Now before the feast of the Passover, when Jesus knew that his hour had come to depart out of this world to the Father, having loved his own who were in the world, he loved them to the end." The imminence of Jesus' death is repeated, followed by the fact that this event will lead to his departure from the world. Because of these forthcoming events the concentration of Jesus' comments will be toward "his own," that is, his disciples. Thus with accuracy many scholars have referred to these final chapters in the fourth gospel as "farewell discourses."

It has long been noted that John's gospel contains no pericope describing the institution of the Lord's Supper. The evangelist has transformed this pericope into a footwashing scene and has transposed it from a position normally found in the passion narrative to the very beginning of the second half of the gospel.[12] This parallels another Johannine transposition: the movement of the temple cleansing scene, also found toward the end of the Synoptic gospels, to the very beginning (2:13–22). This is done intentionally. Placing the temple cleansing scene at the outset of his gospel signals the conflict that surrounds Jesus' public ministry and dominates the first half of the gospel; placing the foot washing scene at the beginning of the instructions to the Johannine church just recently excommunicated from the synagogue reveals much about the ethical style by which this new congregation is to live. To this Johannine concern we now turn.

The action of Jesus is clearly to serve as an example for his followers. Jesus "poured water into a basin, and began to wash the disciples' feet, and to wipe them with the towel with which he was girded" (13:5).

In a manner similar to Mark 8, the pattern of Jesus' life is to influence that of his disciples. John's gospel proceeds in the following way (13:12–17):

When he had washed their feet, and taken his garments, and resumed his place, he said to them, "Do you know what I have done to you? 13 You call me Teacher and Lord; and you are right, for so I am. 14 If I then, your Lord and Teacher, have washed your feet, you also ought to wash one another's feet. 15 For I have given you an example, that you also should do as I have done to you. 16 Truly, truly, I say to you, a servant is not greater than his master; nor is he who is sent greater than he who sent him. 17 If you know these things, blessed are you if you do them.' "

The key is obviously verse 15. The style of Christian discipleship is that of humble service to the other; it is this theme that the evangelist wishes to stress at the very outset as forming the basic characteristic of the Christian community.

As the foot-washing action of Jesus is amplified by the category of "love," so now this theme increases in importance. This is accomplished in two ways. First, the evangelist repeatedly speaks of a disciple "whom Jesus loved." The first reference to this beloved disciple is in John 13:21 and following and he is referred to specifically again in John 19:26–27 and John 20:2 and following. Clearly he serves as a symbolic figure for all disciples. They are to love Jesus in the same way he does. If a historical figure lies behind this idealized portrait of the beloved disciple, he is not easily identifiable and the fact that he is not referred to in the Synoptic gospels offers no assistance from that source. That the apostle John, the probable founder of this Christian community, is intended is a suggestion we made in *Peter in the New Testament* and still remains an attractive possibility.[13] Second, the foot-washing illustration is amplified in John 13:34–35: "A new commandment I give to you, that you love one another; even as I have loved you, that you also love one another. 35 By this all men will know that you are my disciples, if you have love for one another."

The theme of love is found from this point on throughout the gospel and the remainder of the literature of the Johannine community. Some examples include: 14:15, "If you love me, you will keep my commandments"; 15:9–10, "As the Father has loved me, so have I loved you; abide in my love. 10 If you keep my commandments, you will abide in my love, just as I have kept my Father's commandments and abide in his love"; and 15:12–13, "This is my commandment, that you love one another as I have loved you. 13 Greater love has no man than this, that a man lay down his life for his friends." This same theme is repeated several times in 1 John; for example 2:7–10; 3:14, 18; and 4:7, 8, and 19. The specific ethical appeal to love is well illustrated in 1 John 3:17–18; "But if any one has the world's goods and sees his brother in need, yet closes his heart against him, how does God's love abide in him? Little children, let us not love in word or speech but in deed and in truth." The term also occurs in 2 John 1 and 3 John 1 and it occurs in a most interesting manner in Revelation 2:4, "But I have this against you, that you have abandoned the love you had at first." Love in the sense of humble service to the brothers and sisters in Christ is a fundamental characteristic of the Christian congregation throughout the Johannine literature and for this reason it is found in the opening chapter of the second half of John's gospel, that part of the gospel directed to the internal life of the newly separated Johannine community.

The Pauline emphasis of faith active in love (Gal. 5:6) and the Matthean emphasis on the rigor of the Christian life (Matt. 7: 13–27) are found coupled together in the Johannine discourse of the true vine in John 15:1–17. The rigor of the Christian life is portrayed in verse 2, "Every branch of mine that bears no fruit, he takes away, and every branch that does bear fruit he prunes, that it may bear more fruit." This is quite similar to Matthew 7:17–20:

"So, every sound tree bears good fruit, but the bad tree bears evil fruit. 18 A sound tree cannot bear evil fruit, nor can a bad tree bear good fruit. 19 Every tree that does not bear good fruit is cut down and thrown into the fire. 20 Thus you will know them by their fruits."

John 15:5 ("I am the vine, you are the branches. He who abides in me, and I in him, he it is that bears much fruit, for apart from me you can do nothing") is, of course, remarkably close to Paul. The fruit that the new Christian is enabled to bear is love for the other.

In addition to this strong ethical stress in the second half of John, there are other dimensions that are emphasized and to which we must turn our attention.

Since the Johannine church, newly separated from the synagogue, was a small minority in evidently hostile territory, it needed a clear word of encouragement. Having indicated first what was expected in John 13, the evangelist addresses words of hope, especially in chapters 14 and 16. Rather interestingly, this same pattern of first ethical exhortation and then only words of support is exactly what we find in the book of Revelation. Before those who are standing in the threat of persecution are supported beginning in chapter 4, there are three chapters addressing concrete exhortations to the seven congregations describing exactly what it is that God expects of them. Only as Christians are obedient to God's will can they participate in his hope and joy even in the most difficult of situations.

The theme of John 14:1 echoes throughout this section: "Let not your hearts be troubled; believe in God, believe also in me." Here, in strongly apocalyptic language, it is pointed out that Jesus will prepare a place for his disciples in the heavenly world: "And when I go and prepare a place for you, I will come again and will take you to myself, that where I am you may be also" (v. 3). Because of this fact, their hearts need not be troubled.

But the hearts of the Johannine disciples are not to be troubled for other reasons as well. Particularly as suggested in 14:16 and 26, because the Father will send them a "Counselor, the Holy Spirit" (v. 26). Unique to the fourth gospel is this term "Counselor" or "Paraclete"; it is describing, apparently, one dimension of the work of the Holy Spirit. The meaning of the term in this period is that of a legal counselor, an advocate who also will stand beside one in a courtroom defense.[14] In a situation where the term Holy Spirit may well have been used in an imprecise way, the fourth evangelist is trying to communicate to his audience that the Holy Spirit is present in their midst like a legal counselor, as one who is defending them against all the difficulties of their current situation. Despite the fact that this infant Johannine community is a minority and having a difficult time of it, the Holy Spirit is actively in their midst defending them. Although Christ has ascended to the Father and the end has not yet come, the Paraclete will be with them forever.

John 17 contains the last words of Jesus while still with his disciples. It is presented in the form of a prayer and because of its strategic position in the structure of the gospel is intended to communicate an important message. The prayer begins, "Father, the hour has come" and then refers to the fact that Jesus is about to rejoin the Father in heaven. Because of this Jesus prays to his Father for the protection of those of his disciples who must remain on earth and he specifically prays that his disciples will remain "one"; in short, what we have before us is a prayer for the unity of Jesus' disciples.

The first request for the unity of the disciples comes in verse 11: "And now I am no more in the world, but they are in the world, and I am coming to thee. Holy Father, keep them in thy name, which thou hast given me, that they may be one, even as we are one." As the Father and the Son are one so are the disciples to be one; divine unity serves as the example for ecclesiastical unity. This identical request is taken up and elaborated in verses 20–23:

"I do not pray for these only, but also for those who believe in me through their word, 21 that they may all be one; even as thou, Father, art in me, and I in thee, that they also may be in us, so that the world may believe that thou hast sent me. 22 The glory which thou hast given me I have given to them, that they may be one even as we are one, 23 I in them and thou in me, that they may become perfectly one, so that the world may know that thou hast sent me and hast loved them even as thou hast loved me."

These verses go beyond verse 11 in the following ways. Verse 20 has a wider audience in mind. Not only the disciples but also "those who believe in me through their word," that is, subsequent generations. The hope expressed is that disciples in all generations may be one. In verse 21, the request for unity is not based only on the divine example but also on the hope that the world might believe. The credibility of the Word is significantly enhanced by the unity of the Christian disciples. Verse 23 phrases this in a result clause. Perfect oneness is a necessity *"so that* the world may know that thou hast sent me and has loved them even as thou hast loved me." Not only belief in Jesus as the revelation of the Father but also God's love for the world are contingent upon the oneness of the disciples. That this concern for unity within the Johannine church is not merely an abstract concern becomes evident from 1 John 2:19, "They went out from us, but they were not of us; for if they had been of us, they would have continued with us; but they went out, that it might be plain that they all are not of us." From this text as well as from references in 2 and 3 John it is clear that the unfortunate fact of disunity was present in the Johannine community. In all likelihood the present form of John 17 is shaped with such a situation in mind.

The second half of the gospel concludes with a passion narrative, accounts of the resurrection and post-resurrection appearances, all of which are shaped by distinctively Johannine theological themes. The gospel then originally concluded in 20:30–31 with a clear summary of its intentions:

Now Jesus did many other signs in the presence of the disciples, which are not written in this book; 31 but these are written that you may believe that Jesus is the Christ, the Son of God, and that believing you may have life in his name.

At a final stage in the redaction, chapter 21 was added containing further post-resurrection appearances including a dialogue with Peter, a section that has many parallels to the Peter pericope in Matthew 16:17–19.

Although the major event that shaped John's gospel is the

expulsion from the synagogue in A.D. 85, we have also noted that intensive dialogue concerning the identity of Jesus was evident long before this date and much of this material is found throughout the first half of the gospel. Another significant stress in the gospel is the shaping of a new Christian community after the exclusion from the synagogue. Words of comfort, exhortation, and hope are addressed to this community; problems such as unity are discussed. At that point in our discussion we already noted an overlap with the Johannine epistles. There is still one other dimension of concern in this congregation, the problem of false doctrine, a matter that once again draws us closely in the vicinity of the epistles. The specific issue that the final redaction of the fourth gospel has to deal with is that concerning the reality of Jesus having come in the flesh. We know that many second-century Gnostics denied the reality of Jesus' incarnation in the flesh and it is probably a somewhat similar tendency that is infiltrating the Johannine church. We know also that the problem emerges acutely in the Johannine epistles. 2 John 7 refers to the issue in this way, "For many deceivers have gone out into the world, men who will not acknowledge the coming of Jesus Christ in the flesh; such a one is the deceiver and the antichrist." A similar warning, although in an expanded form is found in 1 John 4:1–3a:

Beloved, do not believe every spirit, but test the spirits to see whether they are of God; for many false prophets have gone out into the world. 2 By this you know the Spirit of God: every spirit which confesses that Jesus Christ has come in the flesh is of God, 3 and every spirit which does not confess Jesus is not of God.

This same stress on the reality of Jesus having come in the flesh *(sarx)* is found in the fourth gospel. As we have urged elsewhere, all of these references come from the last stage in the gospel's redaction, that stage in which an anti-heretical emphasis becomes essential. The first reference is in John 1:14, "And the Word became flesh and dwelt among us, full of grace and truth. . . ." In the most precise way possible it is made clear that Jesus' presence among men and women was in the reality of human flesh. To make this assertion so definitively would indicate that it has a polemical intention, presumably against a gnostic-type situation.

Many scholars agree that John 6:51b–58 is also a pericope that was added at a later stage in the development of the gospel. Note the frequency of the term "flesh" in these verses:

"... And the bread which I shall give for the life of the world is my *flesh*." 52 The Jews then disputed among themselves, saying, "How can this man give us his *flesh* to eat?" 53 So Jesus said to them, "Truly, truly, I say to you, unless you eat the *flesh* of the Son of man and drink his blood, you have no life in you; 54 he who eats my *flesh* and drinks my blood has eternal life, and I will raise him up at the last day. 55 For my *flesh* is food indeed and my blood is drink indeed. 56 He who eats my *flesh* and drinks my blood abides in me and I in him."

In addition to the anti-heretical stress of these verses one should also note the reality of John's description of the crucified Jesus hanging on the cross in 19:34: "But one of the soldiers pierced his side with a spear, and at once there came out blood and water." Clearly then the final redactor of John's gospel stresses the physicality of Jesus because of a countercurrent present in the milieu of the Johannine community. It is fully possible that this same redaction was responsible for the addition of John 21, to stress both the reality of the post-resurrection Jesus and to lay a foundation for emerging ecclesiastical authority and the shaping of John 14–15. The inclusion of chapters 14–15 serves to under-score the necessity for ethical seriousness in the community. The similarities both in terms of thesis and language (e.g., "Spirit of Truth") between chapters 14–15 and the Johannine epistles are striking.

We have already had several opportunities to observe overlap-ping of concerns between the final stage of the fourth gospel and the Johannine epistles. This is not surprising since in one view the Johannine epistles are concerned with matters identical to those of the gospel's final redactor. In fact, I have suggested in an essay previously published that the author of the epistles may well have been the final redactor of the gospel.[15] Can we say more about this author?

The writer of 2 and 3 John simply introduces himself as "the elder" *(presbyteros)*. This terse, straightforward introduction, "the elder" (or alternatively, "the presbyter"), indicates that the recipients of these letters would immediately know who was meant and that the presbyter had a specific relationship of authority to his audience. He gives concrete advice and expects to be obeyed. Because a certain Diotrephes has become rebellious, he plans to challenge him upon his arrival. One would hardly risk that unless there was some expectation of success. The presbyter's concerns in 2 and 3 John seem to be identical with that of an elder-bishop as described in Titus 1:9–10, ". . . He must hold firm to the sure word as taught, so that he may be able to give instruction in sound doctrine and also confute those who contradict it. 10 For there are many insubordinate men, empty talkers and deceivers. . . ."

My suggestion is that 2 and 3 John, as well as the final stage of the gospel as previously discussed, were written by the presbyter, who was not only an ecclesiastical officer, but the most important presbyter in a regional network of churches; and, further, that he directed and controlled the missionary activity in that region. The author of 2 John reflects his relationship to one of these congregations in the missionary situation in which he is warning them against the admission of false (gnostic) teachers; in 3 John he is dealing with a different congregational situation in which its ecclesiastical officer, Diotrephes, refuses to acknowledge the presbyter and tries to pull off a coup d'état. We evidence here a political power struggle between two emerging authority figures as the early church enters upon a new stage in its organizational development.

What can be said about the geographical spread of the presbyter's authority? There are basically two options: (1) that he is a presbyter over the church in his city and the area in the immediate vicinity. In this case, the missionaries travel around the various nearby household churches and it is in one of these that we would find Diotrephes. Or, (2) that the presbyter was not only in charge of his own congregation, but because of his own prominence and that of his well-known congregation (Ephesus?) he exercised a wide-ranging moral, but not yet legally defined, influence over other geographically more distant congregations. In this case, one could visualize a series of churches in one region, each with their own elder-bishop. These are subordinate in dignity (not office) to *the* presbyter, in a similar manner to which the elders in Crete are subordinate to Titus. As Titus is concerned with sound doctrine (1:9) and to "exhort and reprove with all authority" (2:15), so, too, is the presbyter of 2 and 3 John.

Option two is preferable for it makes better sense of the supposed geographical distances involved and receives indirect support from the book of Revelation. As R. H. Charles has shown, there are definite linguistic and theological ties between all of the Johannine literature, including Revelation.[16] While Revelation was clearly written by an author separate from that of the epistles, they were probably members of a larger Johanine school operating in the same geographical area with its center in Ephesus. Thus, a not totally improbable conjecture concerning the geographical setting of 2 and 3 John would be that we are dealing with the same area as that of the seven letters in Revelation 1:11.

To locate the epistles in the Johannine trajectory would call for a position alongside what we have designated Stage 3, the antignostic addition to the gospel, and then moving beyond stage 3 to a new stage, 4, which involves a further expansion and sharpening of these ecclesiastical concerns. The Johannine epistles then, represent stage 4 on our schema, with the book of Revelation representing stage 5. Stage 5 overlaps somewhat with stage 4, especially the letters to the seven churches, but then goes beyond it by offering support and encouragement to Christians caught in the midst of persecution.

8. Revelation: A Word about God's Faithfulness and Justice

Let us take a closer look at the last book in the New Testament, the book of Revelation. This document can be divided into two parts: chapters 1–3 and 4–21. The first part consists of some introductory matters and then follows seven letters to the seven churches in the vicinity of Ephesus that we referred to previously. They contain words of praise, exhortation, and warning. As an example we may select the letter to the church at Ephesus (Rev. 2:1–7):

"To the angel of the church in Ephesus write: 'The words of him who holds the seven stars in his right hand, who walks among the seven golden lampstands. 2 " 'I know your works, your toil and your patient endurance, and how you cannot bear evil men but have tested those who call themselves apostles but are not, and found them to be false; 3 I know you are enduring patiently and bearing up for my name's sake, and you have not grown weary. 4 But I have this against you, that you have abandoned the love you had at first. 5 Remember then from what you have fallen, repent and do the works you did at first. If not, I will come to you and remove your lampstand from its place, unless you repent. 6 Yet this you have, you hate the works of the Nicolaitans, which I also hate. 7 He who has an ear, let him hear what the Spirit says to the churches. To him who conquers I will grant to eat of the tree of life, which is in the paradise of God.' "

Verses 2, 3, and 6 are words of praise and the other verses contain words of exhortation and warning. Throughout each of these letters the point is made abundantly clear that only as God's people remain faithful to him and do his will even in the midst of the most difficult of circumstances, can they be counted as faithful servants to whom the Lord of history speaks his word of promise. This majestic picture of God who controls all history and all creation is evident both in the terminology used to describe him and in the imagery used to portray him throughout the entire book. For example, in Revelation 1:4, God is described as the one "who is and who was and who is to come. . . ." By using the verb "to be" God is described as a God who is present to his people now, and it is this same God who acted on their behalf in the past, and who will act decisively in the future. The majesty and sovereignity of God is expressed even more eloquently in verse 8: " 'I am the Alpha and the Omega,' says the Lord God, who is and who was and who is to come, the Almighty." Alpha and omega are the first and last letters in the Greek alphabet and God is described as the beginning and end of all existence.

The major reason that the book of Revelation was written was to support those Christians who were being persecuted by the Romans. The confession that Jesus was Lord often cost Christians their lives. The message of Revelation is simple despite what some consider to be its bizarre imagery: "Hang in there, be faithful," for God is the Lord of history and his righteousness and justice will prevail. But it must not be overlooked that before the author proceeds with this message, he insists that despite the external situation, the churches and their members remain obedient to their call. For this very important reason chapters 1–3 have a chronological as well as a theological priority.

Before we can understand anything of the message of Revelation beginning in chapter 4 we must now say something about the thought-world that produced a document such as Revelation. Scholars refer to it as apocalyptic Judaism; in fact, the term "apocalypse" occurs in the opening verse of this book. What is the meaning of "apocalypse" and what is "apocalyptic Judaism"?[1]

The term "apocalypse" means a revealing, a making known of that which had been previously hidden. Specifically, it is God's future plan for the world that is the subject of the revelation. Why is such a revelation necessary? After Jerusalem had been destroyed by the Babylonians in 586 B.C. and many of the inhabitants of the city were exiled, a great sense of pessimism set in. Had God forsaken his people because of their disobedience? What had happened to the prophets? Was life totally meaningless and controlled by fate? In this kind of an environment God seemed remote and isolated in the heavenly worlds. Increasingly this evil world was contrasted to the distant, but pure, heavenly world. One of the major eschatological expectations of apocalyptic Judaism was that at the end of time a new, heavenly Jerusalem would descend. In the meantime, how was God to be known?

At the heart of the apocalyptic literature, which ranges from about the fourth century B.C. into the Christian era, is a person referred to as a "seer." He gains access to the heavenly world, is shown around, and is given insight into God's plans for the future which usually include the theme of God's triumphant victory over all his enemies and the vindication of his faithful servants at some future date. This seer reveals these insights using very symbolic and mysterious language, but it is a language fully comprehensible to the "in-group."

Only from such a background is it possible to understand the book of Revelation. It is one example of the genre referred to as apocalyptic literature by scholars. Only when one understands both this type of literature and the movement of apocalyptic in general, can one hope to grasp the intention and method of Revelation. When this is done the message of Revelation appears very straightforward indeed. The essential message is summarized in 13:10b: "Here is a call for the endurance and faith of the saints." It is a support document for those who stand close to the threat of persecution. This theme is echoed throughout. Another example is 14:12: "Here is a call for the endurance of the saints, those who keep the commandments of God and the faith of Jesus."

The second half of Revelation opens with typically apocalyptic language, as we find it, for example in 1 Enoch. In Revelation 4:1–2 we read:

After this I looked, and lo, in heaven an open door! And the first voice, which I had heard speaking to me like a trumpet, said, "Come up hither, and I will show you what must take place after this." 2 At once I was in the Spirit, and lo, a throne stood in heaven, with one seated on the throne!

The seer, John, is now in the heavenly world and the remainder of the apocalypse is a communication of what John witnesses. After ascending to the heavenly throne, the elders and the creatures, John reports that the four creatures sing without ceasing:

"Holy, holy, holy, is the Lord God Almighty,
who was and is and is to come!"

(4:8)

It is also reported that the elders fall before the one on the throne and sing:

"Worthy art thou, our Lord and God,
to receive glory and honor and power,
for thou didst create all things,
and by thy will they existed and were created."

(4:11)

In Revelation 5:2 the question is asked, "Who is worthy to open the scroll and break its seals?" The scene is that of God on the throne holding a scroll sealed with seven seals in his right hand. This scroll contains within it God's future plan for history. The answer to the question is Jesus, who is described as the Lamb (5:6-10).

And between the throne and the four living creatures and among the elders, I saw a Lamb standing, as though it had been slain, with seven horns and with seven eyes, which are the seven spirits of God sent out into all the earth; 7 and he went and took the scroll from the right hand of him who was seated on the throne. 8 And when he had taken the scroll, the four living creatures and the twenty-four elders fell down before the Lamb, each holding a harp, and with golden bowls full of incense, which are the prayers of the saints; 9 and they sang a new song, saying,

"Worthy art thou to take the scroll and to open its seals,
for thou wast slain and by thy blood didst ransom men for God
from every tribe and tongue and people and nation,
10 and hast made them a kingdom and priests to our God,
and they shall reign on earth."

Central to this description is the death of Jesus and the kingdom he inaugurated. The exalted position given to Jesus by this author is made evident in verse 12 as everyone in the heavenly world asserts, "Worthy is the Lamb who was slain, to receive power and wealth and wisdom and might and honor and glory and blessing!"

Now that it has been established that the Lamb is worthy to open the seals on the scroll, chapter 6 begins the story of opening the seals. By the end of chapter 6, six of the seven seals have been opened. Let us review the opening of one of these seals, the fifth:

When he opened the fifth seal, I saw under the altar the souls of those who had been slain for the word of God and for the witness they had borne; 10 they cried out with a loud voice, "O Sovereign Lord, holy and true, how long before thou wilt judge and avenge our blood on those who dwell upon the earth?" 11 Then they were each given a white robe and told to rest a little longer, until the number of their fellow servants and their brethren should be complete, who were to be killed as they themselves had been. (6:9–11)

Imbedded in this scene is a question that describes the central problem being addressed throughout this book, "O Sovereign Lord, holy and true, how long before thou wilt judge and avenge our blood on those who dwell upon the earth?"

After the opening of the sixth seal, there is an interruption in chapter 7. The angels who have been given the destructive powers over the earth and sea are instructed, " 'Do not harm the earth or the sea or the trees, till we have sealed the servants of our God upon their foreheads.' 4 And I heard the number of the sealed, a hundred and forty-four thousand sealed . . ." (7:3–4). A protective seal is given to the faithful against this type of destruction that is in the process of being unleashed against the

world. As we shall see in Revelation 13 it is not only those who
are faithful to God who bear a mark or seal, but also those who
worship the beast, the Roman emperor, who are marked—but
their mark will lead to destruction. This is described in 14:9–11:

And another angel, a third, followed them, saying with a loud voice, "If
any one worships the beast and its image, and receives a mark on his
forehead or on his hand, 10 he also shall drink the wine of God's wrath,
poured unmixed into the cup of his anger, and he shall be tormented
with fire and sulphur in the presence of the holy angels and in the
presence of the Lamb. 11 And the smoke of their torment goes up for
ever and ever; and they have no rest, day or night, these worshipers of
the beast and its image, and whoever receives the mark of its name."

The second half of Revelation 7 anticipates the end of history
which is described in chapters 18–21: "Salvation belongs to our
God who sits upon the throne, and to the Lamb" (7:10). Revelation 7:13–17 is an explicit reference to the problem the Johannine congregation is currently experiencing and it portrays the
peaceful and satisfied condition of the martyrs in the presence of
the Lamb and God:

Then one of the elders addressed me, saying, "Who are these, clothed
in white robes, and whence have they come?" 14 I said to him, "Sir, you
know." And he said to me, "These are they who have come out of the
great tribulation; they have washed their robes and made them white in
the blood of the Lamb.

　15 Therefore are they before the throne of God,
　　and serve him day and night within his temple;
　　and he who sits upon the throne will shelter them with his presence,
　16 They shall hunger no more, neither thirst any more;
　　the sun shall not strike them, nor any scorching heat.
　17 For the Lamb in the midst of the throne will be their shepherd,
　　and he will guide them to springs of living water;
　and God will wipe away every tear from their eyes."

The opening of the seventh seal begins in chapter 8 but its
agony is detailed over several chapters with a series of seven

subdivisions. Finally in 11:15–18 the final trumpet is blown and the voices in heaven shout out,

"The kingdom of the world has become the kingdom of our Lord and of his Christ, and he shall reign for ever and ever." 16 And the twenty-four elders who sit on their thrones before God fell on their faces and worshiped God, 17 saying,

"We give thanks to thee, Lord God Almighty, who art and who wast,
that thou hast taken thy great power and begun to reign.
18 The nations raged, but thy wrath came,
and the time for the dead to be judged,
for rewarding thy servants, the prophets and saints,
and those who fear thy name, both small and great,
and for destroying the destroyers of the earth."

Here again we note the twin themes of the second half of the Apocalypse: the triumph of God's kingdom and justice, and the vindication and rewarding of all his servants who have been persecuted and killed.

The subject of God's anger becomes increasingly clear as one moves from the more general statements in Revelation 12 to the highly specific ones in Revelation 18. The Roman empire is the focus of God's destruction. As scholars have recognized, Babylon can only refer to Rome.[2] Not only are the highly allusive references in these chapters part of the apocalyptic style, but they are part of that style for very practical reasons. If one is part of a political minority, life becomes dangerous and one has to be cautious in the expression of one's views. This is especially the case if the author of Revelation is sitting in a prison for political reasons (1:9). In these situations references to the evil and corrupt emperors is expressed by such vague terms as "dragon" or "beast." One of the beasts is referred to even more precisely as "six hundred and sixty-six" (13:18). Since in both Hebrew and Greek letters of the alphabet have numerical values, the suggestion by some scholars is that 666 equals the name of Neron Caesar in Hebrew letters.

Chapters 14–17 prepare for the funeral lament over Babylon

in chapter 18. Brief, joyous announcements are made throughout. Typical is the one found in 14:8, "Fallen, fallen is Babylon
the great, she who made all nations drink the wine of her impure
passion." This great harlot has written on her forehead: " 'Babylon the great, mother of harlots and of earth's abominations.' 6
And I saw the woman, drunk with the blood of the saints and the
blood of the martyrs of Jesus" (17:5b–6).

Chapter 18 contains a taunting, sarcastic lament over the fall
of Babylon. It begins in this way:

> "Fallen, fallen is Babylon the great!
> It has become a dwelling place of demons,
> a haunt of every foul spirit,
> a haunt of every foul and hateful bird;
> for all nations have drunk the wine of her impure passion,
> and the kings of the earth have committed fornication with her,
> and the merchants of the earth have grown rich with the wealth of her
> wantonness."

As William Stringfellow points out, the relevance of a pericope
such as this might be intensified if the reader were to substitute
the word "America" for "Babylon."[3] For example, one does not
have to look too far to note how the kings of the earth have
committed fornication with this nation in order to obtain our
armaments.

In order to focus more sharply on the poignancy of the scene
described in verses 10–24, imagine yourself looking at a major
metropolitan center after a nuclear attack. John the seer writes in
verse 10:

> "Alas! alas! thou great city,
> thou mighty city, Babylon!
> In one hour has thy judgment come."

All the merchants and shipmasters and seafaring men, we are
told, weep and mourn for all their expensive luxuries and delica-
cies will no longer be bought. They all stand around mourning,

> 16 "Alas, alas, for the great city
> that was clothed in fine linen, in purple and scarlet,

bedecked with gold, with jewels, and with pearls!
17 In one hour all this wealth has been laid waste."

And all the shipmasters and seafaring men, sailors and all whose trade is on the sea, stood far off.

The final word of these mourning shipmasters is a word of rejoicing.

"Rejoice over her, O heaven,
O saints and apostles and prophets,
for God has given judgment for you against her!"

(v. 20)

Why has God rendered this judgment against the harlot Babylon? Because "in her was found the blood of prophets and of saints, and of all who have been slain on earth" (v. 24).

Chapter 19 of the Apocalypse begins with the announcement of God's ultimate triumph. This scene communicates one of the basic themes the author deems essential for his persecuted audience to understand.

"Hallelujah! Salvation and glory and power belong to our God,
2 for his judgments are true and just;
he has judged the great harlot who corrupted the earth with her
    fornication,
and he has avenged on her the blood of his servants."

3 Once more they cried,

"Hallelujah! The smoke from her goes up for ever and ever."

The remainder of this chapter as well as chapter 20 gives further support to "those who had been beheaded for their testimony to Jesus and for the word of God, and who had not worshiped the beast or its image and had not received its mark on their foreheads or their hands" (20:4). Then in Revelation 21 comes John's vision of "a new heaven and a new earth" (v. 1). "And he who sat upon the throne said, 'Behold, I make all things new.' . . . 6 And he said to me, 'It is done! I am the Alpha and the Omega, the beginning and the end' " (vv. 5–6).

Finally, the entire purpose for writing this apocalypse is summarized in 22:6–7: "These words are trustworthy and true. And the Lord, the God of the spirits of the prophets, has sent his angel to show his servants what must soon take place. 7 And behold, I am coming soon." The entire point of John's entry into the heavenly world was to encourage his brothers and sisters on the mainland by giving them insight into the future of God's plans, namely, the victory and triumph of his justice.

Having now been exposed to a brief survey of the Johannine school in this and the previous chapter, one can more clearly understand how this body of Johannine literature documents from beginning to end the principle of dynamic actualization we have been discussing throughout this book. From the days of the first proclamation of the gospel through the crisis with the synagogue to the days of persecution, we can see over and over again how this community actualized the Christ event for each new moment on their pilgrimage. It is precisely this that the church in all ages is called to do.

Conclusion: The Dynamic Word

The "dynamic Word"—with that phrase we have attempted to express and illustrate an important dimension in the development of New Testament Christianity. The Word of God, Jesus Christ, is dynamically proclaimed and actualized in different New Testament books. It is for this reason that the early church included twenty-seven documents in its New Testament canon and not simply a few summarizing and static compendia of Christian faith. Because of this basic principle of dynamic actualization we find in the New Testament not one but four gospels, not one Pauline letter but several, and not one emphasis or intention in the literature of the Johannine school, but many.

To recognize that the gospel, the Word of God, is always dynamically and creatively applied in earliest Christianity has important implications at a number of different levels. It should allow us to appreciate God's gift of the historical-critical method of biblical study to the church. For it is precisely the great advances made by Scripture scholars in the twentieth century that have allowed us to see with new eyes the amazingly creative and dynamic character of the first-century church. By allowing us this insight into the reality of the struggles and commitment of early Christians, their faith and fortitude stand out with great vividness. Further, the dynamic way in which the gospel is transmitted by the first-century church forces us to raise some very significant theological questions both about the theological presuppositions of the early church that allowed it to develop the tradition so creatively, and, as a result of these presuppositions, about the way we are to do theology today.

The one thing the New Testament forbids us to do is to treat it as a static document to be used as a set of proof-texts for instant solutions to complex and controversial contemporary problems. To misuse the New Testament in this way is to deny its dynamic character and to fail to realize that the Word has to be applied in a specific context. We must take very seriously the fact that the Word is never found in isolation from a specific historical context. At this point the New Testament is being faithful to the incarnation. Jesus is not some abstract, nonhuman, gnostic redeemer figure, but he is the Jewish man from Nazareth who participated in God's history at a specific time and place. The responsibility of the theological task, therefore, is not to imitate certain static points on the New Testament trajectory but to so understand its process of actualization that it will be involved in a similar process, that is, the actualization of the good news of the gospel to the new realities and circumstances of today's world situation.

To participate in a theological process analogous to that of the early church, however, forces us to take seriously its theological presuppositions. What is it that allowed the early church to develop so creatively and dramatically against what appeared to be unreasonable odds? In today's age, which is often characterized by a high degree of individualism and narcism, it is important to discover that the God of early Christianity is a God who transcends individual needs and personal salvation. He is the God of creation, the God of Abraham, Isaac, and Jacob who in Jesus Christ is reclaiming his entire creation. God's work of redemption in Christ presupposes the radical sinfulness of man, the brokenness of creation, and our inability to change that situation in any significant way. In an age of "I'm OK—you're OK" that particular presupposition of early Christians must be reappropriated as Reinhold Niebuhr, the profound American ethicist and theologian, has demonstrated so cogently. Into this broken and fragmented situation, the New Testament insists that God's kingdom, his new creation, has entered in a preliminary way. Already now his kingdom is present in the form of a new community, but not yet in its final fulfillment, which is yet to be revealed on the last day. Christian existence is therefore lived in eschatological tension, in the tension of "already/not yet," in the paradox of the new present within the old. This Christian existence, it is further asserted, is lived in the midst of a new community, the *ekklēsia,* the church, inaugurated by the great sign of the new age, God's resurrection of Jesus. God's church, established by the resurrection, is sustained and nurtured by the gift of God's Spirit and it is this Spirit that allows it to be faithful until the last day. It is this community that has been given the right and the responsibility for constantly actualizing anew the Christ event so that this event will always become a dynamic Word.

The concept of the dynamic Word in early Christianity is possible only against such a theological background. Only because Jesus is not a dead prophet but the Risen Lord of the church present in her midst is it possible for the church to actualize the Christ event to the new realities confronting it. Therefore, not only one's understanding of *theo*logy (God), *ecclesio*logy (church), but also one's understanding of *Christo*logy (Christ) is critical. A static interpretation of the New Testament is dependent on a frozen Christology, one that views Jesus as limited to the first third of the first century; a dynamic interpretation of the New Testament is based on a Christology that views Jesus not only as the human manifestation of God in first-century Palestine, but also as the Risen Lord of the church present yesterday, today, and tomorrow, who calls his church to obedience until the completion of his salvific purposes on the last day. As the contemporary church remains obedient to the Risen Christ in her midst, the gospel can become a dynamic Word for us as well, and that is an opportunity of great hope and much rejoicing.

Notes

Introduction

1. On the historical-critical method, the following books may prove to be helpful: John Reumann, *Jesus in the Church's Gospels: Modern Scholarship and the Earliest Sources* (Philadelphia: Fortress Press, 1968), especially pp. 18–43; R. S. Barbour, *Traditio-Historical Criticism of the Gospels* (London: SPCK, 1972); Gerhard Lohfink, *The Bible: Now I Get It!* (Garden City, NY: Doubleday, 1979); Richard N. Soulen, *Handbook of Biblical Criticism* (Atlanta: John Knox Press, 1976). On the Qumran documents see: Theodor H. Gaster, *The Dead Sea Scriptures* (Garden City, NY: Doubleday, 1964); Menahem Mansoor, *The Dead Sea Scrolls* (Grand Rapids, MI: Eerdmans, 1964); Frank Moore Cross, Jr., *The Ancient Library of Qumran* (Garden City, NY: Doubleday, 1958). On the Nag Hammadi gnostic documents see: James M. Robinson, *The Nag Hammadi Library* (San Francisco: Harper & Row, 1977); Hans Jonas, *The Gnostic Religion* (Boston: Beacon Press, 1963).
2. See Reumann, *Jesus in the Church's Gospels*, pp. 30–36
3. I am indebted to John Knox for the phrase "Christ event." Knox argues that no "person, however extraordinary he may be, has historical existence, much less historical importance, except as an element in a more inclusive whole. . . ." That more inclusive whole for Knox is the church that both remembered and proclaimed Jesus. See especially John Knox, *The Church and the Reality of Christ* (New York: Harper & Row, 1962), pp. 28–31.
4. Adolf Jülicher, *Die Gleichnisreden Jesu* (Darmstadt: Wissenschaftlicher Buchgesellschaft, 1963).
5. John Dominic Crossan, *In Parables* (New York: Harper & Row, 1973), pp. 8–16.
6. Joachim Jeremias, *The Parables of Jesus* (New York: Scribner, 1963).
7. Crossan, *In Parables.*
8. Edgar McKnight, *What Is Form Criticism?* (Philadelphia: Fortress Press, 1969).
9. Norman Perrin, *What Is Redaction Criticism?* (Philadelphia: Fortress Press, 1969).
10. Karl P. Donfried, *The Romans Debate* (Minneapolis, MN: Augsburg, 1977).
11. I am indebted to Krister Stendahl for this comment. One should note that there is a substantial difference between the early Christian use of the Old Testament and much of the current abuse of the scriptural texts. Early Christians always used the Old Testament texts to illumine and explain the Christ event. Those Christians who play "the game of first-century Bibleland" today employ the texts to support their own positions, which often are not informed by the Christ event.
12. Paul Tillich, *Systematic Theology* (Chicago: University of Chicago Press, 1951). See also my discussion at the end of this introduction.
13. For further literature on the kingdom of God, see two books by Norman

Perrin, *The Kingdom of God in the Teaching of Jesus* (Philadelphia: Westminster Press, 1963) and *Jesus and the Language of the Kingdom* (Philadelphia: Fortress Press, 1976).

14. Paul C. Empie and T. Austin Murphy, eds., *Papal Primacy and the Universal Church* (Minneapolis, MN: Augsburg, 1974), p. 22.

15. See Ernst Käsemann, "Ketzer und Zeuge" in *Exegetische Versuche und Besinnungen*, I (Göttingen: Vandenhoeck & Ruprecht, 1964), pp. 168–187 and Karl P. Donfried, "Ecclesiastical Authority in 2–3 John" in *L'Evangile de Jean*, ed. M. deJonge (BETL 44; Gembloux: Duculot, 1977), pp. 325–333.

16. Hans von Campenhausen, *Ecclesiastical Authority and Spiritual Power* (Stanford, CA: Stanford University Press, 1969).

17. See the discussion in C. K. Barrett, *A Commentary on the First Epistle to the Corinthians* (New York: Harper & Row, 1968), pp. 334–341 and 264–266.

18. What follows is not an attempt to suggest what that relation should be; rather, it indicates that in light of the historical-critical method the entire complex of problems will have to be reevaluated.

19. On the subject of the formation of the New Testament Scripture, see Hans von Campenhausen, *The Formation of the Christian Bible* (Philadelphia: Fortress Press, 1968).

20. von Campenhausen, *Formation of the Christian Bible*, pp. 1–102.

21. See Walter Bauer, *Orthodoxy and Heresy in Earliest Christianity* (Philadelphia: Fortress Press, 1971) and Helmut Koester, *"GNOMAI DIAPHOROI:* The Origin and Nature of Diversification in the History of Early Christianity," *Harvard Theological Review* 58 (1965): 279–318.

22. See Karl P. Donfried, "Justification and Last Judgment in Paul," *Zeitschrift für die Neutestamentliche Wissenschaft* 67 (1976): 90–110.

23. See *Peter in the New Testament: A Collaborative Assessment by Protestant and Roman Catholic Scholars,* ed. R. E. Brown, K. P. Donfried, and J. Reumann (Minneapolis, MN: Augsburg; New York: Paulist Press, 1973).

24. See *Mary in the New Testament: A Collaborative Assessment by Protestant and Roman Catholic Scholars,* ed. R. E. Brown, K. P. Donfried, J. A. Fitzmyer, and J. Reumann (Philadelphia: Fortress Press; New York: Paulist Press, 1978).

25. These terms are used by Jaroslav Pelikan in his book *Obedient Rebels: Catholic Substance and Protestant Principle in Luther's Reformation* (New York: Harper & Row, 1964).

Chapter 1

1. John Knox, *Chapters in a Life of Paul* (New York: Abingdon Press, 1950), especially pp. 74–88.

2. John Reumann, *Jesus in the Church's Gospels: Modern Scholarship and the Earliest Sources* (Philadelphia: Fortress Press, 1968), especially pp. 25–36.

3. See Karl Paul Donfried, *The Setting of Second Clement in Early Christianity* (NovTSup 38; Leiden: E. J. Brill, 1974), p. 7; Strabo, Geog. 8.378 (Loeb 4:191).

4. See especially C. K. Barrett, *A Commentary on the First Epistle to the Corinthians* (New York: Harper & Row, 1968), pp. 264ff and Oscar Cullmann, *Immortality of the Soul or Resurrection of the Dead* (London: SCM, 1962).

5. See Introduction, note 16.

6. See Hans Jonas, *The Gnostic Religion* (Boston: Beacon Press, 1963).

7. James M. Robinson, *The Nag Hammadi Library* (San Francisco: Harper & Row, 1977), pp. 50–53.

8. A comment often made in the classroom. Niebuhr's great contribution to the field of theology and ethics, now a classic, is *The Nature and Destiny of Man: A Christian Interpretation* (New York: Scribner's, 1949).

9. See the discussion in *Peter in the New Testament: A Collaborative Assessment by Protestant and Roman Catholic Scholars*, ed. R. E. Brown, K. P. Donfried, and J. Reumann (Minneapolis, MN: Augsburg; New York: Paulist Press, 1973), pp. 83–101 and 32–36.

10. Barrett, *First Epistle to the Corinthians*, pp. 44–46; Hans Conzelmann, *A Commentary on the First Epistle to the Corinthians* (Philadelphia: Fortress Press, 1975), pp. 33–34.

11. See Victor Furnish, *Theology and Ethics in Paul* (Nashville, TN: Abingdon Press, 1968), pp. 162–180.

12. See Paul Tillich, *Dynamics of Faith* (New York: Harper & Row, 1957).

13. Dietrich Bonhoeffer, *The Cost of Discipleship* (New York: Macmillan, 1963), pp. 45–60.

14. When Paul speaks of "my spirit" in verse 14 he is in all likelihood referring to the gift of the Spirit given to the individual. The phrase therefore does not seem to refer only to one component of being human or to the Holy Spirit, but rather to the working of the Holy Spirit in the believer.

15. For a full discussion see Keith F. Nickle, *The Collection: A Study in Paul's Strategy* (London: SCM, 1966).

Chapter 2

1. For a more complete discussion of what follows, see my article "Justification and Last Judgment in Paul," *Zeitschrift für die Neutestamentliche Wissenschaft* 67 (1976): 90–110. A portion of what follows also appeared in *Interpretation* 30 (1976): 140–152.

2. Now reprinted in Ernst Käsemann, *New Testament Questions of Today* (Philadelphia: Fortress Press, 1969), pp. 168–82.

3. Rudolf Bultmann, "ΔΙΚΑΙΟΣΥΝΗ ΘΕΟΥ," *Journal of Biblical Literature* 83 (1964): 12–16.

4. Käsemann, *New Testament Questions*, p. 180.

5. Käsemann, *New Testament Questions*, p. 176.

6. Käsemann, *New Testament Questions*, p. 170.

7. Karl Kertelge, *Rechtfertigung bei Paulus* (Munich: Aschendorf, 1966).

8. Kertelge, *Rechtfertigung*, p. 133.

9. Kertelge, *Rechtfertigung*, p. 152.

10. Kertelge, *Rechtfertigung*, p. 155.

11. Kertelge, *Rechtfertigung*, pp. 159–225.

12. Kertelge, *Rechtfertigung*, p. 225.

13. A similar point is made in 1 Thessalonians 5:23 and following.

14. C. F. D. Moule aptly comments that ". . . the baptized Christian is no safer in playing fast and loose with his privileges than were the Israelites who had been 'baptized' in the land and the sea." ("The Judgment Theme in the Sacraments," in W. D. Davies and D. Daube, eds., *The Background of the New Testament and Its Eschatology* (Cambridge: Cambridge University Press, 1956), p. 472.

15. Krister Stendahl, "Justification and Last Judgment," *Lutheran World* 8:7 (1961), comments: "Consequently, to be a member of the church is by

definition to be justified, and he who remains in the church will be saved. If someone backslides, he will not be saved."

16. See the further discussion in Karl P. Donfried, *The Setting of Second Clement in Early Christianity* (NovTSup 38; Leiden: E. J. Brill, 1974), pp. 142–144.

17. But not for the Pauline school—for example, Ephesians 2:5, 8.

18. Many scholars argue persuasively that 2 Thessalonians is non-Pauline. For a discussion of the various options see W. G. Kümmel, *Introduction to the New Testament* (Nashville, TN: Abingdon Press, 1966), pp. 187–190.

19. Philippians 1:27ff., 4:1; Romans 14:4; 1 Corinthians 7:37, 15:50, 15:58, 16: 13; Galatians 5:1; 1 Thessalonians 3:8; 2 Thessalonians 2:5.

20. For example, Liselotte Mattern, *Das Verständnis des Gerichtes bei Paulus* (Zurich: Zwingli, 1966), pp. 110f.

21. A phrase coined by Stendahl in his article "The Apostle Paul and the Introspective Conscience of the West," *Harvard Theological Review* 56 (1963): 199 –215.

22. This point is made both in 1 Corinthians 3:13 and 4:15.

23. C. K. Barrett, *A Commentary on the First Epistle to the Corinthians* (New York: Harper & Row, 1968), p. 89

24. Ernst Kühl, *Rechtfertigung auf Grund Glaubens und Gericht nach den Werken bei Paulus* (Königsberg: 1904), pp. 11, 15, 20.

25. That the use of term "spirit" in these verses differs from his ordinary usage is acknowledged by Bornkamm and von Campenhausen in Hans von Campenhausen, *Ecclesiastical Authority and Spiritual Power* (Stanford, CA: Stanford University Press, 1969), pp. 134f., n. 50. Bornkamm is supported by the fact that in 1 Corinthians, Paul, when using the terms *sarx* and *pneuma* with reference to a person, does not use them in a dualistic but a holistic sense —see esp. 1 Corinthians 7:34; also 2 Corinthians 7:1 and 1 Thessalonians 5:23.

26. Hans Conzelmann, *A Commentary on the First Epistle to the Corinthians* (Philadelphia: Fortress Press, 1975), p. 78, n. 92.

27. See the discussion in Markus Barth, *Ephesians 4–6* (Garden City, NY: Doubleday, 1974), pp. 547–550.

28. Ernst Käsemann, *Essays on New Testament Themes* (London: SCM, 1964), p. 126.

Chapter 3

1. This terminology comes from J. M. Robinson and H. Koester, *Trajectories Through Early Christianity* (Philadelphia: Fortress Press, 1971).

2. See Walter Bauer, *Orthodoxy and Heresy in Earliest Christianity* (Philadelphia: Fortress Press, 1971) and Helmut Koester, "*GNOMAI DIAPHOROI:* The Origin and Nature of Diversification in the History of Early Christianity" *Harvard Theological Review* 58 (1965): 279–318.

3. Elaine Pagels, *The Gnostic Paul* (Philadelphia: Fortress Press, 1975).

4. See Eduard Lohse, *A Commentary on the Epistles to the Colossians and to Philemon* (Philadelphia: Fortress Press, 1971), pp. 177–183.

5. Romans 6:5; Philippians 3:10–11.

6. For example, Gilles Quispel, "The Jung Codex and Its Significance" in *The Jung Codex*, ed. F.L. Cross (London: Mowbrays, 1955), pp. 35–78.

7. Colossians 3:1; also 2:12.

8. See the discussion by Hans Conzelmann, "Paulus und die Weisheit," *New Testament Studies* 12 (1965): 231–244.

9. See Martin Dibelius, *A Commentary on the Epistle of James* (Philadelphia: Fortress Press, 1976).

10. Dibelius, *James*, pp. 54–56.

11. *Peter in the New Testament: A Collaborative Assessment by Protestant and Roman Catholic Scholars*, ed. R. E. Brown, K. P. Donfried, and J. Reumann (Minneapolis, MN: Augsburg; New York: Paulist Press, 1973), pp. 149–156.

12. Dibelius, *James*, pp. 163–167.

13. John Knox, *Chapters in the Life of Paul* (New York: Abingdon Press, 1950), pp. 47–73

14. Philipp Vielhauer, "On the 'Paulinism' of Acts" in *Studies in Luke-Acts*, ed. L. E. Keck and J. L. Martyn (Nashville, TN: Abingdon Press, 1966), pp. 33–50.

15. See Jacob Jervell, *Luke and the People of God* (Minneapolis, MN: Augsburg, 1972), pp. 153–207.

16. Jervell, *Luke and the People of God*, pp. 41–132.

17. Günther Bornkamm, "The Missionary Stance of Paul in I Corinthians 9 and in Acts," in *Studies in Luke-Acts*, pp. 194–207.

18. Bornkamm, "Missionary Stance."

19. Bornkamm, "Missionary Stance," p. 205.

20. Samuel Sandmel, "The Ancient Mind and Ours," in *Understanding the Sacred Text*, ed. John Reumann (Valley Forge, PA: Judson, 1972), p. 43.

21. Sandmel, "The Ancient Mind and Ours," p. 42.

22. Charles H. Talbert, "An Introduction to Acts," *Review and Expositor* 71 (1974), pp. 437–449, esp. p. 439.

23. D. R. Stuart, *Epochs of Greek and Roman Biography* (Berkeley: University of California Press, 1928), pp. 158–159, as cited in Talbert, "An Introduction to Acts," p. 440, n. 13. Aristoxenus was a Greek philosopher and musical theorist born between 375 and 360 B.C.

24. Talbert, "An Introduction to Acts," p. 440. *Sitz im Leben* is a German technical term widely used in the English literature to refer to the actual sociological setting of a tradition.

Chapter 4

1. See Ralph P. Martin, *Mark: Evangelist and Theologian* (Exeter, England: Paternoster, 1972), especially pp. 17–50, 140–162; John Reumann, *Jesus in the Church's Gospels* (Philadelphia: Fortress Press, 1968), pp. 18–43.

2. Werner G. Kümmel, *Introduction to the New Testament* (Nashville, TN: Abingdon Press, 1975), pp. 80–101.

3. Among the more creative suggestions see Theodore J. Weeden, Sr., *Mark—Traditions in Conflict* (Philadelphia: Fortress Press, 1979).

4. Kümmel, *Introduction to the New Testament*, pp. 38–80.

5. Martin, *Mark*, pp. 84–205.

6. Willi Marxsen, *Mark the Evangelist* (Nashville, TN: Abingdon Press, 1969), pp. 117–50.

7. Martin, *Mark*, p. 22.

8. Martin, *Mark*, pp. 21–28.

9. Krister Stendahl, *The School of St. Matthew and Its Use of the Old Testament* (Philadelphia: Fortress Press, 1968).

10. See further Kümmel, *Introduction to the New Testament*, pp. 128–130.

11. Raymond E. Brown, *The Gospel According to John (i–xii)* (Garden City, NY: Doubleday, 1966), pp. cv–cxxviii, 3–37

12. Marxsen, *Mark*, p. 138.

13. Concerning the textual history of this verse consult Bruce Metzger, *A Textual Commentary on the Greek New Testament* (London: United Bible Societies, 1971), p. 73.

14. Günther Bornkamm, *Jesus of Nazareth* (New York: Harper & Row, 1960), pp. 226–231.

15. See Martin, *Mark*, pp. 136–138, 142f., 169–171, 175f., 210–214, 214f.

16. *Theological Dictionary of the New Testament*, vol. 2 ed. Gerhard Kittel (Grand Rapids, MI: Eerdmans, 1964) p. 724.

17. See H. D. Betz, "Jesus as Divine Man," in *Jesus the Historian: Festschrift E.C. Colwell* (Philadelphia: Westminster Press, 1968), pp. 114–133.

18. Martin Kähler. See Philipp Vielhauer, *Geschichte der urchristlichen Literatur* (Berlin: de Gruyter, 1975), p. 340.

19. Norman Perrin, *Rediscovering the Teaching of Jesus* (New York: Harper & Row, 1967), pp. 15–53.

20. See Ferdinand Hahn, *The Titles of Jesus in Christology* (London: Lutterworth Press, 1969), pp. 136–239 and Theodore J. Weeden, Sr., *Mark—Traditions in Conflict*, pp. 52–69.

21. Rudolf Bultmann, *The History of the Synoptic Tradition* (New York: Harper & Row, 1963), pp. 209–244.

Chapter 5

1. Krister Stendahl, *The School of St. Matthew and Its Use of the Old Testament* (Philadelphia: Fortress Press, 1968), pp. 20ff.

2. Jack Dean Kingsbury, *Matthew: Structure, Christology, Kingdom* (Philadelphia: Fortress Press, 1975).

3. Karl Paul Donfried, "The Allegory of the Ten Virgins (Matt. 25:1–13) As a Summary of Matthean Theology," *Journal of Biblical Literature* 93 (1974): 415–428.

4. W. D. Davies, *The Setting of the Sermon on the Mount* (Cambridge, Eng.: Cambridge University Press, 1964).

5. Stendahl, *School of St. Matthew*, pp. 11–12, 20ff.

6. See Günther Bornkamm, "End-Expectation and Church in Matthew" in *Tradition and Interpretation in Matthew*, ed. G. Bornkamm, G. Barth, H. J. Held (Philadelphia: Westminster Press, 1963), p. 50, n. 5.

7. See Bornkamm, "End-Expectation."

8. Davies, *Setting of the Sermon on the Mount*, pp. 14–108.

9. W. F. Albright and C. S. Mann, *Matthew* (Garden City, NY: Doubleday, 1971), pp. 45ff.

10. Q is the common designation by scholars of all those places where Matthew and Luke agree but where there is no parallel in Mark. See further Werner Georg Kümmel, *Introduction to the New Testament* (Nashville, TN: Abingdon Press, 1975), pp. 65–80.

11. Joachim Jeremias, *New Testament Theology: The Proclamation of Jesus* (New York: Scribner, 1971), pp. 193–203.

12. A term used by Dietrich Bonhoeffer in *The Cost of Discipleship* (New York: Macmillan, 1963), pp. 45–60.

13. Jeremias, *New Testament Theology*, pp. 199–200.

14. Jeremias, *New Testament Theology*, pp. 201–203.
15. Donfried, "Ten Virgins."
16. John Dominic Crossan, *In Parables* (New York: Harper & Row, 1973), p. 14.
17. Dan O. Via, Jr., *The Parables* (Philadelphia: Fortress Press, 1967), p. 5.
18. Donfried, "Ten Virgins," p. 424.
19. Concerning the identity of "the least of these my brethren" see the discussion in John P. Meier, *Matthew* (Wilmington, DE: Michael Glazier, 1980), p. 304.
20. See Donfried, "Ten Virgins," pp. 427–428.
21. See R. A. Markus, *Saeculum: History and Society in the Theology of St. Augustine* (Cambridge, Eng.: Cambridge University Press, 1970), pp. 121ff.
22. See J. D. Kingsbury, *The Parables of Jesus in Matthew 13* (London: SPCK, 1969).
23. Wolfgang Schrage, *Theological Dictionary of The New Testament*, vol. 7 (Grand Rapids, MI: Eerdmans, 1971), pp. 798–843.
24. *Peter in the New Testament: A Collaborative Assessment by Protestant and Roman Catholic Scholars*, ed. R. E. Brown, K. P. Donfried, and J. Reumann (Minneapolis, MN: Augsburg; New York: Paulist Press, 1973), pp. 83–101.
25. *Peter in the New Testament*, 92
26. Krister Stendahl, "Quis et Unde? An Analysis of Mt. 1–2," in *Judentum, Urchristentum, Kirche: Festschrift für J. Jeremias*, ed. W. Eltester (BZNW 26; Berlin: Töpelmann, 1964): 94–105.
27. Edward F. Campbell, Jr., *Ruth* (Garden City, NY: Doubleday, 1975), p. 121.
28. See *Mary in the New Testament: A Collaborative Assessment by Protestant and Roman Catholic Scholars*, ed. R. E. Brown, K. P. Donfried, J. A. Fitzmyer, and J. Reumann (Philadelphia: Fortress Press; New York: Paulist Press, 1978), pp 289–292.

Chapter 6

1. See Werner Georg Kümmel, *Introduction to the New Testament* (Nashville, TN: Abingdon Press, 1975), pp. 130–147, 160–173.
2. Kümmel, *Introduction to the New Testament*, p. 163.
3. C. K. Barrett, *Luke The Historian in Recent Study* (London: Epworth, 1961).
4. Jacob Jervell, *Luke and the People of God* (Minneapolis, MN: Augsburg, 1972).
5. Henry Joel Cadbury, *The Style and Literary Method of Luke, I. The Diction of Luke and Acts, II. The Treatment of Sources in the Gospel* (Cambridge, MA: Harvard University Press, Harvard Theological Studies 6: 1919–20).
6. See the illuminating treatment in Dan Otto Via, Jr., *The Parables: Their Literary and Existential Dimension* (Philadelphia: Fortress Press, 1967), pp. 162–176.
7. John 4:20ff. See also on the Samaritans the study by R. J. Coggins, *Samaritans and Jews* (Atlanta, GA: John Knox, 1975).
8. For a general discussion of this subject refer to the monograph by William E. Phipps, *Was Jesus Married?* (New York: Harper & Row, 1970).
9. O. Cullmann, "Death of Christ," in *The Interpreter's Dictionary of the Bible*, vol. 1, ed. George A Buttrick (New York: Abingdon Press, 1962), p. 804–808.
10. *Gospel Parallels*, ed. Burton H. Throckmorton, Jr. (Nashville: Thomas Nelson, 1979). This volume compares the three synoptic gospels, Matthew, Mark and Luke, by placing them in parallel columns, section by section, thus allowing the reader to discover both the similarities and the differences.
11. Hans Conzelmann, *The Theology of St. Luke* (New York: Harper & Row, 1960).

12. See F. F. Bruce, "The Holy Spirit in the Acts of the Apostles," *Interpretation* 27 (1973): 166–183.

Chapter 7

1. For a more complete discussion refer to my article "Ecclesiastical Authority in 2–3 John" in *L'Evangile de Jean,* ed. M. deJonge (BETL 44; Gembloux: Duculot, 1977), pp. 325–333.
2. Donfried, "Ecclesiastical Authority," pp. 331–332.
3. R. H. Charles, *The Revelation of St. John,* vol. 1 (Edinburgh: T. & T. Clark, 1920), pp. xxxiii, 43f.
4. See the discussion in Raymond E. Brown, *The Gospel According to John (i–xii)* (Garden City, NY: Doubleday, 1966), pp. ciii–civ.
5. Brown, *John* (i–xii), pp. xxxivff. See also Brown's newest discussion in *The Community of the Beloved Disciple* (New York: Paulist Press, 1979).
6. J. L. Martyn, *History and Theology in the Fourth Gospel* (New York: Harper & Row, 1968; revised edition, Nashville, TN: Abingdon Press, 1979). See also Martyn's newest contribution, *The Gospel of John in Christian History* (New York: Paulist Press 1978).
7. Martyn, *History and Theology,* p. 36.
8. Martyn, *History and Theology,* pp. 40–41.
9. See our previous discussion, pp. 15–18.
10. Martyn, *History and Theology,* pp. 36ff.
11. Brown, *John* (i–xii), pp. 519–524.
12. See Raymond E. Brown, *The Gospel According to John (xiii–xxi)* (Garden City, NY: Doubleday, 1970), pp. 548–562.
13. See *Peter in the New Testament: A Collaborative Assessment by Protestant and Roman Catholic Scholars,* ed. R. E. Brown, K. P. Donfried, and J. Reumann (Minneapolis, MN: Augsburg; New York: Paulist Press, 1973).
14. Brown, *John* (xiii–xxi), pp. 1135–1144.
15. Donfried, "Ecclesiastical Authority," pp. 332–333.
16. See note 3 above.

Chapter 8

1. See the discussion and literature cited in *Mary in the New Testament: A Collaborative Assessment by Protestant and Roman Catholic Scholars,* ed. R. E. Brown, K. P. Donfried, J. A. Fitzmyer, and J. Reumann (Philadelphia: Fortress Press; New York: Paulist Press, 1978), pp. 219–225.
2. P. S. Minear, "Babylon," in *The Interpreter's Dictionary of the Bible,* vol. 1 (New York: Abingdon Press, 1962), p. 338.
3. William Stringfellow, *An Ethic for Christians and Other Aliens in a Strange Land* (Waco, TX: Word, 1973).

Index

Actualization, dynamic, 2–3, 5–7, 9,
  15–16, 21–49, 74–75, 97–99,
  115–17, 127–28, 138–39, 160, 163,
  167, 196–99
Agape. See Love
Albright, W. F., 97, 206 n 9
Alexander the Great, 22
Allegories, 108–13, 123–26, 162,
  177–80
Allegory: of the foot washing,
  177–78; of the rock, 123–26; of the
  temple cleansing, 177; of the ten
  virgins, 107–13, 119, 162; of the
  vine, 179–80
Aphrodite, 22
Apocalypse, 190–96
Apollo, 22
Apollos, 24, 30, 60
Aristoxenus, life of Pythagoras by, 75
Arrogance, 28–33, 35, 43, 62, 145
Augustine, 117
Augustus (Roman emperor), 80

Babylon, 189, 193–95
Baptism. *See* Justification
Barabbas, 159–60
Barbour, R. S., 201 n 1
Barrett, C. K., 140, 202 nn 17, 4,
  203 n 10, 204 n 23, 207 n 3
Barth, Markus, 204 n 27
Bathsheba, 130–31
Bauer, Walter, 202 n 21, 204 n 2
Beatitudes. *See* Sermon on the
  Mount
Benedictions, 170–71, 174
Betz, H. D., 206 n 17
Birth of Christ, 129–35, 143
Boasting. *See* Arrogance
Bonhoeffer, Dietrich, 35, 203 n 13,
  206 n 12

Bornkamm, Günther, 73, 204 n 25,
  205 nn 17–19, 206 nn 14, 6–7
Brown, Raymond E., 168, 202 nn
  23–24, 203 n 9, 205 n 11, 206 n
  11, 207 nn 24–25, 28, 208 nn 4–5,
  11–14, 1
Bruce, F. F., 208 n 12
Bultmann, Rudolf, 50, 206 n 21

Cadbury, Henry Joel, 142, 207 n 5
Caesar, Julius, 22, 80
Campbell, Edward F., Jr., 207 n 27
Catholicism, 15
Charles, R. H., 167–68, 186, 208 n 3
Chloe, 33
Christ: birth of, 129–35, 143;
  conception of, 132–35; false
  concept of, 85–88, 183–84,
  genealogy of, 129–31, 134–35;
  geographic origin of, 129, 135–38;
  identity of, 129, 135–38, 183–84;
  as infant, 135–38, 143; as Jewish
  messiah, 85–87, 131–32;
  relationship of Old Testament to,
  170–76; as Son of God, 81–84,
  103, 123–26, 133–34, 158, 160–61.
  See also Death of Christ
"Christ," meaning of word, 85–88
Christianity, 65–71; after break with
  Judaism, 171–72; conflict of with
  Judaism, 127–29, 131–35, 169–73
Church: authority of the, 120–23,
  126–27; after break of with
  synagogue, 171–72, 177; conflict of
  synagogue with, 169–73; and New
  Testament, 13–15; founding of
  the, 125–28; responsibility of the,
  122–23
"Church," use of word, 122
Coggins, R. J., 207 n 7

Scripture Index